TRUTH

www.penguin.co.uk

Hector Macdonald is an expert in business storytelling. As a strategic communications consultant he has advised the leaders of some of the world's top corporations in industries as diverse as financial services, telecoms, technology and healthcare. He is also the bestselling author of four novels.

www.hectormacdonald.com

TRUTH

How the Many Sides to Every Story Shape Our Reality

Hector Macdonald

BANTAM PRESS

LONDON • TORONTO • SYDNEY • AUCKLAND • JOHANNESBURG

TRANSWORLD PUBLISHERS
61–63 Uxbridge Road, London W5 5SA
www.penguin.co.uk

Transworld is part of the Penguin Random House group of companies
whose addresses can be found at global.penguinrandomhouse.com

Penguin
Random House
UK

First published in Great Britain in 2018 by Bantam Press
an imprint of Transworld Publishers

A CIP catalogue record for this book
is available from the British Library.

ISBN 9780593079324 (hardback)
9780593079331 (trade paperback)

Typeset in 11/15pt Sabon by Falcon Oast Graphic Art Ltd.
Printed and bound by Clays Ltd, Bungay, Suffolk.

Penguin Random House is committed to a sustainable
future for our business, our readers and our planet. This book
is made from Forest Stewardship Council® certified paper.

MIX
Paper from
responsible sources
FSC® C018179

1 3 5 7 9 10 8 6 4 2

CONTENTS

PREFACE

This book looks forward to a backlash.

Written during an epidemic of fake news and alternative facts, it anticipates a revival of public concern for the truth and a widespread insistence that politicians, business leaders, campaigners and other professional communicators be held accountable for the veracity of their words. I have confidence that we value truth enough to fight for it.

But truth is not as straightforward as it seems. There are different ways to speak truth, not all of them honest. On most issues, there are multiple truths we can choose to communicate. Our choice of truth will influence how those around us perceive an issue and react to it. We can select truths that engage people and inspire action, or we can deploy truths that deliberately mislead. Truth comes in many forms, and experienced communicators can exploit its variability to shape our impression of reality.

This is a book about truth, not lies, although much of it is concerned with how truth can be used just like lies. The same instincts, pressures and incentives that lead communicators to say things that aren't true also lead them to use truth in a highly misleading way. By showing how it is done, I hope to encourage more people to spot and call out misleading truths.

Different forms of truth can be used in a more constructive way, to unite, inspire and transform. Selecting the right truth can bring a company together, give courage to an army, speed the development of a new technology, rally supporters to a political party and galvanize the energy, creativity and enthusiasm of whole organizations. Leaders need to understand their communications options and know how to pick and present the most engaging truths.

This book is for anyone who wants to communicate truthfully but understands that they have a choice of truths to use. It's for anyone tired of being led up the garden path by politicians, marketers and PR officers using technically truthful constructions. Which truth will be most effective in making your point? Which truth will inspire your organization? Which truth is the most ethical? What truths might others use to persuade us to act against our own interests? How can we challenge misleading truths? *Truth* should help answer these questions.

A book about truth is an easy target for accusations of inaccuracy or falsehood. In the many stories and topics covered, I have tried hard to get the facts right, but inevitably there will be errors. I welcome corrections from sharp-eyed readers or from all those who know more than I do about the issues discussed. Your feedback now will save my blushes in later editions. I would also like to hear about interesting, sly, outrageous and transformative truths you've encountered in the news, in your organization or in life. Please send me your corrections and suggestions via https://hectormacdonald.com/truth.

London, October 2017

INTRODUCTION

When Truths Collide

There is no worse lie than a truth misunderstood by those who hear it.

WILLIAM JAMES, 'The Value of Saintliness'

The Andean dilemma

For vegetarians and coeliacs, the discovery of quinoa was a kind of miracle. Here was a gluten-free seed, rich in magnesium and iron, that contained more protein than any grain, including all the essential amino acids our bodies cannot produce for themselves. NASA declared quinoa to be one of the most perfectly balanced nutrients on Earth and considered it ideal for astronauts. 'Quinoa tastes great, has a satisfying, "bouncy" texture and is one of the healthiest foodstuffs going,' raved Yotam Ottolenghi in 2007.[1] Grown in the Andes, quinoa had a story that charmed Western consumers: the Incas prized the seed so highly they deemed it sacred and named it 'the mother of all grains'; their emperor would sow the first seeds of the season with tools made of gold. The so-called 'superfood' was even celebrated by the United Nations, which declared 2013 the 'International Year of Quinoa'.

But quinoa fans were in for a disturbing revelation. Between

2006 and 2013, quinoa prices in Bolivia and Peru tripled. At first, the price rise was celebrated for raising the living standards of poor Andean farmers. Then came rumours that local people could no longer afford to eat their traditional food because of the insatiable demand from North America and Europe. The *Independent* warned in 2011 that quinoa consumption in Bolivia had 'slumped by 34 per cent over five years, with local families no longer able to afford a staple that has become a luxury'.[2] The *New York Times* cited studies showing that malnutrition in children was on the rise in quinoa-growing areas.[3] The *Guardian* raised the stakes in 2013 with a provocative headline: 'Can vegans stomach the unpalatable truth about quinoa?' It was now cheaper for poor Peruvians and Bolivians to eat 'imported junk food', the newspaper reported.[4] 'Quinoa: good for you – bad for Bolivians,' ran a 2013 *Independent* headline.[5]

The story echoed around the world, causing healthy eaters a crisis of conscience. 'The more you love quinoa, the more you hurt Peruvians and Bolivians,' claimed a headline in Canada's *Globe and Mail*.[6] On social media, vegan blogs and healthy-eating forums, people asked whether it was still OK to eat the Andean miracle seed. 'I intend to stop eating quinoa,' declared one woman:

> It's a matter of principle . . . the people for which quinoa has been a dietary staple for untold generations can no longer afford to eat it because people like me have created such a demand for its export and driven the price up . . . We will survive without it. I will survive without it.[7]

The idea that high quinoa prices, inflated by global demand, had disadvantaged local people in Bolivia and Peru was credible and widely accepted. But it didn't seem right to economists Marc Bellemare, Seth Gitter and Johanna Fajardo-Gonzalez. After all, a lot of foreign money was now pouring into Bolivia and Peru thanks to the quinoa trade, much of it ending up in some of the poorest parts of South America. Not many other crops grow well 14,000 feet above sea level, so surely the quinoa boom was a blessing for the region?

The economists tracked down Peruvian survey data on household expenditure and split the households into those that grow and eat quinoa, those that eat it but don't grow it, and those that never touch the stuff. They found that between 2004 and 2013 the living standards of all three groups had risen, although the quinoa farmers had enjoyed the fastest growth in household expenditure. Farmers were getting richer, and they were spending their new earnings to the benefit of those around them.[8] The households that ate quinoa but didn't grow it were, on average, already twice as well off as the farmers, suggesting they could afford to pay a bit more. That's not surprising: only around 0.5 per cent of Peruvian household spending goes on quinoa. It never was a critical part of their domestic budget. 'It's really a happy story,' said Seth Gitter. 'The poorest people got the gains.'[9]

But what about that 34 per cent drop in consumption? It turns out quinoa consumption in both countries dropped slowly and steadily over a longer period than the price hike, suggesting the two trends are not significantly connected. A much more likely explanation is that Peruvians and Bolivians just wanted to eat something else for a change. Tanya Kerssen of think tank Food First said of Andean quinoa farmers, 'They get sick of eating quinoa, frankly, so they buy other foods.'[10] A Bolivian agronomist noted, 'Ten years ago they had only an Andean diet in front of them. They had no choice. But now they do and they want rice, noodles, candies, Coke, they want everything!'[11]

I went to see quinoa growing in the Colca Valley, an area of Peru that has been farmed since pre-Inca times. It is a beautiful cereal-like crop, with large seed heads of a deep red or rich golden colour. In this part of the Andes, quinoa is grown in terraced fields alongside unusual local varieties of corn and potatoes. 'The foreign demand is one hundred per cent a good thing,' declared my Peruvian guide, Jessica. 'The farmers are very happy, and anyone who wants quinoa can still afford it.' There's been a further benefit, she explained: previously, metropolitan Peruvians had tended to regard people from her region as 'peasants' for eating quinoa; but now that Americans and Europeans crave it, quinoa is considered fashionable. 'In Lima, finally, they have respect for the people of the Altiplano and our heritage.'

In a remote and inhospitable area of southwest Bolivia dominated by salt flats and dormant volcanos, I was shown much-needed local development and tourism projects that had been funded by quinoa money. Subsistence farmers, who for generations had struggled to feed their families, could now start to invest in a more ambitious future. According to José Luis Landívar Bowles, president of the Bolivian Institute of Foreign Trade, quinoa could 'help lift a lot of people out of extreme poverty'.[12]

The only concern I heard Bolivians voice about the crop in April 2017 was that expanding supply was bringing prices *down*. The area of land dedicated to quinoa cultivation in Bolivia has more than tripled, from around 50,000 hectares in 2007 to 180,000 hectares in 2016. 'For me, that is a sad epilogue, as it is unlikely prices will go back up,' Marc Bellemare told me later. 'The market functioned pretty much in Econ 101 textbook fashion, with the (temporary) extra-normal profits competed away by new producers.'

As the sun set over the picturesque Colca Valley, I asked Jessica if consumers in Europe and North America should feel guilty about eating food that might otherwise have gone to Peruvians and Bolivians. I could guess the answer, but I wanted to hear it from a local. Jessica burst out laughing and extended an arm, as if to encompass the whole bounteous valley. 'Believe me,' she smiled, 'we have a *lot* of quinoa.'

*

This odd tale of food fads, global trade and consumer angst seems, at first glance, to be a story of falsehood corrected. But in fact most of the claims made in the first half are just as true as those made in the second. Quinoa prices did triple, making it more expensive for consumers in Peru and Bolivia to buy one of their staple foods. Quinoa consumption in those countries did drop. The only thing that wasn't true was the conclusion drawn: that healthy eaters in the West were hurting poor Peruvians and Bolivians by denying them their traditional foodstuff. Yet those truths, misinterpreted as they were, might have done real damage to the people of the Altiplano. 'I've seen comments on some of these anti-quinoa articles, like, "Thanks for shining a light on the truth. I won't consume Bolivian quinoa because it's hurting these farmers,"' said Michael Wilcox, a filmmaker who made a documentary about the issue. 'Well, not consuming it is *really* going to hurt these farmers.'[13]

A set of partial truths and misunderstood numbers were strung together in a story without the right context, changing both the desirability of a foodstuff and the morality of eating it. As we will discover, partial truths, numbers, stories, context, desirability and morality are just some of the elements used by experienced communicators in all walks of life to shape reality by presenting a particular view of the world. In this case, the journalists and bloggers steering consumers away from quinoa were doing it for the noblest of reasons: they were genuinely concerned for the welfare of an impoverished people suddenly exposed to the tempestuous winds of global trade. We will encounter plenty of cases where politicians, marketers, activists and even civil servants have shaped reality with far less benevolent intentions.

Truth or truths?

Compare these statements:

The Internet makes the world's knowledge widely available.

The Internet accelerates the spread of misinformation and hatred.

Both statements are true. Yet to someone who had never heard of the Internet, the first statement would give a completely different impression to the second.

There are many sides to every story. To put the old saying another way, there is usually more than one truth to be drawn from any set of facts. We learn this from an early age: every junior debater and errant schoolchild knows how to pick the truths that best support their case. But we may not appreciate how much flexibility these different truths offer communicators. In many cases, there are a variety of genuinely – perhaps even equally – legitimate ways of describing a person, event, thing or policy.

I call them 'competing truths'.

A few years ago, I was asked to support a transformation programme at a global corporation that was going through a particularly tough patch. This was not an unusual assignment. My career in strategic communications has given me the opportunity to help dozens of world-leading companies clarify what they want to do and then explain it to their employees. I interviewed the corporation's top executives to gather their views on the state of their industry and their organization. After consolidating all the facts they'd given me, I sat down with the CEO in a plush Manhattan executive suite and asked him whether he wanted me to write the 'Golden Opportunity' story or the 'Burning Platform' story of his business.

The Golden Opportunity story would describe the exciting

new technological developments that could help the business meet growing demand in key areas of the market and so build a flourishing and profitable future. But the company would miss out on this golden opportunity unless everyone got behind the impending transformation programme. The Burning Platform story, by contrast, would reflect the recent failures of the organization and the deep cultural malaise that had resulted, leading to a vicious cycle of apathy and worsening results that could destroy the organization within five years. The only way to avoid this fate was for everyone to get behind the impending transformation programme.

Both of these stories were true. There really was a great new opportunity to flourish, and if they didn't seize it the very existence of the organization was in jeopardy. The two versions of the truth were both intended to produce the same outcome: employee support for a difficult and painful transformation. But each would create a very different impression of reality in the minds of those employees. Smart people, some of them with multiple degrees, would be persuaded by their leaders to feel either anxious or excited about the future, depending on which story the CEO chose to tell. And that mindset would colour almost everything they did, thought and felt.

The unsettling flexibility of such communications got me questioning how it can be possible to tell more than one truth about a situation, and wondering where else this phenomenon might apply. I started spotting competing truths in the news, in politicians' speeches, in advertisements, in polemical books, in Facebook newsfeeds, in campaigning literature. Some of them were used benignly to achieve shared goals. Others were clearly intended to mislead and dupe. At first, I simply recorded incidences of competing truths in a blog. But gradually I began to see recurring patterns, and that led to a more critical and comprehensive analysis of how competing truths arise. Most importantly, I understood at last how profoundly we are influenced by the competing truths others choose.

*

Wind the clock back a few years and imagine you've never heard of quinoa. You find it on a shelf in your local store and ask the nearest assistant about it. He tells you one true thing about the bag of seeds in your hand. It could be:

Quinoa is really nutritious, high in protein, fibre and minerals, and low in fat.

Or:

Buying quinoa improves the incomes of poor farmers in South America.

Or:

Buying quinoa makes it more expensive for Bolivians and Peruvians to eat their traditional food.

Or:

Quinoa farming is having a serious environmental impact on the Andes.

You are more likely to buy the quinoa if the assistant comes up with one of the first two truths than if he chooses either of the others. He has influenced your action through his selection of a particular competing truth. He has, in a small way, shaped your immediate reality.

In fact, he has done more than that. He has also shaped the way you think about quinoa. He has laid the groundwork for a set of ideas and beliefs about quinoa to crystallize in your mind. This *mindset* may continue to influence the purchases you make, the things you say and the food you eat for a long time to come.

A mindset is *a set of beliefs, ideas and opinions that we hold about ourselves and the world around us.* Our mindsets determine how we think about things and how we choose to act.

Mindsets are flexible in some respects. The part of our mindset that is concerned with quinoa will be very receptive to the first thing we hear about the foodstuff. We are easily influenced when we know nothing about a subject. But once we have established a view on quinoa, once our mindset is settled, it can be surprisingly hard to shift. If, three months after we've been told that quinoa farming is damaging the Andes, someone mentions the nutritional benefits of the seeds, we are quite likely to ignore, doubt or dismiss that information. This is a form of confirmation bias: we tend to be more receptive to new truths that fit with our existing mindsets, and resistant to those that challenge our entrenched views.

Months after that store visit, you might be having lunch with a colleague and see her choose a quinoa salad. If the original truth you heard about quinoa was the environmental-impact issue, you might be inclined to judge her harshly for her lunch choice. You might even try to persuade her to pick something else. Your mindset – shaped by that original truth – is still driving your thoughts and actions all this time later.

We all see the world through different lenses, formed largely by the different truths we hear and read. Whether intentionally or unintentionally, other people regularly steer us towards particular facets and interpretations of the truth. 'Our opinions cover a bigger space, a longer reach of time, a greater number of things, than we can directly observe,' wrote Walter Lippmann, one of the twentieth century's great political journalists and an expert user of competing truths. 'They have, therefore, to be pieced together *out of what others have reported* and what we can imagine'[14] (my emphasis). What others report contributes to our *perceived reality*. But because we act on the basis of our perceptions, what others report also impacts *objective reality*.

Competing truths shape reality.

Competing truths inform our mindsets, and our mindsets determine our subsequent choices and actions. We vote, shop, work, cooperate and fight according to what we believe to be true. Some truths stay with us for life, determining the most important choices we make and defining the very nature of our character. Whether we are faced with a police shooting, a company mission statement, a group of refugees, a presidential candidate, a holy book, a scientific finding, a contentious statue or a natural disaster, our response – which may be dramatic, transformative or violent – will stem from our mindset.

It is therefore no exaggeration to say that much of what we think and do is determined by the competing truths we hear and read. If we care about the influences that drive us to buy a product, support a politician, denounce a public figure or fight for a cause, we need to understand how competing truths work and what we can do about them. This book will answer both questions.

The king's speech

When George VI delivered his radio address to Britain and its Empire at the start of the Second World War, his stammer was not the only reason for brevity. The king's words needed to resonate with people of all backgrounds, cultures and educations. A great number of his listeners were not native English speakers and might struggle to follow a long account of recent events. Many wouldn't understand the geopolitical complexities that had led to Britain's declaration of war. Nevertheless, the king's appeal to his subjects to 'stand calm and firm and united' was surprisingly simple. The full address is just over 400 words long. The factual part is less than half of that:

> For the second time in the lives of most of us we are at war. Over and over again we have tried to find a peaceful way out of the differences between ourselves and those who are now our enemies. But it has been in vain. We have been forced into a conflict for

we are called, with our allies, to meet the challenge of a principle which if it were to prevail would be fatal to any civilised order in the world. It is the principle which permits a state, in the selfish pursuit of power, to disregard its treaties and its solemn pledges which sanction the use of force or threat of force against the sovereignty and independence of other states. Such a principle, stripped of all disguise, is surely the mere primitive doctrine that might is right.[15]

Think about what he's left out: German rearmament, the violation of the Treaty of Versailles, the Nazi pacts with Italy and the Soviet Union, the remilitarization of the Rhineland and the occupation of Czechoslovakia. Astonishingly, he doesn't even mention Germany, Hitler or the invasion of Poland. Instead, the king focuses on a moral claim that has universal appeal.

Despite the obvious factual omissions and the highly selective focus, few would suggest that George VI was misrepresenting the situation. He was voicing a set of truths that were perfectly chosen to steady an empire and prepare his people for war. More information would not have been more honest – it would have merely diluted the message.

So competing truths can be used constructively. Responsible marketers address different messages to different consumer segments, focusing on the product benefits that are most relevant to each segment. Doctors tell their patients the medical facts they need to know to manage their condition, without burdening them with complex details of cell biology or pharmacology. Social justice advocates, environmental campaigners, clerics, public health authorities and leaders of all kinds have to select the right competing truth to win hearts and minds and so achieve their important goals.

Toothpaste and breast cancer

For many years, Colgate-Palmolive ran advertisements claiming that 'more than 80 per cent of dentists recommend Colgate'.[16] Consumers naturally assumed the survey data behind this claim measured the proportion of dentists who recommended Colgate toothpaste *in preference to other brands*. In fact, dentists were being asked which brands (plural) they would recommend, and most named several; a competitor brand was recommended almost as often as Colgate. The thing being measured was not what we had been led to believe, and Colgate-Palmolive's slogan was eventually banned by the Advertising Standards Authority – even though it was true.[17]

Where George VI used competing truths to give a highly simplified but honest account of reality, and the quinoa bloggers innocently cited competing truths that distorted reality, Colgate-Palmolive's marketers deliberately deployed a competing truth that misled consumers. They are not alone. Politicians are adept at spinning truths in a way that creates a false impression. Newspapers bend the truth in attention-grabbing headlines, then straighten it out again in the less-read body of the story. Activists cherry-pick truths that support their campaign, even when they misrepresent a greater truth.

'The only thing I don't believe in is lying,' says Frank Luntz, a master of competing truths whom we shall meet properly later. 'Beyond that, you can use almost anything.'[18]

People are out to mislead you with the truth in all walks of life. Even, in some cases, the people you should be able to rely on for impartial, essential advice . . .

Breast cancer is the second most common cancer among American women, and after lung cancer the second most fatal. So when the Texas Department of State Health Services (DSHS) published a booklet for pregnant women in 2016 making a link between abortion and breast cancer, many pro-choice readers were understandably alarmed. The booklet, entitled 'A Woman's Right to Know', has a section headed 'Abortion risks'. The five risks listed include Death, Future Infertility and . . . 'Breast Cancer Risk'. Here's the official Texas health advice:

> Your pregnancy history affects your chances of getting breast cancer. If you give birth to your baby, you are less likely to develop breast cancer in the future. Research indicates that having an abortion will not provide you this increased protection against breast cancer.[19]

It is true that women who give birth early in life seem to have a lower risk of developing breast cancer. It is *not* true that abortion increases the risk of breast cancer, according to all the best research in the field. The American Cancer Society says, 'The scientific evidence does not support the notion that abortion of any kind raises the risk of breast cancer or any other type of cancer.'[20] The US government's National Cancer Institute agrees: 'Studies consistently showed no association between induced and spontaneous abortions and breast cancer risk.'[21]

But then, the Texas DSHS does not actually claim that abortion causes cancer. It merely implies it. The government officials responsible for the booklet might as well have stated that, 'Avoiding pregnancy altogether will not provide you this increased protection against breast cancer.' The words the Texas DSHS selected are true, but they are clearly intended to suggest something that is not true. A political agenda has superseded the impartial health advice Texans have a right to expect from their state government.

'The wording in Texas gets very cute,' observes Otis Brawley, the chief medical officer at the American Cancer Society. 'It's technically correct, but it is deceiving.'[22]

A powerful tool for good or ill

Everyone has an agenda, and it is only natural for communicators to select truths that further their agenda. But this can be done ethically or deceitfully: communicators can choose whether to convey an impression of reality that is in line with objective reality or one that deliberately distorts it. Moreover, their agenda may be aligned with or opposed to their audience's interests; it may be benign or malevolent. Competing truths are morally neutral: like a loaded gun or a box of matches, the way they are used determines their impact. We will encounter competing truths used in all kinds of ways, for good purposes and bad.

To keep things simple, we can think about three types of communicators:

Advocates: selecting competing truths that create a reasonably accurate impression of reality in order to achieve a constructive goal.

Misinformers: innocently propagating competing truths that unintentionally distort reality.

Misleaders: deliberately deploying competing truths to create an impression of reality that they know is not true.

In the cases discussed, George VI was an Advocate, the quinoa campaigners were Misinformers, and Colgate-Palmolive's marketers were Misleaders.

The Texas DSHS might look like an Advocate to someone with pro-life views. But if the intention of the Texas DSHS was to create a false impression of the best current scientific understanding, then it too is a Misleader. Anyone who deliberately sets out to create a distorted impression of reality is a Misleader, regardless of the righteousness of their agenda or the truthfulness of their words.

'It turns out that lies are often unnecessary,' observed the BBC broadcaster Evan Davis, who has interviewed plenty of Misleaders.

'A remarkable amount of powerful deception can be practised without any lies being told.'[23]

Occasionally, communicators may have good reasons for misleading. Troop commanders may need to gloss over the likely danger of a military manoeuvre to keep morale high. Public health officials may need to downplay the risk of an epidemic to avoid widespread panic. 'Politicians are obliged from time to time to conceal the full truth, to bend it and even distort it, where the interests of the bigger strategic goal demand it be done,' conceded Tony Blair.[24] You may feel the Texas DSHS was right to mislead if it saved unborn lives. It is not my purpose to tell you what is right or wrong but only to point out the need to consider the ethical dimension of such communications. You can decide for yourself whether misleading truths are ever justified.

Briefly, for the philosophers

Truth is a much-debated topic among philosophers. They argue over the relationship between truth and knowledge, the objectivity and universalism of truth, the place of truth in religion, and much else besides. There are plenty of books that cover such matters, but this isn't one of them. I've read a few, and frankly they make my head hurt.

This book is intended to be a practical guide for communicators wanting to use true statements to persuade and inspire, and for anyone concerned that truths are being used to mislead them. It is not a work of philosophy. That said, now might be a good time to clarify what I mean by *truths*.

There are truths that are based in fact, and these ought to be fairly uncontroversial.* The date of India's independence or the boiling point of water are examples of factual truths that can

---

* I realize this is unrealistic in our partisan, post-truth world.

be ascertained through research or scientific measurement. But people make plenty of statements that are not based in fact yet are nevertheless not falsehoods or lies. We talk about whether something is good or desirable, or how much it is worth. These are often subjective judgements, but we treat them like truths and might be inclined to argue with anyone who told us they were not true – at least for us. The same can be said for some of our predictions about the future, and some of our ideological or religious beliefs.

A definition of truth that incorporates subjective judgement, prediction and belief may be too broad for some tastes. But a book limited to factual truths would not give us a full understanding of how communicators shape reality by using true (or at least non-false) statements to persuade people to think and act in particular ways. If a respected food critic tells me that a particular dish is delicious, I'm happy to treat his judgement as a true statement and order accordingly. If an experienced civil engineer shouts, 'This building is going to collapse!' I will take her prediction as a true statement and start running for my life.

This book, then, is concerned not only with factual truths but also with those statements we act on *as if they are true*. For simplicity, I will refer to such beliefs, assertions, judgements and predictions as 'truths', by which I simply mean they are not known to be untrue. Communicators make credible non-factual statements all the time, so it's important to understand when they are valid and how they might be used to influence us. 'There are truths which are not for all men, nor for all times,' wrote Voltaire; this book seeks to include them.

My scope may be broad, but it does not include falsehoods. We will not be looking at lies, alternative facts, conspiracy theories, fake news or all the other suffocating detritus of the post-truth era. The many writers, commentators and journalists busy calling out the liars and fabricators of our age are doing sterling work.

We will concentrate instead on those Misleaders who hide behind a fig leaf of truth.

A last word to any philosophers still reading. My talk of competing truths may have you suspecting I am a diabolical relativist who believes any truth is as good as any other, or that truths are really just opinions. Rest assured, I am not. I take an absolutist view of factual truths: the Truth is out there, even if we can only grasp fragments of it. When it comes to moral and value judgements, however, I take a somewhat more relativist position, as will become clear. Regarding the limits of personal knowledge, I am willing to accept well-reported facts as truths, even if I have not witnessed them myself. So I am perfectly content to say it is true that Ghana is a country in Africa, that David Bowie is dead, and that pigs can't fly. If you are the kind of sceptic who distrusts statements like these, this book is probably not for you.

Four classes of competing truth

Truth will take us on a tour of the wonderfully diverse, creative and occasionally outrageous world of competing truths. Among other illustrative cases, we will look at the way Israeli schools teach history, the portrayal of narcotics over the decades, the strange new appeal of failure, how feminism is best defined, what happened after Hurricane Katrina, how politicians can argue that wages have both gone up and gone down, and why the introduction of autonomous vehicles will be a testing time for legislators. We will encounter numerous kinds of competing truth in politics, business, the media and everyday life. And we'll look at some of the communications tactics used by both Advocates and Misleaders.

By the end, you should be well equipped to spot and neutralize the misleading truths that are all around you, and to communicate more effectively with family, friends and colleagues. Interpreting truth wisely and speaking truth compellingly will almost certainly make you richer, happier, better governed and more attractive (that's a prediction, not a factual truth, so don't hold me to it).

The book has four parts:

Part One: Partial truths

Most of our statements, while true, do not convey the whole truth. Partial truths stem from the **complexity** of even the most mundane subjects and are an unavoidable feature of the way we communicate. Our understanding of **history** is shaped by partial truths, and it in turn shapes us. **Context** can be critical to a proper understanding of things and events, but it can be described in markedly different ways. Statistics and other **numbers** are a rich source of competing truths in a world where many of us don't always understand what those numbers mean. We have evolved to communicate largely in **story** form, but our stories necessarily leave out a lot of relevant detail.

Part Two: Subjective truths

People will fight for what is right. They will crawl over broken glass for the object of their desire. And they will queue around the block for a great price. To say that something is good or desirable or financially valuable is to voice a subjective truth. And because it is subjective, it can be changed. As we are for the most part motivated by perceived **morality, desirability** and **financial value**, understanding how to alter someone's subjective truths may be the key to understanding how to persuade them to act differently.

Part Three: Artificial truths

Language is notoriously flexible. It can mean what we want it to mean if we apply **definitions** that suit us to the words we use.

Similarly, the **names** we give products, events and policies can determine their success or failure. Both names and definitions are man-made – they are artificial truths. Communicators who establish new names or definitions to suit their purposes are in effect forging new truths. Humans are good at forging abstract things, be they currencies, companies, political entities or brands. And because they are human inventions, these **social constructs** are truths that can be easily modified.

Part Four: Unknown truths

When it comes to decisions on investment, marriage, education and much else in life, we act according to the **predictions** that we find most convincing. Such predictions may vary widely, and different people will adopt different ideas about the future. Until time passes and we find out which is right, they remain competing truths. We may never discover the real truth about religious and ideological **beliefs**, yet these are equally important motivators of millions. As long as we can't prove them false, beliefs are for many of us a form of truth.

Select your truth and change the world

In his dystopian novel *Nineteen Eighty-Four*, George Orwell imagined a nightmarish society where bureaucrats from the 'Ministry of Truth' distort reality by disseminating lies and creating fictitious accounts of the past. A restrictive new language and the 'Thought Police' prevent citizens from thinking critically about government propaganda. Orwell's protagonist, Winston Smith, desperately tries to resist the government's lies, telling himself, 'There was truth and there was untruth, and if you clung to the truth even against the whole world, you were not mad.'

Just as Orwell's dystopian vision of omnipresent surveillance seems to be coming true in a rather different form than the one he imagined, thanks to social media and wearable technology, so his fears for the integrity of the truth are turning out to be well founded but misdirected. It is not simply that we are being lied to; the more insidious problem is that we are routinely misled by the truth.

Life feels simpler when, like Winston Smith, we tell ourselves there is a single truth and everything else is a deviation from that truth – an error, a lie, an 'untruth'. It's disturbing to imagine that we can shape reality simply by choosing a different truth. The very idea of competing truths feels slippery, disingenuous, conniving.

Yet their impact can be immense.

Competing truths are found in almost every area of human activity, and the examples I will draw on reflect that diversity. It is in the nature of this subject that some of the examples will, like the Texas DSHS's advice to pregnant women, be political or controversial. It shouldn't matter whether you agree with my point of view in any one example but rather that you see the potential for different truths to be expressed and the consequences when they are.

Shaping reality through competing truths can be disorientating and confusing, especially when we challenge the validity of things we have long taken for granted. It can be exasperating and pedantic, as when statistics and definitions are used in artful but underhand ways. It can be exhilarating and enlightening when our understanding of the world suddenly shifts and new possibilities open up. Above all, competing truths are meaningful and relevant to all of us and, whether we like it or not, they are affecting our lives every day. We owe it to ourselves and our society to get better at recognizing them, using them responsibly and if necessary resisting them.

In practice

There is usually more than one true way to talk about something. We can use competing truths constructively to engage people and inspire action, but we should also watch out for communicators who use competing truths to mislead us. At the end of each chapter, you will find brief practical guidelines on how to do both these things.

Using competing truths frequently raises ethical issues and so, rather than address these in every chapter, let's begin by establishing a simple rule of thumb:

If your audience knew everything you know about your subject, would they think you had portrayed it fairly?

If you can answer yes to that, you're probably on the right track.

Alongside this rule of thumb, I have three criteria for an ethical communication:

1. It is factually correct.

2. It is intended to achieve a constructive outcome which the audience would support.

3. It will not cause members of the audience to act in a way that harms them.

You may have different criteria – my plea is that you have *some* criteria to ensure you don't end up a Misleader . . . unless that is what you are determined to be.

PART ONE

PARTIAL
TRUTHS

Complexity

Truth is the shattered mirror strown in myriad bits; while each believes his little bit the whole to own.

RICHARD BURTON, *The Kasidah of Haji Abdu El-Yezdi*

Reality is complicated

On the table is an egg.

A simple, unambiguous statement.

Can you picture that egg?

Close your eyes for a moment and see the egg on a plain white table top.

How confident are you that you're seeing the same egg as me?

Did you think of a chicken egg?

Why not a duck egg? Or an ostrich egg? How about an egg from a dinosaur, or a frog, or a sturgeon? Why not a human egg?

Or how about a jewelled Fabergé egg, a chocolate Easter egg or Humpty Dumpty?

Go back to the chicken egg. Did you see a whole egg in its shell, or was the egg cooked on a plate? Was it fried, scrambled or poached? If it was a complete egg, fresh from the box, did you see just the shell, or did you visualize the yolk and albumen? Did you think about the scrap of blood, the proteins and fats, the molecular structure of the different materials inside, the DNA and the thousands of genes it bears, the multitude of cellular processes they encode, the trillions of atoms, the astounding complexity of chemical pathways?

What about the symbolism, uses and cultural baggage of that egg? Did you think of a new beginning, a spark of creation? A representation of our entire universe? Perhaps you thought of cakes and meringues, or memorable egg scenes in *Cool Hand Luke* or *Happy Feet*? Did you see the egg as a protestor's weapon or a savings vehicle? Did you see a painting of an egg, and, if so, is that actually an egg?

Eggs, it turns out, are complicated things.

In 1986, the *Guardian* newspaper ran a TV and cinema advert that has stuck in my mind like few others. In newsreel black and white, it showed a skinhead running away from an approaching car. The soundtrack was completely silent except for an authoritative voiceover: 'An event seen from one point of view gives one impression.' The same man is then shown from a different angle: he runs straight at a businessman, seemingly set on attacking him or stealing his briefcase. 'Seen from another point of view it gives quite a different impression.' Another cut, and we see the scene from above. A suspended load of construction material is juddering over the businessman's head, out of control. The skinhead hauls the businessman aside, saving his life as the load crashes to the ground. 'But it's only when you get the whole picture you can fully understand what's going on,' concludes the voiceover.

Created by John Webster of BMP, 'points of view' is still cited as one of the best TV adverts ever made. A sizeable British audience came away with the strong suggestion that only the *Guardian* presents the world as it really is, rather than showing a single, politically motivated side of the story. It's a compelling pitch and proved to be so successful that the newspaper returned to the 'whole picture' theme in a 2012 campaign.

The trouble is, no one really has the whole picture. Life is far too complicated for that.

Look out of the nearest window. What did you see? How many cars were there? What colour and make? How many different species of plants? Were there any manhole covers visible? What materials were the buildings constructed from? How many of their windows were open?

If fully describing the view from your window is hard, try summing up a single individual. Is your daughter, niece or sister doing better than her peers at school? If so, you're most likely thinking of the grades she's getting or perhaps the track races she's winning. But are these really sufficient measures to assess a multi-faceted, fast-changing human being? How is her moral development coming along? Is she choosing healthy lunch options? How many likes do her selfies get?

Our heads would explode if we tried to take in all the available information before forming a practical understanding of our reality. We have no choice but to simplify and select. All of us do it all the time. But the thing about selecting facets of our world to represent reality is that each of us may do it differently. You might look out of the window and see five different species of tree; I might see manhole covers.

We are looking at the same world, but our understanding of it is radically different. We are like the blind men who encounter an elephant in the old Jain story:

the one who touches a leg says an elephant is like a pillar;
the one who touches the tail says an elephant is like a rope;
the one who touches the trunk says an elephant is like the
    branch of a tree;
the one who touches the flank says an elephant is like a wall;
the one who touches the tusk says an elephant is like a pipe;
the one who touches the ear says an elephant is like a hand fan.

How do we decide what to include in our sample of reality? We may select unconsciously, based on our interests or natural biases, or whatever is currently on our mind. We may focus on the things that make sense to us or that fit with our mindset, discarding or downplaying the ideas and data that conflict with our current understanding of the world. Or we may purposefully select those facets of reality that fit our agenda.

Driving test

Sometime soon our legislators will be faced with a question along these lines: 'Should we allow privately owned autonomous vehicles (AVs) on the streets of our cities?'

How should they respond?

So far, driverless cars have been a curiosity for most. Google is doing something, Tesla something else. The big auto companies have their own programmes. You may have seen video of Google's strange pod-like vehicles. Perhaps their design has influenced your opinion? You may have heard that someone died in a Tesla vehicle operating in autopilot mode. Perhaps *that* influenced your opinion?

Responsible legislators would probably ask for more information from civil servants, interested parties and political advisers before making their decision. They might hear a range of competing truths from different people:

An economist: AVs could be a big new industry that will stimulate technological development and consumer demand, boosting economic growth. AVs will also free up billions of hours of drivers' time for more productive work or more consumption of digital entertainment, both of which would contribute to the economy.

A trade union representative: Because AVs don't need drivers, millions of jobs will be lost in the haulage and taxi industries, increasing inequality as profits accrue to Uber and UPS at the expense of ordinary working people.

An environmentalist: AVs will reduce the cost of taxis and increase the attractiveness of alternative mobility models, so fewer people will buy cars, reducing both congestion and energy and resource consumption. AVs also drive more efficiently than humans, reducing emissions and wear.

A safety expert: Every year, nearly 1.3 million people die in road accidents, most of them caused by human error. Although some AV accidents will occur due to software glitches or inadequate perception of hazards, we will still be much safer on the roads if humans are not in control.

A political consultant: Voters are much more tolerant of long-standing problems than new problems. If AV systems failures lead to the deaths of a few hundred people on our streets, that may be politically unacceptable, even if the total number of road deaths is lower than before.

An AV manufacturer: Actually, there are many different types of AV. Some require human participation alongside 'advanced driver-assistance systems', some provide optional human controls, while others have no human interface at all. This is not a binary issue but a question of how much autonomy you are prepared to allow.

An insurance provider: Motor insurance will have to shift from individual driver cover for human error to manufacturer cover for technical failure, potentially wreaking havoc in the General Insurance industry.

A city planner: AVs don't need to be parked in the city centre, so we can turn acres of premium city land currently devoted to parking spaces into profitable developments or amenities such as parks and playgrounds.

A city administrator: We depend on parking revenues to pay for city services. If people no longer need to park their cars, we will have to raise municipal taxes or cut services, hurting the most vulnerable.

A business leader: AVs will one day be standard all around the world. The sooner we allow them on our roads, the greater the head start and competitive advantage our nation's companies will have in the emerging global AV industry.

A security expert: AVs are vulnerable to hacking. We could wake up to find our vehicles have all been disabled or commandeered by terrorists or hostile states.

A moral philosopher: We will need to programme AVs for dire situations where they must choose, for example, between smashing into a child that has run into the road or driving off the road and potentially killing the passengers. As legislators, you will have to decide what AVs should do in a multitude of dreadful situations.

Such wide-ranging consultation might give legislators a reasonably balanced view of a highly complex subject, if not necessarily an easy decision. But suppose, as is common, the legislators were busy with other issues and each of them relied on a single adviser to brief them. They might only get one dominant perspective on the issue. They would be like the blind men encountering the elephant, each gaining only a partial – and possibly misleading – understanding.

Now imagine that the question was put to a referendum. If politicians struggle to take on board all the relevant aspects of an issue, how likely is it that most voters would make the time to research every perspective?

The complexity of issues like this, combined with the speed and short attention span of modern life, means that we can only consider a few facets of any subject in most discussions. But unless we make sure we hear from a range of voices, we will not get anywhere close to a full picture of reality.

Most people do not. We get our news and opinion from a narrow set of sources. We tend to discuss issues with friends or colleagues who agree with us. Confirmation bias is widespread. We subconsciously filter out ideas or data that contradict what we believe. That leaves us vulnerable to highly selective portrayals of vitally important issues. On far too many issues, we hear only a small proportion of the available competing truths.

A photograph is a handy analogy for a competing truth.

When you take a picture, your camera will capture exactly what is in front of it. But you have the opportunity to shape photographic reality in so many ways. You choose what to include in the frame. You can use zoom to change the scale relationship between the elements in the frame, focus on one element rather than another, illuminate with flash or deliberately under-expose. After the photograph is taken, you can use digital processing tools to lighten one part of the picture and darken another, to change colours, to add contrast, to make the picture more or less grainy.

The camera never lies . . . but you can take a thousand different pictures of the same scene.

Just as you must choose what to include in a photograph, so you can choose to leave out undesirable elements. Don't like Aunty Doreen? Move the camera or crop the image and it's as if she never existed. We do the same thing in our communications.

Our busy legislator consults her special adviser, who has read everything there is to know about autonomous vehicles. The adviser would have to be heroically unbiased to give appropriate weight to all of those different perspectives, rather than favouring those which support his own agenda. An adviser who has invested in AV manufacturers is unlikely to dwell on the hacking threat or the expected job losses. On the other hand, an adviser married to a taxi driver may well play down the environmental and safety benefits of AVs.

Similarly, once the legislator has made up her mind, how will she defend her position in Parliament, Congress or the media? She might briefly acknowledge one or two of the issues on the other side of the debate, but she will devote most of her speeches and briefings to the points that support her position.

Complexity tactic #1
Omission

Omission is a natural tactic for all of us. We don't post unflattering pictures on Facebook. We don't tell first dates about our snoring or our troublesome relatives. The more complex a subject, the greater the opportunity to omit unhelpful truths – there is just so much else to say!

All too often, as we will see, omission is used to hide important truths and distort reality. Asset managers set up a range of different funds but only publicize the growth rates of the best-performing ones. Medical administrators celebrate a reduction in cancer deaths but don't mention a rise in hospital-acquired infections. Food packaging boldly declares healthy ingredients while relegating the unhealthy stuff to the small print on the back.

But omission doesn't have to be misleading. Manufacturers and retailers of PCs could bewilder us with a million highly technical features and design details that distinguish their models from those of their competitors. But they know we couldn't cope with that much information. So they omit most of it and focus on a few simple metrics like memory capacity and processor speed. All the other subtle differences between one product and another are invisible to us, and for that we are grateful.

The complexity store

'Is Amazon Really the Devil?' asked *Publishers Weekly* in 2014,[1] when publisher Hachette went to war with the retail giant over the right to set its own prices for e-books. 'Some book professionals and publishers,' noted the industry magazine with admirable balance, 'take issue with the conventional wisdom that Amazon is the devil incarnate.'

Bookstores have, quite understandably, long detested Amazon. The online retailer has contributed to the demise of many of them. James Daunt, managing director of British chain Waterstones, characterized Amazon as 'a ruthless, money-making devil'.[2] Authors who have built large readerships through the handselling efforts of many a bricks-and-mortar bookseller decry their loss. 'Amazon aggressively wants to kill us,' said author and bookstore founder Ann Patchett.[3] Scott Turow, then president of the US Authors Guild, called Amazon 'the Darth Vader of the literary world'.[4]

Meanwhile, publishers who once welcomed the extra sales Amazon brought them now fear the dominance the online giant has achieved in their industry. The dispute with Hachette was only the most public of a number of battles fought over sales terms. When Amazon began 'sanctioning' Hachette authors, delaying shipping of their books and guiding shoppers away from their pages, more than 900 authors signed a protest letter. The campaign group Authors United called on the US Department of Justice to investigate the retailer: 'Amazon has used its dominance in ways that we believe harm the interests of America's readers, impoverish the book industry as a whole, damage the careers of (and generate fear among) many authors, and impede the free flow of ideas in our society.'[5]

On the other hand, many authors and small publishers see Amazon as their saviour. The Kindle Direct Publishing (KDP) platform allows authors, plenty of whom had been rejected or dropped by conventional publishers, to publish their own e-books and keep 70 per cent of the sales price – a far bigger share than they would ever have received from the likes of Penguin Random House or Hachette. Such authors, according to Jonathan Derbyshire of *Prospect* magazine, regard Amazon as the 'midwife to a gigantic democratization of the means of literary production and distribution'. A survey of members by the UK's Society of Authors received 'many more replies praising Amazon than attempting to bury it'.[6]

'More people are buying more books than ever, and more people are making a living by writing them,' observes author Barry Eisler. 'Why do millionaire authors want to destroy the one company that's made this all possible?'[7]

Small publishers can also use the KDP platform for their e-books and can sell their printed editions to readers across the globe, receiving payment within 30 days, something few other booksellers and distributors offer. Any author or publisher whose titles end up in the 'long tail' of publications that would never normally appear on bookstore shelves has reason to be grateful to Amazon. Similarly, while some readers mourn the loss of their local bookstores, others rejoice in the lower prices and greater choice Amazon brings. With its popular Kindle series of e-readers, the retailer has done more to promote e-books than any other company and in the process has arguably encouraged millions more people to read books.

Of course, I'm simplifying. There are many other things one could say about Amazon's impact on the book industry. Did you know that Amazon also operates an e-book 'lending library' and has now become a publisher? Such is the complexity of the business that authors, publishers, booksellers and readers can form entirely different opinions – and convey entirely different messages – about Amazon, depending on which of the many competing truths they hear and choose to propagate.

And that's just books.

What about all the other things Amazon sells?

What about all the other things Amazon *does*?

Amazon Marketplace allows millions of other businesses and individuals to sell directly to Amazon customers, opening up a valuable route to market for budding entrepreneurs. Amazon will even store their inventory and fulfil orders on their behalf.

Amazon streams video and music and makes its own TV shows and movies.

Amazon owns Whole Foods.

Amazon operates the biggest public Cloud, with 34 per cent of the Cloud Services market in 2017 (Microsoft was second with just 11 per cent).[8] Amazon Web Services (AWS) is able to offer Cloud storage so cheaply and reliably that even companies like GE and Apple are using it in place of in-house servers. Countless Internet start-ups depend on AWS, making the service as important to web entrepreneurs as Marketplace is to early-stage retailers. All kinds of industry-disrupting businesses will, like Airbnb and Netflix, transform our world from Amazon's Cloud. Even the CIA uses it.

We don't have time to talk about the way Amazon operates, but its working conditions and tax affairs would add a plethora of further truths to this brief portrait of the company. What lies ahead? Delivery by drone, a marketplace for services, a consumer logistics business, a new global payment system, 3-D printing, artificial intelligence – more complexity that might challenge even Alexa's understanding of her company.

So what is Amazon? That depends on which truths you

prioritize. Bookstore destroyer, saviour of authors, monopolistic bully, small-business enabler, grocery store, tax avoider, reading promoter, movie studio, tech innovator, tyrannical employer, virtual marketplace, global distributor or consumer champion. Take your pick. The chances are you won't have the time or inclination to recall all the many facets of the company when you next hear its name or see its branded packaging on your doormat. One or two key truths will predominate. What is Amazon? You choose.

Exploiting complexity

Haters of Amazon may be seething by now. They may feel I am watering down or confusing their particular concern by talking about all these other facets of the company. So what if Amazon provides cheap Cloud services to start-ups? That doesn't make up for the damage they've done to my local bookstore!

This is another key tactic communicators use to shape reality. Rather than omitting uncomfortable truths, they bury them in a mass of other truths. *It's true that our tax reform policy will disadvantage disabled people, but let me talk about all the groups who will be better off.*

An Advocate might use this tactic to dilute an unfavourable truth with a number of *equally relevant* but more agreeable competing truths. An impartial listener could then conclude that, on balance, the unfavourable truth was outweighed by the other points.

A Misleader might use *irrelevant* truths to achieve the same outcome. *Yes, it's true that our tax reform policy will disadvantage disabled people, but more people with disabilities are employed than ever before, and technology is increasingly helping people overcome their disabilities.* All three statements are truths, and they seem related; the interpretation might be that because of better employment and technological prospects, disabled people need less government help. But in fact, the second and third truth do nothing to mitigate the first: disabled people will be disadvantaged by this policy, end of conversation.

Complexity tactic #2
Obfuscation

One of the most dramatic and damaging cases of obfuscation in recent years occurred in South Africa, where the extraordinarily wealthy Gupta family had come under investigation by the media for its apparent power and influence over national politics. The Guptas' close ties to President Jacob Zuma had led to allegations of 'state capture' – systemic political corruption where private interests largely control government activities. The nation was shocked to discover that the Guptas had been permitted to make personal use of a South African air force base. By 2016, President Zuma was forced to deny in parliament that he let the Guptas select government ministers.

In early 2016, a Gupta-owned company, Oakbay Investments, hired Bell Pottinger, a British PR firm notorious for working with some deeply unsavoury clients. The firm's truth-omitting tactics had been revealed a few years earlier when research by the Bureau of Investigative Journalism showed that someone using a Bell Pottinger computer had been deleting negative content on their clients' Wikipedia pages.[9] Oakbay commissioned Bell Pottinger to promote across South Africa 'a narrative around the existence of "economic apartheid"* and the need for more "economic emancipation".'[10] The cynical purpose of this £100,000/month assignment was, it seems, to divert attention from the Gupta

---

* *Apartheid* was the system of racial segregation enforced until 1991; it remains a highly emotive word in South Africa.

state-capture scandal. Bell Pottinger was to get the whole country thinking about something else and focusing on a different enemy: 'White Monopoly Capital'.

Whether or not Bell Pottinger deliberately rebooted this old but still toxic term is as yet unclear. But leaked emails between Bell Pottinger and Oakbay reveal the PR firm's intention to 'strategise the appropriate engagement tactics, be this radio, social media and/or slogans e.g. #Endeconomicapartheid'.[11] From the outset, the historically charged language was central to their campaign.

Bell Pottinger has since been accused of creating fake news, but in fact much of the incendiary material the firm promoted was factually accurate. More than a quarter of a century after the end of political apartheid in South Africa, the majority of the country's wealth is still in the hands of the white minority. Studying South Africa's income distribution in 2015, economist Thomas Piketty found the 'same structure of racial inequality'[12] as during the apartheid era. In the words of Victoria Geoghegan, the partner who ran the campaign, Bell Pottinger would 'utilise compelling research, case studies and data which illustrate the apartheid that still exists'.[13]

So the speeches, social media posts and slogans that Bell Pottinger manufactured were, in the main part, truths. But the reason why the firm was being paid so handsomely to circulate them was to deflect attention away from the Guptas. They were truths deployed deliberately to muddy the waters in a highly charged political environment.

Tragically for a country already beset by social and political problems, the economic-apartheid narrative was all too successful. A surge of anger against 'White Monopoly Capital' spread across South Africa, and by 2017 Bell Pottinger was facing accusations of running a racially divisive campaign that had undone the painstaking work of years of reconciliation. After prestigious clients started to abandon the firm, Geoghegan was fired, the CEO resigned and Bell Pottinger went into administration. A firm re-nowned for its ability to shape reality was ultimately unable to save its own reputation. The lesson for other Misleaders is clear: if you must obfuscate, be very careful what extraneous truths you bring into play – they might come back to haunt you.

> **Complexity tactic #3**
> *Association*

If obfuscation allows Misleaders to bury bad news in a deluge of other truths, association enables them to give the impression of a meaningful connection between two or more truths where none exists.

This text accompanied the photo of a former British cabinet minister in a 2017 *Times* article critical of a certain green energy policy:

> Green subsidies for wood pellets were championed by Chris Huhne when he was energy and climate change secretary. Mr Huhne, 62, was jailed in 2013 for perverting the course of justice.[14]

Chris Huhne was convicted for lying about a driving offence. It had absolutely nothing to do with green subsidies. By combining the two unrelated truths, *The Times* creates the impression that Huhne was acting malignly, or even criminally, in promoting this policy. A more relevant truth appears three paragraphs down: Huhne 'is now European chairman of Zilkha Biomass, a US supplier of wood pellets'. Had *The Times* used that truth in their photo credit, they could have more honestly cast aspersions on the former cabinet minister's motivation; perhaps the editors felt the industry job wouldn't have hammered home their point as robustly as the unrelated jail term.

When George W. Bush wanted to make the case for war against Iraq in a televised address delivered one year after the 9/11 attacks, he chose to link al Qaeda and Iraq like this:

> We know that Iraq is continuing to finance terror and gives assistance to groups that use terrorism to undermine Middle East peace. We know that Iraq and the al Qaeda terrorist network share a common enemy – the United States of America. We know that Iraq and al Qaeda have had high-level contacts that go back a decade. Some al Qaeda leaders who fled Afghanistan went to Iraq. These include one very senior al Qaeda leader who received medical treatment in Baghdad this year, and who has been associated with planning for chemical and biological attacks. We've learned that Iraq has trained al Qaeda members in bomb-making and poisons and deadly gases.[15]

Each of these statements, as far as I know, was true. Taken together, they gave the impression that Iraq was financing al Qaeda, that al Qaeda was operating out of Iraq and that al Qaeda was cooperating with Iraq on shared plans to attack the United States. None of those things were true, and Bush did not actually say them. He didn't need to. By intertwining carefully selected truths from a highly complex situation, he let his audience across the nation reach their own conclusions.

Association can be used by Misleaders to wreck entire projects and campaigns. Rudy Giuliani's bid for the 2008 Republican presidential nomination was badly hurt by the personal misdeeds of several key allies. For most of 2007, Giuliani led the field in the Republican primary race. But in June, his state chairman in South Carolina, Thomas Ravenel, was indicted on charges of distributing cocaine. The following month, Southern Region campaign chair David Vitter was accused of using a prostitution service. Later. in the year, another long-time ally, Bernard Kerik, was indicted for tax fraud. Giuliani could not be blamed for – or be expected to have known of – any of these activities, and yet they provided powerful ammunition for his opponents. 'Cocaine, corruption and prostitution,'[16] began a *New York Times* piece on Giuliani in July 2007. The association of these partial truths with the presidential hopeful's campaign undoubtedly contributed to its collapse.

A similar pattern of guilt by association nearly destroyed Barack Obama's presidential candidacy the following year. ABC News drew attention to select passages from the sermons of his then pastor, Jeremiah Wright. The passages were highly critical of the US government and included the phrase 'No, no, no, not God Bless America. God damn America.'[17] Although Obama himself had never expressed such views or used such poisonous language, he was forced to disown the pastor and resign from his church in order to rescue his campaign.

Neither Obama nor Giuliani was guilty of any aspect of these scandals. Yet their political opponents were able to do them great damage by publicizing partial truths about people close to them. Similar tactics are used to damage brands, discredit scientific findings and destroy the reputations of numerous people in the public eye. At a time when more and more information is publicly available about the people and organizations around us, we are all increasingly vulnerable to unfair disparagement through association with others' partial truths.

Everything is complicated

You might object that I've chosen some particularly complex examples for this chapter. Autonomous vehicles and Amazon are both multi-faceted, fast-evolving products of our modern tech economy; the Bell Pottinger scandal and the invasion of Iraq were far from straightforward. Not everything in life is so complicated.

But remember that egg. There is complexity everywhere. There are more sides to the people we know, the places we visit and the stuff we depend upon than most of us will ever bother to think through. Certainly, we don't have time to describe them all. Next time you hear someone start a sentence with, 'Women prefer . . .' or 'Bankers are . . .' or 'Muslims want . . .' or 'The gay community feels . . .', just think about the many diverse, complex and contradictory people being wrapped up in the impending declaration. Maybe it will be a truth of sorts, but we can be sure plenty of competing truths could be drawn from the same constituency.

The subject of this chapter is complexity, but the argument is simple: most of the issues and entities we deal with are too complex to describe in full; we have to communicate in partial truths because life is too convoluted for us to offer anything more comprehensive. That allows Advocates and Misleaders alike to shape reality by selecting only those truths that support their agenda. We should be wary of politicians, commentators and activists who, far from giving us the whole picture, will inevitably present that part of the canvas that best suits them. But it also gives us an opportunity to select simple truths from a complex subject to express ourselves more effectively. So long as the facets of truth we choose to highlight give a reasonably accurate sense of the facts as we know them, then simplification and selectivity can be good for both communicator and audience.

Complexity-driven partial truths come in a variety of flavours. In the following chapters, we will explore four of them: History, Context, Numbers and Story.

In practice

• Consider the many different sides to any issue of importance and seek a balanced range of views.

• Select truths that will strengthen your argument without distorting the impression of reality you convey.

• Omit truths to make an issue clearer but be careful not to mislead.

But watch out for . . .

• Misleaders who bury important truths in a sea of irrelevance.

• Misleaders who attack people and projects on grounds of association alone.

2

History

Who controls the past controls the future. Who controls the present controls the past.

GEORGE ORWELL, *Nineteen Eighty-Four*

The invention of Fanta

To celebrate a milestone anniversary in 2011, Coca-Cola produced a 27-page 'Short History' entitled '125 years of sharing happiness'.[1] Beautifully illustrated with colourful advertisements from decades past, it has a fact for nearly every year since 1886. Coca-Cola's second biggest international brand, Fanta, makes one appearance in the history, under the year 1955: 'Fanta Orange is introduced in Naples, Italy, the first new product to be distributed by the Company. The Fanta line of flavored beverages comes to the United States in 1960.'

Oddly, Coca-Cola's history doesn't record the invention and launch of Fanta, which actually took place fifteen years earlier. The entry for 1940 reads only, 'Booklets on flower arranging by Laura Lee Burroughs are distributed to consumers. More than 5 million booklets reach American homes.' Why omit such an important milestone?

Perhaps because Fanta was invented in Nazi Germany.

Prior to the Second World War, Germany was Coca-Cola's most successful international market. But when war led to a trade embargo, the German arm of Coca-Cola was unable to import the necessary ingredients for Coke. So they set about developing an alternative sugary drink using food waste products like whey and apple fibre. The name comes from *Fantasie*, German for imagination; the boss of Coca-Cola GmbH had run a contest to name the drink, telling his employees to let their imaginations run wild.

The new product was a hit: nearly three million bottles were sold in 1943. With sugar rationed, some Germans even used Fanta to sweeten soups and stews. It's a really interesting story of innovation in difficult times, but it's not one that you'll find in Coca-Cola's 'Short History'.*

> **History tactic #1**
> *Forgetting the past*

There are certain things kings can do that not even Coca-Cola would dare try. The Edict of Nantes (1598), a proclamation by King Henri IV of France, begins like this:

> We have, by this perpetual and irrevocable edict, established and proclaimed and do establish and proclaim:
> I. First, that the memory of everything done by one side or the other, between March 1585 and our accession to the crown, and during the preceding troubles and because of them, shall remain obliterated and forgotten, as if they had never happened.

---

* Coca-Cola declared: 'Fanta was invented in Germany during the Second World War but the 75-year-old brand had no association with Hitler or the Nazi Party.'

This policy of *oubliance*, or *oblivion*, was introduced to prevent a recurrence of the devastating Wars of Religion, which pitted Catholics against Protestants (Huguenots) for more than 30 years. Henri IV sought to bring peace to his traumatized state by commanding his subjects to forget what had happened.* All official documents and memoirs of the conflict were destroyed on the orders of the king. Murders and other crimes linked to the religious clash were left untried. Prisoners were released. Reference to the recent wars in plays and poetry was forbidden. Lawsuits from the conflict years were annulled and their written records and evidence destroyed. A 'perpetual silence' was imposed on royal prosecutors with regard to anything done by Huguenot political assemblies. 'Forgive and forget' was no mere folk proverb; in seventeenth-century France, it was literal royal command.

As a policy of reconciliation, *oubliance* was only partially and temporarily successful. Henri IV, a Huguenot, was assassinated in 1610 by a Catholic fanatic, and religious conflict resumed a few years later. The Edict of Nantes was revoked by Louis XIV in 1685, leading to a mass emigration of Huguenots from France. Memories of the wars of the previous century were, it turned out, not so easy to obliterate.

Omission of sins

If it is impractical to mandate forgetfulness, communicators can nevertheless steer us away from those historical truths that don't suit their needs. As Coca-Cola's booklet demonstrates, the simplest way to mould history to meet a modern agenda is to leave

---

* South Africa's Truth and Reconciliation Commission took the opposite approach following the many crimes and abuses of the Apartheid era. 'Amnesia is no solution,' said Archbishop Desmond Tutu. 'Without memory, there is no healing.'

out the inconvenient bits. Historical omission is widely practised in school textbooks, where the civil servants and politicians who decide national curricula choose to ignore the more embarrassing or shameful aspects of their country's history.

To many Americans, slavery and the subsequent treatment of black people in the Southern states is a fundamental part of US history. According to Pulitzer Prize-winning historian James M. McPherson, 'The Civil War started because of uncompromising differences between the free and slave states over the power of the national government to prohibit slavery in the territories that had not yet become states.'[2] Following the abolition of slavery, the Southern states enacted the notorious Jim Crow laws to segregate black and white Americans in all public facilities. This segregation, which extended to schools, buses and drinking fountains, remained in force until 1965. Over the same period, the white supremacist Ku Klux Klan movement terrorized African Americans, Jews and civil rights activists.

In 2015, Texas issued new guidelines for teaching American history that made no mention of the Jim Crow laws or the Ku Klux Klan at all.[3] The five million public-school students using the new Texas textbooks read that the Civil War that killed over 600,000 Americans was fought primarily over 'states' rights'. Slavery was a 'side issue to the Civil War', according to Patricia Hardy of the Texas State Board of Education. Of course the 'rights' that the Southern states were most concerned to protect were the rights to buy and sell people. One textbook even euphemistically referred to the Atlantic slave trade as bringing 'millions of workers' to the plantations of the Southern states.[4]

The omission and downplaying of slavery and racial oppression in the history being taught in some US schools will have long-lasting consequences. Gaps in our historical knowledge are already bad enough without state boards of education deliberately entrenching them. In a 2011 survey conducted by the Pew Research

Center, only 38 per cent of Americans polled thought the Civil War was 'mainly about slavery'.[5] 'A lot of white Southerners have grown up believing that the Confederacy's struggle was somehow a noble cause rather than a war in the defense of a horrific institution that enslaved millions of human beings,' said Dan Quinn of the Texas Freedom Network.[6] Such distorted impressions of US history can only give strength to those white supremacists whose hatred and bigotry were so grossly manifested in 2017 in Charlottesville, Virginia.

Israel has faced a similar controversy over the Palestinian exodus known to Arabs as the Nakba, or 'catastrophe'. In 1948, as the state of Israel was founded, over 700,000 Palestinian Arabs left – or were forced to leave – their homes. Most ended up as refugees in the West Bank, Gaza, Jordan, Lebanon and Syria. These refugees and their offspring now number more than four million people. Israeli laws have prevented them from returning home or claiming their property, most of which was acquired by Jewish Israelis.

For many years, Israel's elementary-school history textbooks did not mention the Nakba. Then, in 2007, Israel's ministry of education announced that a new set of history books aimed at eight- and nine-year-olds would for the first time make mention of the formative Palestinian tragedy.[7] This was seen around the world as a very positive step towards reconciliation and greater understanding between the two embittered communities. In fact, the revised textbooks were only printed in Arabic, for use by Israel's large Arab population. Hebrew textbooks were not revised, and Jewish children continued to learn a different version of their shared history. Two years later, with a new government in power, the reference was removed from the Arabic textbooks. The new education minister, Gideon Sa'ar, argued that no state could be expected to portray its own foundation as a catastrophe. 'Including the term in the official curriculum of the Arab sector was a mistake,' he said.[8]

On the face of it, it's not unreasonable to avoid confronting eight-year-olds with a horrendous tale of suffering bound up in the nation's origins. It's not lying to leave something out. Yet the omission of the Nakba from Israeli textbooks has fundamental consequences for Israel's Arab population, as well as the conception of historical reality in the minds of young Jewish Israelis. Children who are not taught that their great-grandparents forced hundreds of thousands of people from homes their families had occupied for generations may less readily empathize with the continuing plight of four million Palestinian refugees.

Misleaders can sidestep criticism by omitting mention of past sins. They can also weaken opponents by ignoring and downplaying their successes.

The many detractors of George W. Bush are quick to cite the invasion of Iraq and the patchy response to Hurricane Katrina. Few of them recall the President's Emergency Plan for AIDS Relief (PEPFAR). Founded in 2003, it was the largest ever global health initiative dedicated to a single disease. Bush managed to secure $15 billion of US government funding over five years to support HIV/AIDS prevention and treatment programmes in developing countries. Before PEPFAR, 50,000 people had access to anti-retroviral drugs in sub-Saharan Africa; by the end of Bush's presidency, the number was over 1.3 million.[9] Bush also set up a $1.2 billion initiative to fight malaria. Over the course of his presidency, Bush channelled more financial assistance to Africa than any other president. He did not do this to win votes. One of his predecessors, Democrat president Jimmy Carter, was moved to praise for his ideological opponent: 'Mr President, let me say that I'm filled with admiration for you and. deep gratitude for you about the great contributions you've made to the most needy people on Earth.'[10]

An earlier Republican president gets insufficient credit for his contribution to the environment. By the late 1960s, concerns about oil spills, chemical dumping, toxic pesticides, radioactive fallout and wilderness depletion were mounting across the United States, and the sitting president decided radical measures were needed. He introduced the National Environmental Policy Act, which required federal agencies to assess the environmental effects of building highways and power plants, granting land-use permits, and a host of other actions. He extended the Clean Air Act, targeting airborne pollutants such as sulphur dioxide, nitrogen dioxide and particulate matter. He signed into law the Endangered Species Act, the Marine Mammal Protection Act and the Ocean Dumping Act, and he proposed the Safe Drinking Water Act. Most significantly of all, he created the Environmental Protection Agency, one of the world's most effective government organizations dedicated to safeguarding and policing the environment.

That president was the infamous and much maligned Richard Nixon.

Long-term grudge

If omission is the simplest form of truthful historical manipulation, biased selection is perhaps the most common. We are all naturals at this. No one needs an instruction manual to craft a résumé that draws the recruiter's attention towards our most favourable past activities. Ask a 12-year-old what he's been up to since he got back from school, and he is likely to focus more on the homework completed than the computer games played.

Selective accounts of history can be extremely misleading. I could describe a certain historical event quite truthfully like this:

Important technologies were developed, especially in transport, cutlery and personal hygiene. Democracy flourished, with many more people joining unions and gaining the vote. Social equality increased. Diets for many poor people improved, making them fitter and stronger. Infant mortality dropped and life expectancy rose. Drunkenness decreased. More jobs were available, especially for women, opening the way for greater gender equality.

What event am I talking about?

The First World War.

Technologies developed during the war included aeroplanes, stainless steel and sanitary towels. In Britain, universal suffrage was introduced for men, and around 40 per cent of women were given the vote for the first time. In Germany, Austria, Russia and Turkey, empires collapsed, paving the way for more democratic forms of government. Enlisted soldiers were given more nutritious meals than many were accustomed to, with 'meat every day' for British troops. As millions of men were sent to the Front, munitions and agricultural production jobs were given to women. Full employment allowed many families a better standard of living than they had ever known before. New laws cut alcohol consumption and led to a reduction in domestic violence. The British Labour politician and later prime minister Ramsay MacDonald, who had opposed the war, observed that it had done more for social reform in Britain than all the efforts of unions and humanitarians in half a century.

Yet to focus on these truths alone would be an appalling way to depict a war in which over 15 million people died.

History tactic #2
Selectively remembering the past

Charles de Gaulle was president of France when the UK first tried to join the European Economic Community, forerunner to the European Union. He vetoed the British application. Four years later, the UK tried again. Once more, de Gaulle objected. France alone among the EEC members vetoed British accession.

Coming just two decades after British and American forces had sacrificed immense quantities of blood and treasure to liberate France from Nazi rule, this looked like astronomical ingratitude. Britain had even given de Gaulle and his Free French Forces a home in London during the Second World War and provided him with political, military and financial support. Without Britain, there would have been no Free France for de Gaulle to rule, nor any EEC to join.

Many were outraged by de Gaulle's attitude towards the country that had done so much for him. One of them was Paul Reynaud, a close colleague and a former French prime minister, who wrote to de Gaulle to protest. In reply, de Gaulle sent an empty envelope, on the back of which he had written, 'If absent, forward to Agincourt or Waterloo.' Thus did de Gaulle make clear his historical frame of reference. 'Our greatest hereditary enemy was not Germany: it was England,' he once declared. His choice of historical truths led him to act in a way that had (and perhaps still has) colossal repercussions for the UK's relationship with the rest of Europe.

To build the future, look back

Ericsson is a telecommunications multinational with a rich and impressive history. In the 1990s, the Swedish company was one of the world's largest manufacturers of mobile telephones but within a few troubled years had exited the business to focus on building communications networks. Now Ericsson is embarked on an exciting mission to connect up the Internet of Things. Already they have created 'the world's largest floating network' with Danish shipping company Maersk, and they are working with Scania and Volvo to connect up road vehicles. But the transformation Ericsson must go through to build its new businesses in Cloud, TV, IP networks and the Internet of Things is not easy for its more than 100,000 employees.

I worked with one of Ericsson's biggest divisions to help prepare employees for this demanding transformation. The best approach, we decided, was to position Ericsson as a *technology pioneer*. There are many other ways one could describe this giant organization, but by focusing on the adventurous, groundbreaking side of the company, we hoped to encourage employees to embrace new challenges and be open to whatever changes of role or direction might be necessary. To establish the high-tech, futuristic company's credentials as a pioneer, we looked to its history.

We recalled that the founder, Lars Magnus Ericsson, started designing telephones in 1878, long before most people were aware of the technology. Ericsson's 500 switch, first deployed in 1923, connected callers all over the world. Ericsson launched the first modern mobile telephony system in 1981. Erlang, the programming language first deployed in 1986, is now used by WhatsApp, Facebook and Amazon, as well as millions of smartphones. Ericsson either launched or created the standards for GSM 2G, 3G and LTE 4G. Ericsson engineers invented Bluetooth in 1998.

By highlighting selective elements of the company's history, we were able to show that Ericsson really is a technology pioneer – and ready for all kinds of new adventures in uncharted territories.

At the same time, Ericsson had another, trickier challenge: one of its biggest markets was Russia, and that country had recently fallen foul of the European Union by invading Crimea, fomenting war in Eastern Ukraine and supplying the weapon used to shoot down Malaysia Airlines Flight 17. Although the EU had applied sanctions against Russia's banking, energy and defence sectors, trade in telecommunications was still permitted. But Russian mobile operators were wary about continuing to invest for the long term with a European provider; a Chinese rival, Huawei, might be less likely to pull out of the country. Ericsson needed to reassure its Russian customers and employees that it was fully committed to the market.

Again, we turned to history to make the point. Ericsson had begun operating in Russia over 130 years earlier, when it supplied the equipment for the Russian Post and Telegraph Administration and built a factory in St Petersburg. At the beginning of the twentieth century, the Russian market seemed to offer greater growth potential than Sweden, and Lars Magnus Ericsson even considered moving his company's headquarters to St Petersburg. Ericsson had continued trading in Russia despite the 1905 revolution, the war with Japan, the First World War and a maritime blockade. The Swedish company's Russian roots ran deep. A short-term political dispute was not going to threaten their long-standing commitment to a great nation of over 140 million citizens.

For one of the most prominent companies currently bringing us the future, history is proving to be a valuable asset. It is a selective history – we did not mention the fact that Ericsson, like most other foreign businesses, was expelled from Russia in 1917 following the Bolshevik revolution, nor that its St Petersburg factory was nationalized without compensation – but that age-old Russian connection nevertheless has helped reaffirm contemporary trading relationships with this important market.

A big bowl of competing truths

A schoolteacher of mine once compared history to a bowl of spaghetti. There are many strands, all mixed up together, he said. Historians have to select a strand and pull it free from the rest to paint a coherent picture of the past. I still think it's a great metaphor. Each strand of spaghetti is a competing truth: the one you choose to pull out will determine your understanding of the past, which in turn will drive your actions in the present.

It's not just geopolitical or corporate history that matters. Who hasn't tried to reinterpret the history of a relationship or an argument? What is understood to have happened in the past matters immensely in our present and future. Our history moulds our identity. It shapes the way we think.

But histories can be extremely complicated bowls of spaghetti, with thousands of different strands to choose from. Even when we have no present-day agenda, we have to choose from a range of portrayals of past events because no account could incorporate all the people, actions, details and external factors that might influence our interpretation of the past. Misinformers can convey a very skewed impression of history by talking only about the one strand they have discovered.

One thing we can say for sure about the last few thousand years is that there were just as many women around as men. You wouldn't know it from the history books. Aside from Joan of Arc, Anne Boleyn, Elizabeth I, Florence Nightingale, Marie Curie and a few other rare remembered figures, traditional history is about men. It's not that historians were deliberately excluding women from their accounts (although some may have done) – they just didn't consider them as important as the men ruling nations, commanding armies and leading rebellions. The same can be said for most ordinary people: history books rarely bother to include their stories, even where their letters, journals and records are preserved. You might notice the preponderance of war references in this chapter; wars get a lot more historical attention than all the years of peace in between.

Recount the history of a place or organization you know well, and you too will be forced to leave out most of the possible elements of that history. There just isn't time to describe every meeting, transaction, report, achievement, failure, disruption and proposal – even if you could remember them all. So quite naturally you select; and by selecting you shape history.

Add a present-day agenda and the reshaped past can take on almost any form.

Glorying in humiliation

Consider how differently the United States, Britain and China view three historic national failures: the fall of Saigon, the evacuation from Dunkirk and the so-called Century of Humiliation.

On 30 April 1975, the US ambassador to South Vietnam was evacuated by helicopter from the embassy in Saigon as North Vietnamese troops entered the capital. Even before the fall of Saigon, Vietnam had become a miserable embarrassment to the United States. Unprecedented reporting from the war, with vivid photography that included a monk's immolation, executions, the My Lai massacre and a child burnt by napalm, made many Americans question the moral foundations of the war. Some called US soldiers 'baby-killers'. Others despaired of their military's failure to win against an apparently inferior force. Until Vietnam, the United States had never lost a war.

The release of the 'Pentagon Papers' in 1971, which revealed secret bombings in Cambodia and Laos, was said by the *New York Times* to show that President Johnson's administration had 'systematically lied, not only to the public but also to Congress' during a war in which nearly 60,000 Americans were killed.[11] Talk show host Dick Cavett called the war 'a hideous, world-shaking case of criminal political ineptitude and miscalculation'.[12]

So it is perhaps only natural that many Americans would rather not remember the final US retreat from Saigon at all. Yet as a military operation, it was a remarkable achievement: helicopter crews worked doggedly round the clock to evacuate 1,373 Americans and 5,595 Vietnamese and other nationals from Saigon, ahead of the arrival of the victorious North Vietnamese army. There were plenty of stories of heroism beyond the call of duty in which a demoralized nation might have taken pride. Instead, the over-whelming response was shame.

'I was crying and I think everyone else was crying. We were crying for a lot of different reasons,' said Major James Kean of the embassy evacuation. 'But most of all we were ashamed. How did the United States of America get itself in a position where we had to tuck tail and run?'[13]

They should not have been surprised: President Richard Nixon and his national security advisor Henry Kissinger had known more than two years earlier, when they withdrew US troops and left South Vietnam to fight alone, that their ally would not survive. In negotiations with China, Kissinger was said to have sought a 'decent interval' between the US withdrawal and the collapse of South Vietnam.[14] With public opinion soundly against the war and Congress voting down further military assistance for South Vietnam, the administration probably had no choice. Still, many would now characterize the US withdrawal of troops and, ultimately, its defense attaché and embassy staff as not only a failure but a grievous betrayal.

The consequences of this characterization for America and the world have been bleak. Some argue that the retreat from Vietnam has shaped American foreign policy ever since. The *Guardian*'s former foreign editor Martin Woollacott wrote:

> Everything the US has done in the world since then has been conditioned by its fear of the consequences of trying to reassert itself militarily – and by its compulsion to do so. The fear is of another Vietnam, another quagmire, another debacle. The compulsion, though, constantly seeks out other places where something like Vietnam can be taken on again, but this time won, cleanly and conclusively. The US has sought this compensatory victory again and again, most recently in Afghanistan and Iraq. Vietnam, like Hamlet's ghost, refuses to go away.[15]

How different is the British memory of Dunkirk.

The British Expeditionary Force had been sent to France, following the outbreak of the Second World War, to help French and Belgian forces hold back the advancing German army. In that aim, they completely failed. Between 27 May and 4 June 1940, more than 300,000 British and French troops had to be rescued from the beaches and harbour of Dunkirk in northern France, following their humiliating rout by German forces. Thousands more were captured or killed. A mountain of supplies, weapons, vehicles and ammunition were lost to the Third Reich. Hitler was left in near total control of France for the next four years.

Fighting in the weeks leading up to the Dunkirk evacuation had been extraordinarily intense. Many British units held impossible positions with great bravery, despite the capitulation of the Belgian army which left their eastern flank disastrously exposed. Nevertheless, the result was undeniable: British and French forces had been outmanoeuvred and outgunned. As the German magazine *Der Adler* put it:

> For us Germans the word 'Dunkirchen' will stand for all time for victory in the greatest battle of annihilation in history. But for the British and French who were there, it will remind them for the rest of their lives of a defeat that was heavier than any army had ever suffered before.[16]

Yet that's not what happened. Ask most British people what Dunkirk represents and they will talk about the flotilla of fishing vessels, pleasure boats and private yachts that set out for the French coastline, and the thousands of plucky soldiers that they rescued. Although the Royal Navy's own ships carried out much of the evacuation, it is the 'little ships' that are best remembered. These were manned by tiny crews, in some cases a single skipper. Many were just 10–15 metres in length. Some of the boats were deployed to ferry soldiers from the Dunkirk beaches to the larger naval vessels waiting offshore, operating in waters bombarded by German artillery. Others collected as many men as they could hold and sailed them back to England, under repeated Luftwaffe attack, before going back for more. Their brave efforts helped save the British army from annihilation. Winston Churchill called it a 'miracle of deliverance'; with a battered but still largely complete army to defend Britain against invasion, he was able to dismiss any suggestion of surrender.

So the Dunkirk evacuation really was a great achievement. But it might easily have been seen by the country and history as just the positive coda to a truly disastrous military adventure. Instead, 'The "spin" given to the evacuation of the British army was almost too successful, setting off a wave of euphoria throughout Britain,' wrote Dr Duncan Anderson, head of the War Studies Department at the Royal Military Academy Sandhurst:

> Increasingly concerned at the air of unreality that seemed to permeate Britain, on 4 June Churchill addressed the House of Commons in terms that spelt out clearly the truly desperate nature of Britain's situation. He reminded his countrymen that wars were not won by evacuations, and that 'what has happened in France and Belgium is a colossal military disaster'. But the British people didn't really believe him; they much preferred the myth to the reality, and they were not prepared to listen to anyone who sought to puncture their belief, not even Churchill himself.[17]

The term 'Dunkirk spirit' has entered the English language to denote great courage, unity and determination in the face of adversity. Dunkirk, in Britain, is seen as a kind of victory, despite the complete defeat of British forces in the Battle of France. Britain has chosen to celebrate an event that a different nation might have preferred to forget. In doing so, it has arguably shaped British culture. It certainly helped Britain win the war.

If Americans look back with shame on Saigon, and the British look back with pride on Dunkirk, the Chinese look back with deliberate and purposeful anger on their Century of Humiliation.

It began with the First Opium War, when Britain sent an expeditionary force to China in 1840 to protect its opium trade, after China had confiscated large quantities of the drug and blockaded British traders. British gunboats and troops easily defeated a numerically larger imperial Chinese army, thanks to superior weaponry and naval technology. China was forced to sign the Treaty of Nanking in 1842 – known as the first of the 'unequal treaties' because all the obligations were on the Chinese side. China had to pay reparations, open up 'Treaty ports' to foreign trade and cede Hong Kong Island to the British.

The Second Opium War was worse. This time, with still less justification, Britain and France joined forces to invade China. The war culminated in the vindictive destruction of the emperor's Summer Palace near Beijing. Known as the Garden of Perfect Brightness, this magnificent complex of palaces was filled with exquisite treasures. The buildings now lie in ruins, and many of the palace's treasures are in British and French collections.

While China was fighting the Second Opium War, Russia took advantage of the country's difficulties and threatened invasion. In the resulting Treaty of Aigun, China was forced to cede a great slice of territory to Russia. Meanwhile, China was being torn apart by the civil war known as the Taiping Rebellion, which consumed an estimated 20 million lives.

Other wars and invasions followed, leading to the cataclysm of Japanese domination. The First Sino-Japanese War was fought over Korea, formerly a vassal state of China. Japan won decisively and would later take possession of Korea and Formosa (Taiwan).

In the following years, Japan gained increasing control over Manchuria (northeast China), finally invading in 1931. The Second Sino-Japanese War began in 1937, with the Japanese army seizing Beijing, Shanghai and Nanjing. The National Revolutionary Army of China was forced to retreat from Shanghai after months of bloody house-to-house combat with the invading Imperial Japanese Army. The epic battle cost over 200,000 Chinese lives and was to be followed a few weeks later by the massacre of an estimated 50,000–300,000 civilians in Nanjing.

It was indeed an abysmal century for China. One might expect a proud, ascendant nation to play down the worst aspects of its history. On the contrary, the Chinese government has ensured every detail is seared into the consciousness of the nation. A 'patriotic education' programme brings busloads of Chinese to the ruins of the Summer Palace to see the evidence of British and French atrocity. The Nanjing Massacre memorial is the most-visited tourism site in the former capital city.

Some suggest that the Chinese Communist Party chose to re-open these grievous historical wounds following the Tiananmen Square protests and massacre of 1989, in order to convince its people that strong, unchallenged government was necessary to prevent a repeat of such foreign outrages. In fact, Chinese leaders have been talking about the 'Century of Humiliation' since the 1920s. Historian Dr Julia Lovell suggests China has fashioned a founding myth from the Opium Wars, casting China – one of history's great nations – as a victim.

But the government's rationale for fanning this burning resentment is mostly one of motivation. The long sequence of humiliations is blamed on the failure of imperial China to keep up with the technological development of the West. That failure, by implication, must never happen again. In this way are the Chinese motivated to build, to progress, to invent, to triumph.

We are our history

What gives an individual, an organization or a nation their identity? Culture, perhaps, or personality, values and capabilities. But all of that depends on our history. We see ourselves as good or capable or determined based on our understanding of our individual and collective past. Entire nations such as Israel, Italy and Germany have been forged on the basis of a selective recall of events that took place before living memory. 'We reach into the past for foundation myths of our tribe, our nation,' observed historical novelist Hilary Mantel, 'and found them on glory, or found them on grievance, but we seldom found them on cold facts.'[18]

History shapes our identity; and people, organizations and nations act according to the identity they adopt. 'We are made by history,' said Martin Luther King, Jr. That is why George Orwell had the bureaucrats of Oceania expend so much effort rewriting history in *Nineteen Eighty-Four*. Everything we do stems at least in part from our understanding of the past.

A past that can be infinitely rewritten.

In practice

• Draw on relevant historical events and achievements to shape the current identity of organizations.

• Recount successful past actions and events to inspire action in others today.

But watch out for . . .

• Misleaders who ignore relevant and important history to save themselves embarrassment or weaken opponents.

• Misleaders who use highly selective accounts of history to promote violence, discrimination and ethnic conflict.

3

Context

To the jaundiced honey seems bitter, to those bitten by rabid dogs water is a terror.

MARCUS AURELIUS, *Meditations*

How bad can it get?

Imagine you have been stripped down to your underwear and dropped in a lake. You have no idea where in the world you are, and when you exhaustedly crawl ashore there is no sign of human habitation or agriculture. You seem to be in the middle of nowhere.

Terrifying?

Not if you're the astronaut hero of the movie *Gravity*, and against all the odds you've just made it back to Earth after being stranded in space, facing the imminent prospect of death by collision, incineration or asphyxiation. It is a testament to the narrative skill of the filmmakers that when Sandra Bullock pulls herself on to that alien shore and lies there clutching at wet sand, we rejoice in the conviction that all her troubles are over. She's breathing fresh air! She's on solid ground!

Yet exactly the same scene could have been the chilling start to a survival adventure. A lone woman with no food, map, shoes, matches, phone or knowledge of the wilderness has to find her way back to civilization. A daunting prospect. But because we know how much worse her situation was just a short while earlier, and we anticipate a NASA rescue mission, we see this scene as a happy ending.

Context makes all the difference to our impression of reality. I've worked with companies that celebrated wholeheartedly when they made a loss of several million dollars, because the previous years had been so much worse. A modest gift from a child may be much more precious than the same gift from a wealthy adult. A cold beer tastes different after a long, hot day of manual work. Party leader Jeremy Corbyn claimed Labour had 'won' the 2017 UK general election, despite taking 56 fewer parliamentary seats than the governing Conservative Party, simply because everyone had expected Theresa May to do so much better. Context changes meaning.

Such context is part of the complexity of the world we are trying to understand. It is easy to say we should know the context of any actions and events we evaluate but harder to say *which* context is relevant or appropriate. Hearing a story in one context will give a very different impression to hearing the same story told within a different context. Deciding which contexts to highlight and which to downplay is a critical part of shaping reality.

A thing is not just a thing

The psychologist Paul Rozin earned a certain notoriety in academic circles when he created a colourful experiment to test human disgust responses. He would show his test subjects a brand-new bedpan, fresh out of the manufacturer's packaging. He would reiterate that the bedpan had never been used, and his subjects would cheerfully agree. Then he would fill the bedpan with apple juice and invite them to drink it.

Most would refuse.

This is not some innate aversion encoded in our genes; our ancestors would have willingly drunk from this conveniently shaped, pristine vessel. But we have come to associate the object so strongly with urine that we can no longer bear to drink from it. Rozin's subjects felt disgusted at the idea, 'even though they know it's brand new, there's no urine, there's no contamination'.[1]

The object is not just an object – it has context, which shapes how we see it.

Conversely, if one of Rozin's subjects was stranded in a desert with no water and he happened upon a bedpan full of apple juice, he would likely drink it without a second thought. The context is different, so his actions are different.

Our responses to many objects are more dependent on context than on the objects themselves. Imagine you own a designer watch. How would you feel about it if five other people at work bought the same watch? What if you discovered it had been made by a company notorious for tax evasion? What if you saw a news clip of a celebrity you loathe sporting the same watch? The object hasn't changed, but it has been compromised by its context. In the same way, an antique silver fork might have greater or lesser appeal for a collector if it was once used by Hitler.

A black and white cat named Humphrey used to live at 10 Downing Street in London. Humphrey shared the address at various times with three prime ministers, including Conservative Margaret Thatcher and Labour's Tony Blair. In a telling experiment, British voters were shown a picture of Humphrey and asked to say whether they liked or disliked him. When described as 'Thatcher's cat', Humphrey received a net approval rating of 44 per cent from Conservative voters and only 21 per cent from

Labour voters; as 'Blair's cat', Humphrey scored 27 per cent with Conservative voters and 37 per cent with Labour voters.[2] Same cat, different context.

If the physical description of an object (or a cat) is one truth, the various possible contexts of that object are competing truths that may provoke in us very different responses. Perhaps the clearest way to show this is by looking at an industry which prices objects largely according to their context: the art business.

Better than Matisse

Europe in the years immediately after the Second World War was a chaotic place. Cities lay in ruins, millions had been displaced by the fighting, borders had shifted and the Soviet Union had seized control of much of the east. It was a time of great hardship and misery, but it was also a time of opportunity.

In February 1947, a man claiming to be a dispossessed Hungarian aristocrat checked into a hotel in Copenhagen. His story was tragic: his high-born family had been murdered by the Nazis, and their extensive landholdings and property had been confiscated by the Russians. A homosexual Jew, he himself had spent much of the war in a German concentration camp. He had suffered a broken leg during a Gestapo interrogation and had only made it out of the Soviet-controlled eastern bloc by bribing border guards with some diamonds he had sewn into his coat. All he had left in the world were five Picasso drawings – the last remnant of his noble family's once-great wealth.

Driven to desperation, he had to sell.

A local dealer was immediately interested. The drawings seemed to be from Picasso's Classical period and would now be worth a great deal. The gracious but forlorn refugee's story made sense: a lot of valuable art had been hurriedly packed up and dispersed around Europe under threat of Nazi looting or bombing.

Savvy collectors could pick up real bargains as the works began to emerge from the rubble. This was a chance to be seized.

The dealer arranged for the drawings to be inspected by an expert, and they were soon pronounced genuine. By the end of the day, a Stockholm gallery had agreed to buy the drawings for $6,000. The refugee was presented with a cheque. It was made out to the name he had given: Elmyr de Hory.

Unfortunately for the Swedish gallery, and for a great number of other art buyers over the following decades, the man calling himself de Hory was a master forger. The drawings were not by Picasso; de Hory had created them himself in a matter of hours. He was still new at the game, having sold his first 'Picasso' rather by chance the previous year, when a friend misidentified one of his own drawings and asked to buy it. So goes the story, at least; although everything surrounding de Hory and his biographer Clifford Irving – another great fabricator, best known for writing a fake autobiography of eccentric billionaire Howard Hughes – is open to doubt.

Believed to have been born Elemér Albert Hoffmann in Budapest, a very ordinary middle-class child who developed a remarkable artistic ability, de Hory went on to forge hundreds of works of art bearing the signatures of Matisse, Picasso, Modigliani, Monet and Degas among others. He and his associates conned galleries and private art collectors out of millions of dollars during a criminal career that lasted nearly 30 years. Living in the United States for over a decade, he dubbed himself Baron de Hory to add lustre to his dispossessed aristocrat story. 'I never offered a painting or a drawing to a museum who didn't buy it,' he claimed. 'They never refused one – never.'[3] Long after he had been exposed by suspicious US dealers and pursued by the FBI, he continued to create his forgeries on the Spanish island of Ibiza, where his charm, talent and notoriety earned him a comfortable villa and the company of celebrities like Marlene Dietrich and Ursula Andress.

De Hory did not copy existing works of art. His method was to create something new that famous artists *might have* drawn or painted. He was always careful to use aged canvas, frames and paper, sometimes buying an old painting to reuse the canvas, or tearing blank pages out of antique books for sketches. His ability to imitate the style of Modernist masters was so good that few experts were able to tell the difference. A living artist, Kees van Dongen, was convinced that he himself had painted a work created by de Hory. One New York art gallery owner declared, 'When it came to doing Matisse, de Hory was better than Matisse.' Indeed, it is widely claimed that many of de Hory's works are still on show in galleries around the world, misattributed to more famous artists.

'If my work hangs in a museum long enough, it becomes real,' he once said.[4]

That's debatable, but what's not in question is the absolutely minimal physical difference between a real Picasso and a de Hory Picasso. Yet one is worth millions of dollars, the other considerably less. As de Hory himself asked, why should his forgeries be considered inferior to the drawings and paintings of the artists he imitated, when most experts couldn't tell them apart? Art connoisseurs appreciated his Matisse paintings just as much as real Matisse paintings, until they discovered what they actually were. So where does the true value of a painting by a great master really lie?

To put it another way, imagine that you were offered an exact atom-for-atom replica of Picasso's *Les femmes d'Alger* (Version O). The original sold at auction in 2015 for $179.3 million. The painting in your hands is not the original, and you will never be able to pass it off as the original, but it is physically identical to the original. How much would you pay for it?

Probably not much. You might offer a few thousand dollars if you have a healthy bank balance and you really like the image.

Surely not more than $300,000. Which implies that the immense value of the original painting lies not in the physical object itself but in the context of that object – its provenance, its story, its brand name, its rarity, its uniqueness. Where the canvas and paint are worth at most a few thousand dollars, the context is worth over $179 million.

This is not as crazy as it sounds. We actually get more pleasure from art which we believe has been created by a respected artist than by someone mimicking their skill. Recent developments in neuroscience have allowed researchers to monitor activity in parts of the brain associated with 'hedonic value'. One team asked test subjects to rate a series of abstract paintings while in an fMRI scanner. Half of the paintings they were shown were labelled as coming from a prestigious art gallery. The other half were labelled as having been generated by the researchers on a computer.

No one was surprised that on average the subjects gave the 'Gallery' pictures a higher subjective rating than the 'Computer' pictures, even though the labels had been allocated randomly; it would be hard for anyone not to be influenced by such strong contextual signposts when making an aesthetic judgement. But the real eye-opener lay in the fMRI data. Those parts of the brain associated with hedonic value showed greater activity when subjects viewed the 'Gallery' pictures: they really did enjoy looking at artworks they believed were painted by real artists more than those they believed were created by the researchers.

So while the inflated price of *Les femmes d'Alger* (Version O) is a function of a whole range of factors, not least what the buyer believes they could sell it for, part of it must be the added pleasure we get from looking at any picture we think was painted by Picasso. It is therefore not unreasonable for art galleries to pay more for works by artists whose names their visitors recognize. The context of the name adds measurable hedonic value to the canvas and paint.

Forgers like de Hory have already raised the question of where an artwork's value lies. Progress in additive manufacturing techniques – commonly known as 3-D printing – might make the question routinely pertinent. What will happen to our understanding of art value if we can print off perfect replicas of the *Venus de Milo* or van Gogh's *Starry Night*? As the context changes, will objects identical to the paintings and sculptures that people currently queue to see in national museums become as worthless as the art posters taped to students' walls?

As for Elmyr de Hory, he has to some extent been vindicated in his provocative question about the inferior value of high-quality forgeries. His fake Picassos, Modiglianis and Monets now sell, unmasked, for many thousands of dollars each. Ironically, fake de Hory fakes have turned up in various corners of the art market; the de Hory name is sufficiently famous context to make it worth fabricating. Art collectors now ask, 'Yes, but is it a *real* de Hory?'

Sadly, de Hory did not live to see himself subjected to his own medicine. Facing extradition to France in 1976 on charges of fraud, he took an overdose of barbiturates and died on Ibiza.

Or so, at least, we are led to believe.

From Monet to meat

Art, for all its hedonic value, remains a niche concern for many. Far more pressing is the issue of how we feed ourselves, but here again context may come to play a critical role.

Our current consumption of meat is unsustainable. Delicious and nutritious as much of it is, farmed meat imposes a high cost on our environment as well as on the animals themselves. Around a third of harvested grain and 8 per cent of the world's fresh water supply is consumed by farm animals, which are also responsible for 15 per cent of human-caused greenhouse-gas emissions.[5] Large parts of the Amazon rainforest have been obliterated to make room for cattle ranches. Modern 'Concentrated Animal Feeding Operations' (CAFOs), which keep animals confined in window-less buildings or crowded areas with no vegetation for weeks on end, are considered by some to be the animal equivalent of concentration camps; developed in the United States, CAFOs are proliferating around the world, ensuring unrelentingly miserable lives for unimaginable numbers of sentient mammals. The immense quantities of urine and faeces emanating from such 'mega farms' pollute groundwater and cause dangerous algal blooms. As millions more people in Asia join the middle classes, demand for meat is expected to rise substantially, exacerbating our impact on the environment and animal welfare.

That is the context of the tasty steaks and burgers we enjoy today.

Many of us do our grocery shopping, cooking and eating largely without considering this context. We concern ourselves with the more immediate truths of meat quality, nutritional value and price, ignorant of – or deliberately ignoring – the competing truths of animal suffering and environmental degradation. I am as guilty of this as any other meat-lover. Our blindness to the less appealing competing truths of our purchasing behaviour is encouraged by the messaging we experience day to day. Most of it concerns the succulence of this particular meat product or the risk to our arteries of that meat category. Occasionally, there is a food scare, but such alarms are quickly forgotten in the flurry of new messaging about mouth-watering recipes or irresistible prices. The environmental and animal welfare context is almost entirely hidden from us.

For anyone concerned about the health of the planet or the suffering of billions of animals, the most urgent task is to acquaint more people with the wider context of the meat we consume.

However, the context may one day be very different. Scientists and entrepreneurs have begun to *grow* meat.

In 2013, a research team at the University of Maastricht led by

Professor Mark Post created a burger out of beef they had grown from a small sample of cow stem cells, the natural templates from which specialized cells develop. The Dutch team manipulated the cells to grow muscle fibre and fat. The world's first burger made from meat that did not have to be cut out of an animal required beetroot juice to make it look the right colour and cost around $300,000 to produce. Nevertheless, it was an extraordinary achievement and potentially marked the founding of an entirely new food industry.

Cultured meat, or 'clean meat' as some Advocates are calling it, could require half as much calorific input as regular meat and only a tiny fraction of the water and land, while producing far less greenhouse gas and waste materials. The meat is safer to eat because it's grown in a sterile environment, with no risk of anti-biotic, bacterial or faecal contamination.

Already, several start-ups are trying to make cultured meat economically viable. California's Memphis Meats is developing cultured meatballs. At the unveiling of its first product, CEO Uma Valeti declared, 'This is the first time a meatball has ever been cooked with beef cells that did not require a cow to be slaughtered.'[6] Israeli start-up SuperMeat is developing machines to grow chicken meat and has suggested that these could be used in restaurants or supermarkets, or even at home.

It will be some years, if not decades, before cultured meat can be produced cheaply enough to rival the farm-grown stuff, and we are yet to see whether it can taste as good. But let's imagine that one day you are presented with a cultured meat burger that costs the same and tastes the same as a regular burger. The object, in other words, is identical, but the context is completely different. Would you eat it?

Your response might be a resounding *Yes!* If you love meat but have given it up on ethical grounds, this might be the answer to your prayers. Or you might be too freaked out by the idea of meat grown in a factory to go near the stuff. Or your response might depend on how this new context is explained to you, how you see others behave, how the media portrays cultured meat. For Advocates of cultured meat – which should include anyone concerned about animal welfare and the environment – communicating this new context in the right way will be critical. The future of the planet may depend on it.

I began that discussion of cultured meat by talking about the threats to the environment from expanding meat production. A different writer might have started by talking about theology: who are we, he might have asked, to play God with biology? He might have pointed to the moral or spiritual dangers of interfering in God's domains. Yet another writer might have started with a discussion of the ideal of nature: surely we can all agree that natural food is better than artificial food? She might have referenced problematic food technologies already in our grocery stores, such as olestra, nitrates and hydrogenated fats.

The three of us are setting three different contexts or 'frames' for the ensuing discussion of cultured meat. By foregrounding one context and discounting others, we are effectively shifting the mindset of our audience before they begin to think about the issue at hand. If a randomly selected group were to be asked to assess the value of cultured meat, they would likely come to different conclusions depending on which of these contexts they had been exposed to. A group influenced by either of those other two writers might be far less inclined to eat or promote cultured meat than one that had focused on its environmental and animal-welfare benefits.

> **Context tactic #1**
> *Framing*

This *framing effect* can take many forms, but setting a context that favours your agenda is a particularly powerful communications tactic. Gifted speakers can sometimes win an argument before they've even made it, just by setting a context that will predetermine how people respond to an issue. Parents who want to encourage generosity in their children will sometimes talk to them about less fortunate children who don't have any toys or enough to eat – just before they hand over their pocket money. Politicians arguing for greater welfare allowances might start by describing the awful plight of a particular constituent. Company leaders will preface the announcement of job cuts or a salary freeze by describing the harsh competition or price pressures the business faces.

Setting the right context creates the frame for a convincing argument. The frame influences how people process the information presented within that frame.

But framing can also forestall agreement. If two sides come at a complex issue with completely different frames, they are unlikely to find common ground. A tragic example is the Israel–Palestine conflict: many Jewish Israelis see the issue in terms of the sacred land they believe was promised to them by God, or in terms of hard-won security in a hostile neighbourhood; Palestinians see it in terms of the injustice they suffered when they were forced from their homes and lands. Both sides have their own context, their own competing truths, and the framing mismatch makes compromise largely impossible. Sometimes we struggle even to hear information that doesn't fit with our current frame.

We may not actually be aware of the frames that shape our thoughts and behaviour. They are part of our mindsets, built up over years of information input and lived experiences. Some people call this our world view or *Weltanschauung*. I come from a Western, omnivorous context, so it was quite natural for me to write about beef in the previous section; had I grown up a Hindu or a vegan I might have chosen a different example. If some of the ideas or stories in this book strike a dissonant chord with you, it may be because we have different world views.

We even apply frames to ourselves subconsciously as our context changes. Introduce yourself to a man on the touchline of a school football match, and he may say something like, 'Hello, I'm Danny's father', even if he is a top surgeon or TV presenter. The context has changed, and so the man's self-image has changed.

Frames are essential to help us interpret events, but they can also be used to manipulate and persuade us. If we don't like the way a debate or an interaction is unfolding, we may be able to alter its course by reframing it for ourselves and the other participants. We can introduce different context – we can use different truths – to reorient a negotiation or a dispute. Reframing – changing the context – is a vital skill in conflict resolution, innovation and change management.

All the boys

In the summer of 2014, a picture circulated on social media that quickly drew a storm of derision and protest. The picture seemed at first glance quite mundane: it showed a panel of speakers at a conference, not normally the kind of tableau to provoke the ire of the Twitterati. But there were a couple of details that, in combination, made it viral dynamite. The sign above the panel read 'Global Summit of Women 2014' . . . and all of the panellists were men.

'A picture is worth a thousand words,' wrote the conference attendee who originally posted the image to Twitter.[7] Nevertheless, the many outraged women and men who retweeted it were happy to add plenty of words of their own. 'Is this a joke? This must be a joke' was one of the kinder responses. 'Because men know better. Truly preposterous' was another.[8] The fact that all the panellists were older white men in dark suits didn't help. 'I don't know whether to laugh or cry,' wrote feminist novelist Kathy Lette.[9]

I remember briefly sharing that sense of scorn and dismay when I saw the picture. But that first impression was quickly dispelled, because I recognized one of the men on the panel. His name was Michel Landel, he was the CEO of French contract services and facilities management company Sodexo, and I had worked with him just a few weeks earlier on a major transformation programme. He had been forthright in insisting that our communications should stress the importance and value of diversity. He was, I knew, a man who sincerely believed in gender equality. Six of the thirteen members of his executive committee were women. I did not believe for a second that Michel Landel would be party to any kind of patriarchal 'mansplaining' endeavour.

So I checked the context.

The Global Summit of Women is hosted by GlobeWomen, an organization 'conceived as the nexus at which all sectors – public, private and non-profit – would come together under the common vision of dramatically expanding women's economic opportunities globally'.[10] As one would expect, it is run by women, and its summits are organized by an all-woman planning committee. Most of the speakers are women, as are most of the attendees. The gender issue, if there is one, is a shortage of men. Here's the first item in GlobeWomen's newsletter of 18 December 2013, six months before that incriminating picture was taken:

I. VOICES OF MALE CEOS AT THE 2014 GLOBAL SUMMIT OF WOMEN
In response to a challenge from Taj France CEO Gianmarco Monsellato to include more men in women's events as part of their own 'continuing education' in gender relations, the 2014 Global Summit of Women has invited several male CEOs, mostly French, to its June 5–7th gathering in Paris where 1,000 women from 70+ countries will be attending.[11]

The whole point of the panel was to hear from men in business who had experience of supporting female advancement. Such a sensible and inclusive move to bring like-minded men into the gender-equality conversation should have been welcomed.

> **Context tactic #2**
> *Ignoring relevant context*

Most of the people reacting with outrage and scorn to the all-male panel at the Global Summit of Women were Misinformers unaware of the context. They should have checked their facts before weighing in, but they weren't guilty of deliberate misrepresentation of the truth. Unfortunately, many professional communicators manipulate or ignore context intentionally to mislead.

Politicians like to misrepresent opponents' positions by quoting them out of context, making it easier to refute them. This is sometimes called a *straw man* argument: the politician sets up a straw man – a deliberate misrepresentation of another's point of view – and then knocks it down. For example, a British Labour politician might selectively quote a Conservative health minister talking about outsourcing hospital facilities management so as to imply that he is in favour of privatizing the NHS – a hanging crime in the UK. Or an AfD politician might quote the German chancellor out of context to imply that she wants to let *all* foreign migrants into the country rather than just the desperate refugees she had in mind.

A related trick is to claim support for an argument by quoting some well-respected figure out of context. Such an *appeal to authority* is one of the first rhetorical devices that children learn: 'But Mummy said I can watch TV after my bath,' the little boy earnestly tells his confused babysitter, leaving out the context that this concession only applies on Saturdays. Business consultants do something similar when they tell prospective clients about the latest neuroscience research and imply it supports their leadership development pitch, ignoring the fact that the research applies only to prisoners, or toddlers, or rats.

When Ted Cruz was running for the Republican presidential nomination, he approved a television advertisement that included a clip of Donald Trump saying, 'Planned Parenthood serves a good function'.[12] Planned Parenthood is a US non-profit that provides a range of reproductive services, including STI testing and contraception, but it is best known for conducting around half of all US abortions. For many conservative voters, abortion is anathema, so the Cruz advertisement may have cost Trump a lot of votes. Yet Cruz's team were deliberately misleading viewers on a couple of levels. First of all, this is what Trump actually said in the 2015 Fox News interview:

> I've had many Republican conservative women come up and say, 'Planned Parenthood serves a good function, other than that one aspect [abortion].'

By leaving out all but six of Trump's words, Cruz's team entirely changed his meaning. It was as misleading as if they'd cut Trump's contribution to 'I've had many Republican conservative women' – which would at least have been entertaining.

The Cruz advertisement was doubly mendacious, however, because not only did it omit the immediate context of Trump's quote, it also left out the wider context of the rest of the interview. Before uttering the words Cruz's team exploited, Trump had gone to great lengths in the Fox News interview to burnish his pro-life credentials:

There's two Planned Parenthoods in a way. You have it as an abortion clinic – now that's actually a fairly small part of what they do, but it's a brutal part and I'm totally against it [. . .] I'm totally against the abortion aspect of Planned Parenthood, but I've had many women . . . I've had many Republican conservative women . . .

Whatever we may feel about Donald Trump and his own appalling relationship with the truth, there's no question that in this case he was being deliberately misrepresented by Ted Cruz's team.

Contextual competence

We like our information bite-sized these days. Long-form journalism has given way to news tickers and Twitter feeds. Where once a politician's speech would have been reported in full, now she will be lucky to see ten seconds of it on the evening news. We're just too busy to digest long articles or sit through detailed explanations of policy or world events. Memos at work get deleted unread if they demand too much of our attention. There isn't time to absorb even a fraction of the information available to us.

The inevitable consequence is that we lose context. We respond to events, comments, announcements and hearsay without really knowing what's going on. Our accelerating world and diminishing attention spans are making us dangerously quick to act in situations we don't fully understand. To avoid unfairly pillorying people, or being duped by misleading politicians and commentators, or hurting ourselves through misinformed choices, we need to make sure we are aware of the most relevant context.

In practice

• Always check the context!

• Strengthen your arguments by framing them with the most helpful context.

• Change attitudes to objects, people and issues by changing the context.

But watch out for . . .

• Misinformers who share seemingly shocking news without understanding the full context.

• Misleaders who deliberately leave out critical context, especially when quoting others.

4

Numbers

Torture numbers, and they'll confess to anything.
GREGG EASTERBROOK

Sinister statistics

Left-handers don't always have an easy time. Potato peelers and scissors are designed for right-handers. Boxing classes get disrupted by 'southpaws'. Writing in a chequebook or ring binder can be a struggle. Try eating soup left-handed at a tightly packed dinner table, and you're liable to cause an accident. Even the humble trouser zip favours the right-hander.

But left-handers seemed to face a drawback of an altogether greater magnitude when in 1991 two reputable psychologists published research that suggested left-handed people die on average nine years younger than right-handers.

Dr Diane F. Halpern of California State University at San Bernardino and Dr Stanley Coren of the University of British Columbia reviewed the deaths of 1,000 Californians and found that, on average, the right-handers died aged 75 and the left-handers died aged 66. In their article entitled 'Left-handedness: a marker for decreased survival fitness', they claimed that 'Some of the elevated risk for sinistrals is apparently due to environmental factors that elevate their accident susceptibility.'[1] Tools and vehicles are designed for right-handers, the logic went, therefore left-handers are more likely to have car or chainsaw accidents. As the *New York Times* gloomily noted, 'The proportion of left-handers is 13 percent among people in their 20's, but only 1 percent among those in their 80's.'[2] Being left-handed, it seemed, was as bad for your health as smoking.

The notion that left-handers are doomed to an early death spread rapidly, and as late as 2013 the BBC felt the need to revisit the question: 'Do left-handed people really die young?'[3]

The answer is no. It's complete nonsense. Coren and Halpern had misinterpreted the truth they found in their numbers. They had become Misinformers.

Growing up in the easy-going 1970s, I was positively encouraged to embrace my left-handedness. Previous generations were not so open-minded. Suspicion attached to 'sinister', 'gauche' left-handers, who were once supposed to have been touched by the devil. Left-handers were shunned and discriminated against. Consequently, parents did their best to raise their children as right-handers. Infants that picked up eating or writing implements with the wrong hand were swiftly corrected. Although the natural rate of left-handedness is around 10–12 per cent, a far smaller proportion of the population identified as left-handed in the nineteenth and early twentieth centuries. Only in more recent years have natural left-handers been likely to grow up left-handed.

As a result, the population of left-handers in 1991 was on average younger than the right-handed population. Those who died were therefore likely to be younger than their right-handed cemetery neighbours. This is most easily understood with an analogy. Digital natives who have already died did so at a younger average age than non-digital natives: this has to be true, because people born into a world of widespread Internet use are all under 25 years old. That does not mean that being a digital native is bad for your health.

It was true in 1991 that those left-handers who died did so at a significantly younger age than right-handers. But that truth was widely misinterpreted, causing unnecessary alarm for left-handers everywhere. Any left-handers still anxious about their longevity should be consoled by the competing truth that left-handers and right-handers of the same age enjoy approximately the same life expectancy.

Numbers are wonderful. They give us a clarity about our world that words often fail to provide. They allow us to compare things, to rate things, to measure change, to sum up a galaxy in a single figure. They can speak to anyone of any culture. They are a universal language. But the problem with numbers is that so many of us misunderstand them so much of the time. If even two scientists with statistical training couldn't see what their own numbers were telling them, is it any surprise that so many people get confused about what numbers mean?

This is not a question of mathematical ability. Few of us have any need these days to multiply or divide in our heads. It really doesn't matter if you don't know what a quadratic equation is. What matters, to anyone managing a household budget or voting for a responsible government, is that we understand what a particular number *means*.

But because so many of us find it hard to look at a statistic, or the cost of a new school, or the size of a population, and know what it really means, Misleaders have the opportunity to shape reality by suggesting their own meanings. Numbers ought by rights to be the most transparent form of communication in existence and therefore the hardest to abuse. Instead, we find competing truths co-opting numbers in every walk of life.

Apples, oranges and Chicago murders

Before we get to the numbers themselves, we need to check what they actually represent. Is a business boasting of its employment record talking about full-time employees, contractors, unpaid interns or 'full-time equivalents' (FTEs)? Is the demagogue quoting numbers of migrants, illegal migrants, economic migrants or refugees? Are all those people 'on welfare' unemployed or just eligible for child or low-income support? Do 7 out of 10 people really prefer Product Y, or is it 70 per cent of the people polled in a single town recently flooded with advertisements for Product Y? Are those government statistics referring to corn grown or corn sold, households or individuals, taxpayers or residents? Huge variation can be found in these distinctions, and therein lie opportunities for competing truths.

Canada and Australia have the highest rates of kidnapping in the world. Really, it's true. Not because they are more dangerous than Mexico and Colombia but because their governments include parental disputes over child custody in kidnapping statistics. Similarly, Sweden is said to have the second highest incidence of rape in the world, with more than 60 cases reported per 100,000 inhabitants each year (the rate for India is 2 per 100,000).[4] Yet this reflects not only Sweden's better reporting of sexual crime but also a broader definition of rape.

In 2001, Vice President Dick Cheney tried to make the case for oil exploration in the Arctic National Wildlife Refuge by arguing that only 2,000 acres would be affected, or 'one-fifth the size of Dulles Airport'. It transpired that he was only counting land on which 'production and support facilities' were built, not land required for roads and related infrastructure, nor land close enough to the drilling for wildlife to be disturbed or contaminated. Moreover, where a pipeline was built above ground, only the stanchions on which it rested would be included in the designated acreage, not the ground beneath the rest of the pipeline. Cheney's number was highly misleading, and the proposal was subsequently blocked by the Senate.

Numbers tactic #1
Choosing helpful units

When President Donald Trump told Congress in 2017 that '94 million Americans are out of the labor force',[5] he gave the impression that all these people were involuntarily unemployed. In fact, this Bureau of Labor Statistics figure includes all students over 16 years old, as well as retired people and those choosing not to work. The real US unemployment figure – those people who want to work but can't find a job – was about 7.6 million in early 2017, less than a tenth of Trump's figure.[6]

Similarly, when Trump claimed, 'Places like Afghanistan are safer than some of our inner cities',[7] he was either misremembering or deliberately misrepresenting a comparison of Chicago homicides with *American* deaths in Afghanistan. Between 2001 and 2016, 7,916 murders were recorded in Chicago; over the same period, 2,384 Americans were killed in Afghanistan.[8] The *total* number of violent deaths in Afghanistan was far higher (one academic estimate suggests over 100,000 people have been killed in the Afghanistan war since 2001),[9] and the violent death rate among the relatively small number of Americans in Afghanistan significantly exceeded that of Chicago. Trump's statement was only true in as much as more Americans were killed in Chicago (where many more Americans live) than in Afghanistan. With that logic, he could have said it was safer to live on the sun.

Is that a big number?

The marketing material for one shower gel product claims, '7,927 tingling real mint leaves are packed into Original Source Mint and Tea Tree'. The number 7,927 is printed in large font on the bottle. Is 7,927 mint leaves a lot? I have no idea. It takes thousands of roses to make a few millilitres of essential oil, so perhaps not. Yet the clear suggestion is that this is a *big number*.

In the context of a playful branding concept, it doesn't matter much. But how about these statements?

We're hiring a thousand new nurses.

Our new delivery vehicles use one million gallons less fuel per year.

Are these big numbers? They are clearly meant to be. But unless we know the context, we can't say. A thousand new nurses would be a highly significant development in Estonia, which has approximately 8,000 nursing professionals; in Germany, with a nursing workforce of around 900,000, the new recruits would barely be noticed. For a company like UPS, with over 100,000 delivery vehicles, a million gallons of fuel per year would be a rounding error.

It is now very difficult for young people to buy a home in the UK, largely because of a shortage of 'affordable' house-building. During a major speech in October 2017, prime minister Theresa May declared, 'I will dedicate my premiership to fixing this problem.'[10] She went on: 'Today, I can announce that we will invest an additional £2 billion in affordable housing.' It was meant to sound like a big number, but the media were quick to burst May's bubble: £2 billion ($2.6 billion) is enough to build an extra 25,000 homes, a drop in the ocean in a country with 1.2 million households on council waiting lists for housing.[11]

> **Numbers tactic #2**
> *Making numbers look bigger or smaller*

When someone tries to persuade you that a number is especially significant, the first thing to do is to translate it into a more revealing truth that incorporates relevant context. Percentages are often more informative than the actual numbers. Impressed by Total's investment of $1.4 billion in solar panel manufacturer SunPower Corp? Don't be too hasty to predict a renewable revolution at the French oil and gas giant: the stake represents less than 1 per cent of Total's assets. Wyoming saw just 145 road deaths in 2015, compared to Texas where 3,516 people died in vehicle accidents; but with a population of only 586,000, Wyoming had an alarming annual rate of 24.7 road deaths per 100,000 people, compared to 12.8 in crowded Texas.[12]

In 2010, 18 Chinese employees of the electronics manufacturer Foxconn tried to commit suicide; 14 of them succeeded. The story made headlines in the West because Foxconn manufactured Apple's iPhone and a range of products for global brands like Samsung, Dell and Sony. Immediately, accusations of labour abuse and poor working conditions were thrown at Foxconn and Apple. The suicides were a tragedy, but were they indicative of a real problem at Foxconn? The company employed close to a million people in 2010, implying an annual suicide rate of around 1.5 per 100,000. The average suicide rate in China was 22 per 100,000.[13] In other words, the suicide rate at Foxconn was less than 7 per cent of the national average. Fourteen highly visible deaths had obscured a much more positive competing truth.

Barack Obama was criticized for saying that terrorism costs fewer lives in America than bathtubs, but he was absolutely right. According to the National Safety Council, 464 people drowned in American baths in 2013; 1,810 drowned in natural water, 903 were accidentally suffocated or strangled in bed, and more than 30,000 died by falling.[14] That same year, just three people were killed in America by Islamist terrorists, during the Boston marathon[15] – less than one per cent of the bathtub death toll.

But we can also be led astray by relative numbers. Misleaders who want to disguise a big figure may characterize it as a small proportion of something even bigger. It's easy to dismiss something that is only a tiny fraction of something else, even when the absolute number is substantial.

'Three percent of all Planned Parenthood health services are abortion services,' declared the US non-profit on its website.* The vast majority of their services, according to the 2014–15 annual report, are related to STI testing and treatment (45 per cent) and contraception (31 per cent).[16] Three per cent makes abortion sound like a marginal activity for Planned Parenthood. But how did they get to that figure? Their annual report records 9,455,582 'services' delivered in 2014–15. Almost one million of these involve the provision of emergency contraception kits. More than one million are pregnancy tests. Over 3.5 million are STI tests. None of these services are remotely comparable to abortion, either in terms of cost, labour or impact on the individual. Yet the high numbers of such routine activities dwarf the 323,999 abortion procedures conducted in the same year. Nevertheless, this figure† represents nearly 50 per cent of all reported US abortions.[17]

The UK government spends 0.7 per cent of Gross National Income (GNI) on Overseas Development Assistance, or overseas aid. This has been a UN target for developed countries since 1970,

---

* The claim has since been removed, but lives on in the 2014–15 annual report.
† Assuming each 'abortion procedure' results in an abortion.

but the UK is one of only six nations to meet the target. Should British taxpayers be proud of this generosity, or are we paying too much? As a tiny percentage, 0.7 per cent of GNI sounds a harmless kind of commitment. In fact, this translated into £13.6 billion ($18 billion) in 2016.[18] That really is a big number. It is more than the UK government spends on universities. It is more than it spends on police.

The sum of £13.6 billion may be appropriate for a rich country to spend every year on the very substantial health, nutrition and infrastructure needs of other nations, but few commentators seem to have given the absolute cash value – as opposed to the GNI percentage – very much thought. During the 2017 UK election, there was endless debate around the Conservatives' plan to cut free school lunches for pupils aged 4–7 (expected saving: £650 million) and replace them with free school breakfasts (expected cost: £60 million) but almost no discussion of that far greater £13.6 billion expenditure on overseas aid.

As if we don't have enough trouble with the basic numbers, politicians, marketers and journalists have become adept at making them look bigger or smaller than they really are. One favourite trick for minimizing perceived government expenditure is to talk about the cost per day rather than per year, or even the cost per taxpayer or citizen. 'What a bargain! How the Royal Family costs you just 56p a year,' read a headline in the loyal *Daily Express*[19] (cost to taxpayers that year: £35.7 million). One cancer drug 'costs just 43p per day for every patient,' according to a supportive newspaper, apparently uninterested in the total cost to the state.[20] 'Free 4-year college for every American would only cost taxpayers 70 cents a day,' claims a numerate campaigner.[21] To make a number look bigger, just make the timescale longer: 'The Government recently reaffirmed its commitment to cycling and walking by investing over £300m over the life of this Parliament'[22] sounds more generous than £60 million per year. 'Federal government announces additional $81 billion for infrastructure'[23] is a more exciting headline than 'Canada to invest an extra $7.36 billion per year for 11 years'.

Alternatively, communicators can make something look cheap or expensive by converting it into some unrelated unit of measurement such as nurses or hot beverages. 'For less than the cost of a coffee and a piece of cake each week, you can have our hospital treatment insurance,' promised one recent healthcare offer. Or why not use hospitals themselves as your unit of measurement? Eurosceptic MEP Daniel Hannan claimed that the amount of money misspent by the EU in 2013 was 'Enough to build 10 state-of-the-art NHS hospitals.'[24]

Leaving aside the huge variation in the price of both cake and hospitals, such creative financial conversions can dangerously muddy the waters. A thing costs what it costs in dollars, euros or pounds. Any adaptation of that cost is a competing truth, most likely serving a particular agenda.

Brexit by numbers

One number dominated the Brexit referendum. It was this: 'Britain sends £350 million a week to the EU'. Leading Brexiteer Boris Johnson even took a 'battle bus' around the country with this claim emblazoned on the side. It was a straightforward lie. There is nothing more to say about it in this book on truth.

But other, truer numbers were cleverly used to mislead. The chancellor of the exchequer, George Osborne, made the case for Remain with one particularly striking number. The Treasury published a forecast suggesting that by 2030 British GDP would be 6 per cent less outside the EU than in. Osborne's press release read, 'Britain will be worse off by £4,300 a year per household if Britain votes to leave European Union.'[25]

What's wrong with this? Firstly, Osborne's press release gave the impression that Britain would be 'worse off' than it is *now*. In fact, the Treasury forecast shows Britain will have significantly higher GDP in 2030, whether inside or outside the EU. A more complete and honest headline would have read, 'Britain will be *less well off than it otherwise would have been, but will still be better off than now.*'

Then there is the issue of the households. The press release implies (although it does not actually say) that each British household will have £4,300 less to spend (newspapers interpreting the press release said exactly that). But the Treasury analysis is not talking about household income – GDP is a very different beast, as it includes factors such as corporate investments and government expenditure. With GDP at £1,869 billion and 27 million households, the UK's GDP per household in 2015 was over £69,000. As the median household disposable income in 2014–15 was just over a third of that figure, at £25,700, it is immediately apparent that the very concept of GDP per household is pretty meaningless. George Osborne and his Treasury team were well aware of all this; their headline was a truth, but a deliberately misleading one.

What's new?

In 2016, Children with Cancer UK issued a distressing press release: 'Cancer cases in children and young people up 40 per cent in past 16 years.'[26] This prompted a downright crazy headline from the normally sober *Telegraph*: 'Modern life is killing our children'.[27] The *Telegraph*, apparently unaware that children's cancer death rates in the UK had dropped by a stunning 24 per cent in the previous decade,[28] quoted the charity's 'scientific adviser' blaming all kinds of things from domestic electricity to hairdryers.

It is true that the number of UK childhood cancer cases has gone up. But there are two very good reasons for this. The number of children in the UK has increased over the same period; with more children we would expect more cases. Moreover, diagnostics have improved substantially, allowing many more cases of cancer to be diagnosed and treated earlier;[29] previously, cancer arising in children would often not have been identified or recorded in health statistics until adulthood. The charity knows both of these facts, so their press-release headline must be considered misleading even if it's true. Cancer Research UK, a different charity, estimates cancer incidence rates in children have increased by a much more realistic 11 per cent since the early 1990s.[30]

Some of our most significant truths derive from the way in which important numbers change over time. Is a social issue getting better or worse? Is a government spending more or less? Is a company growing or declining? The numbers should be able to give us a straight answer. But a Misleader may be able to tell a different story by choosing a related number. Are more teenagers getting arrested? If the population is growing, perhaps the *proportion* of teenage arrests is actually decreasing. How about the number of under-16s? Or the proportion of black teenagers? Or the number of teenage arrests for violent crime? Or teenage arrests in a particular city? Or teenage repeat offenders? One of those metrics is bound to be heading in the right direction.

Picking a different start year for the period under consideration may change the truth about any change observed. In January 2011, American businesses could celebrate two years of stock-market growth, with the S&P 500 rising 36 per cent since January 2009. Or they could mourn three years of stock-market decline, with the S&P 500 falling 10 per cent since January 2008.

'The crime figures this week were pretty bad,' admitted Labour spin doctor Lance Price in his private diary entry for 20 January 2000. Price was a key member of Tony Blair's Downing Street team. 'We had one mad meeting in advance in which somebody helpfully pointed out that if you took out the areas where crime was going up then crime was going down! It occurred to me that we could apply the same principle to hospital waiting lists.'[31]

Two years later, a group of researchers examined a set of statistical 'indicators' published by the Labour Party, under the heading 'What Labour's done in your constituency'. These measured progress in areas such as education, the NHS, policing and the economy. 'What drew our attention,' said the researchers, was the impression given by Labour's numbers that 'everything appeared to be getting better everywhere'.[32] Surely no government was that good? The researchers examined each of the indicators in detail to figure out how Labour had managed to make it look like every single one was improving:

> If an indicator had not improved for one timescale then the timescale was changed for that constituency to one during which conditions had improved. Indicators are also reported at different spatial scales . . . in the case of crime figures, for example, for some constituencies indicators are given which are averages for the whole of England and Wales if those constituencies are in police force areas and regions where crime had increased. Thus, on the Labour Party's website crime had fallen under Labour everywhere.

That 'mad meeting' in Downing Street, it seems, had translated into serious communications policy.

Numbers tactic #3
Concealing or exaggerating trends

Graphically, Misleaders can transform truths by changing the scale of a graph or using axes that don't start at 0. Downward trends can be made to look flat, and insignificant growth can appear significant, if the data are plotted on a favourable axis. If the number of hospital beds available in your region has risen from 15,134 to 15,326, that trivial 1 per cent increase can be presented as a stellar achievement on a graph whose y-axis begins at 15,000.

Poor sales of your leading product can be disguised for that awkward investors' meeting by plotting cumulative sales figures – the total number of products you have sold ever, not just this year. For Misleaders, the great thing about cumulative graphs is that they can't go down. It is impossible to have sold fewer products cumulatively this year than last year, unless you operate a very generous returns policy. Tim Cook, Apple's CEO, presented a chart of 'Cumulative iPhone sales' in 2013, thus concealing two quarters of declining sales. He did the same thing a month later for iPad sales, which had also declined for two quarters. Business news website Quartz concluded, 'Apple is either terrible at designing charts or thinks you won't notice the difference.'[33]

There is a lovely graph on the Web that plots the decline in the number of pirates since 1820 against the rise in global average temperature. The correlation is uncanny: as the pirate population has decreased, the world has got warmer. Clearly, the fall in crime on the high seas has allowed more intercontinental trade, which has caused global warming!

That conclusion, of course, is ridiculous. As any fool can see, it's the other way round: rising temperatures cause the alcohol in ships' rum to evaporate, weakening the morale of pirates and driving them into more honest trades.

This spoof analysis warns us against assuming that an observed correlation between two number sets implies some kind of causal relationship. It has been noted that the more ice creams are sold in beach resorts the more people seem to drown. That does not mean that ice cream is causing fatal cramp; people tend to eat ice cream when it warms up, and people also tend to go swimming when the weather improves. There is no causation between ice cream consumption and increased cases of drowning; both are caused by a third factor.

It's an easy trap for Misinformers. One worrying recent phenomenon is the apparent link between poverty and obesity in developed nations. 'You can almost now tell somebody's background by their weight,' said UK public health minister Anna Soubry in 2013.[34] The poorest children in the UK are nearly twice as likely to be obese as the richest. Does this mean poverty causes obesity and therefore puts lives at risk?

Some politicians have suggested as much, citing the low cost of junk food, and campaigners have used the correlation to argue for policies to reduce poverty. Yet the causality is not clear. Cheap food does not have to be high in sugar and fat. Obesity may be caused more by educational and cultural factors that are associated with areas of deprivation. Simply increasing financial support to poor families will not necessarily improve their diets. The money may be better spent on public awareness campaigns, sports facilities or nutritious school meals. Poverty alleviation measures might be needed, but arguing for them on the basis of the obesity correlation is probably a misuse of a competing truth.

Lies and damned lies

It's a popular saying: 'There are three kinds of lies: lies, damned lies, and statistics.' Yet we depend on statistics to make the right choices in health, politics, investment, education and numerous other fields. Statistics aren't lies; but as truths, they can be much more malleable than one might expect from simple numbers.

One of the best-known statistics is the average. To estimate the average height in a population, we might measure the height of 75 people and take the average for the sample. One might not think that it was possible to generate competing truths around something as simple as the average – but there is more than one kind of average. There is the *mean*, which we obtain by adding up all the heights in our sample and dividing by 75. And then there is the *median*: if we line up the 75 people in order of their height, the person halfway along the line is the median height. These two averages will be different numbers.*

The choice between the mean and the median can be exploited by Misleaders addressing audiences who may not know the difference. In 2014–15, the UK *median* income before tax was £22,400. The *mean* income before tax for the same year was £31,800 (both figures apply to taxpayers only).[35] The higher mean should not surprise us in a society where a small number of people earn many millions: they make almost no difference to the median, but their vast compensation packages skew the mean substantially upwards.

So in 2015 both of these statements would have been true:

A teacher on a salary of £28,000 is earning below the average income.

A teacher on a salary of £28,000 is earning above the average income.

Most commentators don't bother to specify what kind of average they are using. Smart politicians, union leaders and activists will choose the type of average that suits their agenda.

> **Numbers tactic #4**
> *Cherry-picking statistics*

---

* There is a third, less common, average called the *mode*, which identifies the value in a sample that occurs most frequently.

The mean can be slippery in other ways too. Many parents are concerned about class sizes at their children's schools, generally preferring smaller classes where teachers have more time to devote to each child. So politicians are keen to show that class sizes on average are small. However, this does not mean that the average child is in a small class.

To illustrate this counter-intuitive phenomenon, imagine that there are only two school classes in your town. One has 10 kids, the other has 50. The mean class size is 30, which sounds reasonable. But the majority of children are in the 50-strong class. So the 'average' child will be in a class size of 50. To be more precise, the mean number of kids in a child's class will be just over 43.

So when politicians talk truthfully about the average class size in a state or country, that figure will be lower than the number of kids in the average child's class. The same trick can be applied to overcrowding in prisons, on trains, in hospitals and so on. The national or state mean will always underestimate the average person's experience.

Consider this riddle. A man with longer-than-average hair enters a bar and the average length of hair in the bar decreases. How is that possible?

It's a simple riddle, but it encapsulates a problematic aspect of statistics known as Simpson's Paradox. It is problematic because the same numbers can convey two very different truths. Before we answer the riddle, let's look at a real-world example.

Between 2000 and 2012, the median US wage, adjusted for inflation, rose by 0.9 per cent.[36] This might seem like good news. Yet over the same period, the median wage for high-school drop-outs declined by 7.9 per cent, the median wage for high-school graduates declined by 4.7 per cent, the median wage for people with some college education declined by 7.6 per cent, and the median wage for people with at least one degree declined by 1.2 per cent.

Put simply, every economic group in the US experienced a wage decline, even though overall the average wage went up.

You can see why they call it a paradox.

Back to that riddle. The answer hinges on what we mean by 'longer-than-average'. We aren't talking about 'average' for the whole population; the man had hair that was longer than average *for men*. But of course there are also women in the bar, and the newcomer's hair is shorter than the average for women. The average length of hair for the subgroup of men in the bar has increased and the average for the subgroup of women has not changed; the overall average has decreased.

The key to Simpson's Paradox is recognizing the difference between the group and the subgroup.

Look again at those wage declines. Did you assume that each of those subgroups (high-school drop-out, college educated, etc.) was fixed over time? We know that isn't true: many more American workers are now college graduates. In other words, the best-paid subgroups are bigger relative to the worst-paid subgroups than in 2000. So although the median wage for college graduates has decreased, their greater number has pulled the overall average up.

This matters because the different conclusions at the group and subgroup levels allow American politicians to argue, truthfully, that wages have gone up *and* that wages have gone down. Most people have never heard of Simpson's Paradox and lack the statistical training to understand that two such contradictory truths can co-exist. As a result, they will believe the version they hear, or – if they hear both – they may lose trust in statistics altogether.

Wages have gone up, and here are the statistics to prove it!

Wages have gone down, and here are the statistics to prove it!

Both true.

It's easy to see why people get cynical.

Grossly misleading?

When it comes to understanding the economic health of a nation, there is no more closely watched measure than Gross Domestic Product (GDP). A single number is supposed to capture the size and performance of an economy formed of billions of transactions and investments. GDP measures the value created in an economy, adjusted for inflation. It is used to determine interest rates, sovereign credit ratings, pension payments, tax rates and government expenditure. If GDP rises, we expect living standards for ordinary people to increase; if it falls for two quarters in a row, we declare a recession and cut important expenditure. GDP impacts us all.

In 2015, the GDP of Ireland grew by 26 per cent. A staggering achievement, one might think, for the small Eurozone country. GDP growth in India was 7.6 per cent and in China it was 6.9 per cent. The Eurozone average was a paltry 1.7 per cent. How did the Irish do it?

Sadly, the people of Ireland had very little to do with their GDP surge. They didn't create it, and they will not benefit much from it. Instead, a small number of foreign companies have moved some chips around the global gaming table for tax reasons, and a set of valuable assets have landed in Ireland, where they are now generating substantial income. Ireland imposes a corporate tax rate of just 12.5 per cent, making it an extremely attractive jurisdiction for global businesses able to move their domicile through corporate inversions and other arrangements. Over 700 US companies are now officially headquartered in Ireland. Three hundred billion euros of productive assets were transferred to Ireland in 2015, including €35 billion of aeroplanes belonging to Dutch leasing company AerCap and a range of intellectual property belonging to tech giants like Apple.

But what do all those extra assets and that extra national income mean for the people of Ireland? Not much, it seems. Officially, exports rose in 2015 from €220 billion to €295 billion, but most of the goods and services that made up that staggering increase were not produced in Ireland. The operations and management of US companies that have relocated their domicile in Ireland tend to remain in the US. There has been an increase in corporate tax revenues, easing Austerity-struck government budgets somewhat, but incomes for most Irish citizens will be unaffected. According to Ireland's Central Statistics Office, the level of employment hasn't changed much. The wealth and prospects of most people in Ireland will be more or less the same as before.

What is the point, then, of the GDP metric? If a country can see such significant growth on paper yet experience no material improvement for most of its citizens, can we really say that the measure of Gross Domestic Product is fit for purpose? In Ireland's case, it may become positively misleading. In early 2016, there was celebration that the country's Debt:GDP ratio had fallen from over 125 per cent in 2013 to less than 100 per cent. That achievement looks hollow in the context of an artificially inflated GDP. Ireland is still the world's second most indebted nation per capita.

Ireland is an exceptional case of GDP distortion, but the measure is problematic for all of us. When a motorcyclist in Colorado takes a tumble and breaks a leg, it's bad news for her but good news for GDP: she or her insurer will have to pay for an ambulance, for medical treatment, for a hospital bed, for physiotherapy, perhaps even for lawyers and a new motorcycle; her misfortune means an increase in economic activity, which boosts GDP. Similarly, if a rural African community suffers a drought and must buy food rather than growing it, GDP increases as a direct result of their hardship. And if primary rainforest is plundered for timber, or an earthquake necessitates new construction, GDP goes up. On the other hand, if an auto manufacturer invents a cheaper, more efficient car, expenditure on both vehicles and fuel may fall, causing a decline in GDP. So although GDP is seen as the best measure we have of the economic health of a nation, an increase in GDP does not necessarily imply increased happiness and well-being. The truth that GDP has gone up may well coexist with the competing truth that many people are worse off in terms of their health and happiness.

This discrepancy between GDP and human well-being is becoming increasingly important as technology changes our activities and the things we value. GDP has been largely stagnant in most developed countries for several years, and commentators have taken this to mean our living standards are also stagnant. Yet in that time the quality of our machines, communications and medicines has improved substantially, and we have gained access to almost unlimited knowledge, music, TV, book, networking and games resources. Young people who once might have craved a car or a wardrobe of clothes may now be more interested in adding friends on Facebook or posting selfies on Instagram. We obtain immense value from streaming music, accessing online information, playing multiplayer games, searching for jobs and partners, and building our networks, but because we can do all of it without spending a cent, much of that value is ignored in GDP statistics. An app that helps you coordinate a car share or mutual childcare is likely to add significantly to your quality of life; it is also likely to decrease GDP, by reducing your expenditure on taxis and child-minders.

Recognizing the problem, the deputy director of China's National Bureau of Statistics called in 2016 for services offered for free to be included in GDP reporting. 'The digitised economy gives birth to new business models, and creates a great deal of non-currency transactions,' said Xu Xianchun. 'Most of their revenue comes from online ads, not from the users who actually enjoy their services. So the value of the final services, free to consumers, are often underestimated or neglected.'[37] Britain's Office for National Statistics has been tasked to investigate how to include the sharing economy in GDP estimates. The question of how to quantify the real value of WhatsApp messages, Google maps or YouTube videos is yet to be resolved.

Even if statisticians find a way to incorporate the free digital goods and sharing economy services of our age into GDP, we should still recognize its limitations when we next hear a politician trumpet a slight increase in the measure. As Robert F. Kennedy said in 1968 of the closely related Gross National Product, 'It measures neither our wit nor our courage, neither our wisdom nor our learning, neither our compassion nor our devotion to our country; it measures everything in short, except that which makes life worthwhile.'[38]

Number-crunched

The researchers critiquing the Labour Party's performance indicators in 2002 drew this conclusion:

> It is fair to say that nothing presented on the Labour Party website is untrue in the strict sense of the word. It is just that the way in which the statistics have been put together – mixing and matching years and areas to present the best possible picture of improvement – is disingenuous overall.

Such manipulation of statistics may seem so commonplace as to be fair play. If you're naive enough to believe the numbers published by a partisan organization, some might argue, you deserve to be taken for a ride. The trouble is that many people are so uncomfortable with numbers that they suspend critical thinking in their presence. If the man from the ministry holds up a set of figures, who are we to question them? If rival think tanks present us with contradictory numbers, how are we to establish which set represents the greater truth?

How we understand the world depends on how we measure it. Our understanding, in turn, determines our votes, our actions and our attitudes. Numbers matter. We mustn't lose trust in them. But we have to get better at interpreting them and holding Misleaders to account when they use numerical truths to lie to us.

In practice

• Dig deep to understand what each number in a debate really represents.

• Make sure you're using the most relevant units and comparing like with like.

• Put numbers in context by comparing them to other relevant numbers to show how big they actually are.

But watch out for . . .

• Misleaders who try to make a number look bigger or smaller, or a trend more significant, than it really is.

• Misinformers who assume causation between two correlated datasets.

• Misleaders who cherry-pick statistics or are vague about which average they've used.

5

Story

To hell with facts! We need stories!

KEN KESEY

The most complicated story in the world?

When setting out to explain how the 2008 global financial crisis happened, the former governor of the Bank of England, Mervyn King, titled his text 'The story of the crisis'.[1]

'We should start,' he wrote, 'at the key turning point – the fall of the Berlin Wall.' Lord King describes how the 'demise of the socialist model of a planned economy' encouraged China, India and other countries to embrace the international trading system, with the result that the pool of labour supplying that system more than trebled. He explains how this led to large trade surpluses in Asia, which ultimately led to a global excess of savings. As long-term interest rates are determined by the global balance between saving and spending, the 'savings glut' caused interest rates to plummet and asset prices to rise. Borrowing money became very cheap, incentivizing businesses to invest in more borderline projects. Meanwhile, asset managers and banks were desperate to find investment opportunities that would give a better return than low-interest bonds and loans.

King recounts how this resulted in bank balance sheets expanding rapidly, filled with increasingly risky investments, often in newly devised financial instruments that few people understood. Together with the imbalance in the world economy, this produced a highly unstable economic powder keg, just waiting for a spark. This came when banks stopped trusting each other to be able to repay loans, because of the pile of high-risk, opaque investments they had taken on. Financial institutions could no longer be sure their counterparts would be able to find the cash when needed, so they stopped lending to each other, exacerbating the liquidity problem. What followed – the collapse of Lehman Brothers, the plunging stock markets and multi-billion-dollar government bail-outs – is painfully familiar to us all.

The three essential components of a story

Why did Mervyn King call this account of such a serious and world-shaking set of events a 'story'? To answer that question, we need to understand what a story is. Many people, on hearing the word, think first of fairy stories and novels, of dragons and spies and romance. 'Tell me a story' is the nursery plea. Stories are for fun, for children, for the movies, for escapism and for journalists in search of a scoop. Stories, many people might feel, are only loosely related to the truth.

After a decade of writing stories for companies and government organizations, I would like to offer a different definition:

A story is a coherent and selective account of a process of change, which emphasizes causal relationships between situations and events.

I know . . . it sounds like I've taken a fun concept and ruined it with boring terminology. But stories are so fundamental to the way we communicate that it's worth trying to understand what makes them work. These are the indispensable elements of any story:

A process of change

If nothing changes, there is no story. If your hero ends up exactly as they are in the beginning, there is no story. Michael Corleone is transformed from a clean-living serviceman into the most ruthless of Mafia dons. Dorothy gets back home from Oz, but she herself has changed irreversibly. The run-up to the 2008 financial crisis took us from a period of global economic balance and conservative bank balance sheets to a time of increasing disequilibrium and swollen, risky balance sheets. By contrast, a description of banks taking the same deposits and making the same loans year after year would be no story at all.

Causal relationships

Cause and effect are at the heart of any story. Because Tintin finds a scroll of parchment hidden in a model ship, he embarks on a treasure hunt in the Caribbean. Because the Trojans decide to bring a giant wooden horse inside their walls, the Greeks are able to overrun the city. Because interest rates were so low, investors took greater risks in the search for yield. This is what makes a story logical, and therefore credible to an audience: the storyteller makes clear *why* things happen.

Trigger

Bring causation and change together and you generate what screen-writers refer to as the 'inciting incident': the reason why a process of change begins. Mervyn King calls it 'the key turning point' in his story: the fall of the Berlin Wall. Every story needs this first trigger that sets events in motion. Dracula hires a law firm to oversee the purchase of an English estate. Mr Darcy's friend rents the big house near Elizabeth Bennet's home. Princess Leia obtains the plans of the Death Star and hides them in the droid R2-D2. Of course things have happened beforehand (as a recent *Star Wars* prequel about the stealing of those plans illustrates), but this point marks the beginning of the story proper. The trigger is the original cause in an account of multiple causes and effects.

There are many other elements that contribute to a good story – a hero, a villain, a mentor, tricksters, allies, setbacks and obstacles, twists and dramatic reveals – but these three are the defining foundations that every story must have. Here they are in Shakespeare's *Hamlet*:

The trigger: the appearance of the ghost of Hamlet's father, the former king, who reveals that he was murdered by Hamlet's uncle, Claudius, now in possession of both throne and queen.

Causal relationships: because Hamlet is filled with doubt over the ghost's claim, he devises a test of Claudius's guilt; because Ophelia's father is killed by the man she loves, she goes mad and is drowned; because Claudius fears Hamlet, he plots his death; because Ophelia dies, her brother seeks revenge.

Process of change: Hamlet learns the truth about his father's death; Ophelia goes mad; most of the main characters are killed; the Danish throne passes to the Norwegian crown prince.

A process of change, causal relationships and a trigger: Mervyn King's account of the origins of the 2008 financial crisis has all three.

Making sense of our world

But why a story in the first place? What is it about this age-old cognitive structure that makes the former governor of the Bank of England choose it to communicate such a complex subject?

The answer lies in those causal relationships. Human beings crave explanation. If something important happens, we want to understand *why* it happens. Because stories seem to show how one thing leads to another, they help us make sense of a chaotic world. A huge amount of stuff happened during the financial crisis, much of it frightening, destructive and mystifying. King's story draws a coherent and comprehensible thread of logic through the mire of events.

In the simplest stories, there is a single cause for every effect, and each effect in turn becomes the cause of the next effect. King's story is not so simple. He describes multiple causes for multiple effects, and his story of complex economic and banking inter-relationships lasts for several pages. Nevertheless, a focused reader will come away from it with the feeling that they understand why the crisis occurred. This is the real value of stories as a means of communication: they make complex stuff coherent and clear.

But we pay a price for that clarity and coherence. The trouble with stories is that they are highly selective. Stories, bluntly, do not give the whole picture. They are partial truths. We can see this literally in movies, with cuts between scenes that skip over substantial periods of time, and camera angles that exclude much of the action. Screenwriters, directors and editors choose what to show from a multiplicity of options. Charles Dickens, writing the life of David Copperfield, recounts only a few episodes from that life. David Nicholls, in his novel *One Day*, paints a portrait of two lives over two decades by narrating only the events of a single day in each year.

So it is with nonfiction stories. When we describe a sequence of

113

events, we make choices about our starting point, the moments we recount, the ways in which we portray people. Crucially, we simplify cause and effect. Stories are very tidy in this way: *because* Paris steals Helen from Menelaus, Greece declares war on Troy; *because* Heathcliff overhears Cathy saying that marrying him would degrade her, he leaves home and wins the fortune that will make him master of Wuthering Heights. Real life is rarely so black and white. Events often have multiple causes. It may well be that X was one of the causes of Y, but so were U, V and W. Politicians routinely explain the sovereign debt crisis or the emergence of Islamic State with simple cause-and-effect stories that favour their own agenda. Rival politicians tell alternative stories with different causal links which may be just as true. Scholars like Nassim Nicholas Taleb even talk of a 'narrative fallacy' – our 'limited ability to look at sequences of facts without weaving an explanation into them, or, equivalently, forcing a logical link'.[2]

Katrina's story

In her polemical book *The Shock Doctrine*, Naomi Klein told a story about the response to Hurricane Katrina.[3] President George W. Bush's administration saw Katrina as an opportunity, she wrote, to apply neoliberal policies such as privatization, deregulation, smaller government and free trade to the decaying public infrastructure of New Orleans. The devastating hurricane (the trigger in her story) caused such an upheaval in the city's demographics and municipal operations that some saw the city as a blank slate on which to test their free-market ideas. 'Within weeks, the Gulf Coast became a domestic laboratory' for a 'government-run-by-contractors'.

Inspired by the work of Nobel Prize-winning economist Milton Friedman, the Bush administration withheld emergency funds from public sector organizations, directing $3.4 billion instead to private 'disaster capitalism' contractors such as Halliburton, Bechtel and Blackwater. The City of New Orleans, stripped of its tax base by the catastrophe, had to fire 3,000 workers; in their place, the federal government hired private consultants to plan the reconstruction, favouring real-estate developers over New Orleans citizens. Public housing units sitting on prime land long coveted by developers were marked for demolition as soon as their residents were evacuated. Public schools were converted into 'free-market' charter schools. President Bush introduced new tax incentives for big business in the region and waived regulations protecting workers and their pay.

The (overwhelmingly black) poor of New Orleans were too battered and traumatized by the hurricane to oppose these blatantly neoliberal measures. They were 'shocked' into submission. And so 'people who don't believe in governments', as Klein characterizes free-market enthusiasts, were able to use a natural disaster to build a 'corporate shadow state' funded 'almost exclusively with public resources'. The rich and middle classes, she suggests, will thrive inside gated communities, served by private security firms, schools and hospitals, while the poor are displaced or live wretched lives under the weakened protection of an increasingly diminished public sector.

Klein's book is an impressive and well-researched work, and it is not my intention to dispute her New Orleans story. The facts she presents are true, as far as I know. But other facts from Katrina can be used to tell a very different story:

> *The public-sector response to Hurricane Katrina was*
> *completely inadequate. FEMA (the Federal Emergency*
> *Management Agency) was disorganized and slow to act.*
> *Hundreds of volunteer firefighters from other cities were*
> *left idle in Atlanta. New Orleans mayor Ray Nagin failed*

to order an evacuation until less than 24 hours before Katrina made landfall and then refused to allow a fleet of school buses to be used to transport elderly and disabled residents out of the city. Police were unable to control widespread looting. National Guard units in Louisiana had a shortage of troops and were distracted by protecting their own headquarters from flooding and rescuing soldiers who could not swim. Overall, according to the 2006 Congressional Report, the government's response was marked by 'fecklessness, flailing and organizational paralysis'.

Luckily, the private sector was equipped and ready to step in and do the job the public sector could not. Companies like Halliburton, Bechtel and Blackwater had the manpower, experience and leadership to respond swiftly and effectively in a very difficult environment. They were able to organize food and water supplies, medical services, temporary housing and a clean-up operation far faster than the beleaguered city authorities or FEMA could. A Dutch company, De Boer, was contracted to provide a massive temporary mortuary, as state facilities were insufficient for the expected fatalities. The Army Corps of Engineers hired four companies to clear debris in deals worth a total of $2 billion because they didn't have the capacity to do it themselves. It is a credit to the Bush administration that they were willing to make use of private enterprise to meet the great public need. Moreover, they took appropriate steps to ensure federal funds were spent wisely: 30 Homeland Security investigators and auditors were dispatched to monitor contractors' work on the Gulf Coast. In drawing on all available resources, the Bush administration showed a flexibility and pragmatism that were sorely needed following the woeful initial public response to the disaster.

Both stories present a set of more or less accurate facts, yet the tone and message could not be more different. Neoliberal conspiracy or well-intentioned pragmatism? Without seeing into the souls of George W. Bush and his advisers, it's hard to be sure. So, in the absence of a definitive truth, we can only fall back on the partial truths these stories represent.

You may be more inclined to accept one story over the other, depending on your view of the Bush administration, of privatization or of conspiracy theories. Your mindset or worldview may predispose you to believe one version of events. Nevertheless, both stories are truths, in as much as the facts they present are true. How those facts are linked together in a set of causal relationships that coalesce to form an ultimate message . . . well, that's storytelling.

> **Story tactic #1**
> *Linking facts to imply causation*

While Mervyn King's 'story of the crisis' rings true and makes sense, other commentators have told a different story. Where King begins his story with the fall of the Berlin Wall, others choose as their trigger the deregulation of the financial services industry, the invention of collateralized debt obligations or the US housing bubble. Some focus on the greed of bankers, others the recklessness of consumers, others the incompetence of politicians or the corruption of ratings agencies. These storytellers choose triggers and prioritize causal relationships that support their themes. Some blame policymakers like King, and their stories describe disastrous effects resulting from the deregulation that King and other central bankers oversaw. By contrast, King's story of overwhelming macroeconomic trends helpfully implies that central banks and regulators had little power to prevent the coming disaster.

The sheer complexity of the financial crisis makes it possible to tell any number of stories about it that serve all kinds of agendas.

I don't wish to suggest that stories necessarily distort the truth or are inherently misleading. Most of us explain stuff by telling stories, whether we mean to or not; the structure of our presentations or accounts of events often takes the form of a story, with a trigger, causal relationships and a process of change. That's just the way we're wired, after millennia of telling stories to each other about gods, beasts, enemies and relationships.

But if we're going to tell a story, we ought to tell the right story. We need to be aware of the different ways a story can be constructed out of the facts available, and the different conclusions we can elicit in our audience.

The purpose of a garden

Royal Botanic Gardens, Kew, is a British organization dedicated to plant and fungi research and conservation. Perhaps you've heard of Kew Gardens; perhaps you've even visited. If so, my first sentence may surprise you. Isn't Kew just a beautiful heritage garden in southwest London?

That's what many people think. Crucially, it's what many British politicians think. This matters because Kew is partly dependent on public funding: it receives about £20 million ($26 million) per year from the UK government. That sounds rather a lot to give a garden, especially one that draws a healthy crowd of paying visitors. On the other hand, if Kew helps conserve biodiversity, mitigate the effects of climate change, secure global food supplies and reduce the risk of pandemics, then £20 million per year is a laughably small price to pay.

In 2015, Kew faced a funding shortfall of over £5 million per year. Government budget cuts in Austerity Britain looked set to slash Kew's public funding still further. Employees were laid off and critical infrastructure investments were put on hold. Richard Deverell, the director of RBG, Kew, needed to clarify his organization's vital international role and make the case for continued public funding.

As a former BBC controller, Deverell understood the power of storytelling, and he invited me to help craft a new narrative for Kew. To kick things off, we sat down to talk about Kew, and he began by recounting the early days of the gardens. A history enthusiast, he spoke with passion about Princess Augusta, the mother of George III, who developed the royal gardens around Kew Palace. The two royal estates of Richmond Gardens and Kew Gardens were combined into a single estate by George III and then given to the nation in 1841. We had an hour together, and this historical account took up the first 15 minutes. I was not surprised. Deverell's staff had already supplied me with the transcripts of a couple of his recent speeches to important stakeholder groups; both began with Kew's history.

My single most important contribution to Kew in 2015 was to point out that an organization attempting to position itself as a twenty-first-century cutting-edge research powerhouse should not anchor its narrative in sepia-tinted history. Everything Deverell said about Princess Augusta and George III was true, but it told the wrong story. Reminiscing about royal estates and benevolent bequests only reinforced the 'heritage garden' image that Kew was trying to shake off. Of course, in his speeches Deverell also talked about conservation and unique plant collections and scientific partnerships with leading institutions, but the risk was that by then his audience had mentally assigned Kew to a box marked 'Past Glories'.

Our new narrative for Kew began far away from the gardens in southwest London.

The first part did not mention Kew at all. It described the critical importance of plants to many of our greatest global challenges, including climate change, sustainable energy provision and food security, as well as the tragic reality that many species, which might hold the key to new foods, materials, medicines and fuels, are being wiped out before we can even discover them. In short, plants matter immensely, and we need to learn more about them before they are lost, for the sake of our own survival.

Only then did the story turn to Kew. And the Kew it described was not the dusty treasure of historical accounts. It was a global scientific resource of unique importance, with the biggest botanical dataset in the world: a living collection in the gardens, a dried specimen collection, a DNA collection and a seed collection in the renowned Millennium Seed Bank. In a world that has come to idolize big data, these resources represented a valuable asset for Britain and international science. Coupled with the datasets, Kew also held some of the finest skillsets in botanical science, with leading experts in plant identification and cultivation. Finally, the relationships Kew had built up with research institutions around the world were the match of any diplomatic relationships the British government could boast.

Kew, in other words, was perfectly positioned for the challenge of learning about and conserving the plants that will contribute to our own species' survival.

The rest of the story set out how Kew intended to meet that challenge: digitizing the collections so the whole world could access Kew's data, guiding international conservation efforts and targeting resources at biodiversity projects with relevance for human welfare and development. This would lead ultimately to better understood and protected genetic diversity, and new food, material, fuel and drug discoveries.

The story began with the trigger of species loss. It described a journey of change for Kew as well as the world's biodiversity. It showed causal relationships between Kew's endeavours and a brighter future for humanity. It was coherent, and above all it was selective, describing only those aspects of Kew that positioned the organization as a modern scientific asset.

Story tactic #2
Using stories to define identity

There are a few things to note about this story.

It presents only one version of Kew. Kew has some of the best gardeners in the world. Hearing this story, they might rightly feel put out by the focus on science: Kew is *also* a very fine and beautiful garden, thanks to their great skill and dedication. Furthermore, Kew has some remarkable historic buildings, including the Victorian Palm House, the Georgian Pagoda and Kew Palace. To an audience of gardeners or historians, one would tell a quite different story, perhaps starting with Princess Augusta and her celebrated gardener William Aiton, or focusing on the pleasure and educational value the gardens bring more than a million visitors every year. Each of these possible stories is a competing truth about Kew.

It makes causal links that downplay other possible causal links. The essence of the story is the connection between a great need for plant research to solve humanity's challenges and Kew's data resources and research and identification capabilities. There is a global need, and Kew is best placed to meet that need, it implies. But one could write a similar story that made a different botanical institution the hero. Or one could argue that because the need has not yet been met by existing institutions, the governments of the world should come together to form a *new* botanical research organization. Different stories with other causal relationships form competing truths.

It looks to the future. The story begins in the present, with the challenges of climate change and food security, and continues into the future, plotting a course whereby Kew helps to solve some of those challenges. People think of stories as taking place in the past, but in fact most of the corporate stories I write set out the future trajectory of the business. This is a powerful way of inspiring stakeholders with a sense of where an organization is heading and how it might get there. But it also introduces further potential for competing truths. Gazing into the future, we can tell a variety of different, equally valid stories about where we might be going.

There is so much one *could* say about Kew. The question is what one *should* say. For an audience of MPs and civil servants already predisposed to view Kew through heritage lenses, the answer was definitely not more history. Instead, the story focused on the science and the data, looking to the future rather than the past. The gardens themselves played only a small part in a story that portrayed Kew more like a science department in a leading university than an assembly of shrubberies, elegant buildings and centuries-old trees. The following year, Kew secured a new financial settlement, with the government guaranteeing its £20 million annual grant for the next four years, despite widespread Austerity cuts, and finding an extra £50 million to spend on capital projects.

Short story, long reach

Business storytelling has now become a sizeable industry, thanks in part to the pioneering work of The Storytellers, a British company with which I have worked for many years. But most business storytelling takes a different form to the future-oriented organizational story exemplified by the Kew case. When HR or marketing executives talk about storytelling, they generally mean using anecdotes or origin stories to share best practices, encourage particular behaviours or build a brand.

Company origin stories are popular devices to bond employees or engage customers. The North Face and Patagonia brands are much enhanced by their founders' stories of devising kit and clothing to meet their own adventuring needs. Barclays is proud of its Quaker founders, and their principles of honesty, integrity and plain dealing are useful watchwords for the bank's current employees. These are, of course, selective histories, recounting only those elements of the corporate past that make the present-day organization look good.

Nike has built a complex mythology around co-founder and running coach Bill Bowerman, who – so the story goes – poured melted rubber into his family waffle iron to make better athletic shoes for his team. Nike launched a storytelling programme in the 1970s and tasked senior executives to serve as 'corporate storytellers'. Storytelling ambassadors known as 'Ekins' ('Nike' backwards) visit key locations from the Nike origin story as part of their training and run at the Hayward Field track where Bowerman coached.

Anecdotes are a powerful tool in any organization. They are partial truths told about specific people or events that are intended to change mindsets and behaviours more generally. Here's an example of a typical corporate anecdote:

Sally Fauset had met the old couple staying in room 406 while she was cleaning, and she had noticed that Mr Bradshaw needed to take insulin injections. On Tuesday morning, she spotted the Bradshaws heading out to the pier for the day trip to Turtle Island. When she went to clean their room, she found Mr Bradshaw's insulin kit still lying on the bed. Had he meant to take it? She didn't want to risk Mr Bradshaw being stuck on the island without essential medication.

So Sally scooped up the kit and ran down to the pier. The boat had already left, but Sally had a friend with a motor launch on the next beach. She borrowed her manager's car, drove along the coast and persuaded her friend to take her out to Turtle Island. They got there to find the Bradshaws searching anxiously for the insulin kit. 'I'm incredibly grateful for the initiative Sally showed and the efforts she took on my behalf,' Mr Bradshaw said later. The Bradshaws have already booked another two weeks at Golden Sands next year.

This story is fictitious, but it is closely modelled on the anecdotes used by many businesses to inspire employees and guide behaviour. The story illustrates the virtues of putting oneself in the shoes of the customer, being proactive, using resources creatively and going beyond the call of duty. It draws a direct line from attentive customer service to business success and employee recognition. By sharing Sally's story with other employees, managers would hope to encourage them to follow her example. A literary critic might take issue with the story's banality, but in a business context a straightforward and true account of this kind can serve a useful motivating purpose.

> **Story tactic #3**
> *Using example stories to inspire or change behaviour*

You may be thinking that such simple, literal stories would only influence mindsets in low-skill environments. But I have written stories like these about research scientists using protein crystallography to design pharmaceutical compounds, about banking experts foiling fraud in Hong Kong, about healthcare professionals creating new therapeutic pathways, and even about nuclear specialists repackaging plutonium. All were successfully used to inspire and guide highly sophisticated employees. Simple anecdotes can be immensely powerful, even in the most complex fields.

But anecdotes take on a different resonance when they are used by politicians and journalists to make a controversial argument:

On Monday, 23 January, shortly after 3pm, the regular din of children turning out of the Capital Academy secondary school in north-west London was interrupted by a sudden hush. 'All the kids were running around like usual,' said one neighbour. 'But then it just went quiet. I got up to draw the curtains and saw kids running away, screaming.'

Quamari Barnes, a 15-year-old student, had been stabbed several times. He fell just yards from the school gate. A woman cradled him in her arms as paramedics rushed to the scene before whisking Quamari away to hospital.

So begins a major 2017 *Guardian* article on teenage knife crime in Britain.[4] Quamari Barnes did not survive his injuries. His death at the hands of another boy was a tragedy, but in this article his story serves a specific function: a child stabbed outside his own school is a far more arresting opening than a balanced presentation of the dry facts about knife crime.

But is such an emotive story a responsible way to frame this difficult and politically charged subject? The article's author, Gary Younge, goes on to blame cuts in government funding of youth services, child mental-health services, policing and education for a recent surge in knife crime and teenage knife possession. 'Efforts to make a positive intervention are dwarfed by all the things the government is doing that are making the situation worse,' he writes. Does the story of Quamari Barnes in any way support these assertions?

You can read the article online ('Beyond the blade: the truth about knife crime in Britain') and decide for yourself, but in my view the opening anecdote bears little relation to Younge's main arguments. No causal link between Barnes's murder and diminished public services is established. It is just a tragic event, co-opted to prick our emotions long enough to win us over to the journalist's point of view.

Opening anecdotes are such a common journalistic technique that we barely notice them any more. I've picked on this particular article because it is well written, thoughtful and nuanced; there are thousands of lesser articles that depend on the same device. And it is not only journalists who use anecdotes to convince. The BBC's 'Writing to persuade, argue and advise' guide for school-children provides a 'Persuader's Toolkit' in which the top item is *Anecdotes*.[5] TED talks begin with a story that underlines the speaker's theme. Fundraisers showcase the story of a single bene-ficiary whose life has been transformed by their work.

Politicians love to recount stories of constituents in dire circumstances before going on to argue for a new policy. Tony Blair transformed the ideology and character of the left-wing Labour Party on the basis of an anecdote about a single voter:

> I met a man polishing his Ford Sierra. His dad voted Labour, he said. He used to vote Labour, too. But he'd bought his own house now. He was doing very nicely. 'So I've become a Tory,' he said. That man polishing his car was clear. His instincts were to get on in life. And he thought our instincts were to stop him.[6]

This book is full of stories, deployed in support of my various arguments. Some of the best-loved nonfiction writers of our age have built whole books on a foundation of compelling anecdotes. Writers, TED speakers, politicians, charities and journalists who want to argue their case are responding to a fundamental characteristic of human psychology: people love stories and – even more importantly – *people find stories convincing.*

> **Story tactic #4**
> *Positioning stories as evidence*

But stories are not proof of anything. At best, they are individual datapoints that, in sufficient numbers, constitute a form of evidence for an argument. A single anecdote tells you no more about the human condition, voting behaviour or teenage knife crime than a single event would. It is a logical fallacy to extrapolate from a specific case to a general rule.

So when is it legitimate for an Advocate to use a story in support of an argument? The best application of a story is to show how something *might* be rather than attempting to prove it *is* so. A true story illustrates possibility. The story of left-hander mortality shows how numbers *can* be misinterpreted; it doesn't prove anything more definitive than that. It certainly doesn't show that all scientists are statistically illiterate or that all experts are wrong.

I am a storyteller. Stories infuse and inform my writing. But I try to use anecdotes only as datapoints and illustrations, never as the basis of an argument. Throughout these chapters, I have sought to suggest interesting ideas to you, colour them in with stories, but stick to cold numbers and facts when I have wanted to prove something.

A happy ending?

Stories are immensely powerful. They convince easily, sometimes unjustifiably. Because they help us make sense of a complex world, because their structure taps into ancient psychological patterns, we are inclined to accept them as *the truth* when they may only be *one truth*.

We communicate through stories all the time. It would be hard to get through the day without using a story format to describe some event, explain some circumstance or predict some outcome. So it's worth remembering, as we hear stories and tell stories, quite how flexible the truth they portray can be.

In practice

• Use stories to clarify why things happened or how things might happen.

• Carefully select the story you tell about an organization to help shape its identity.

• Share best-practice anecdotes to inspire others to behave the same way.

But watch out for . . .

• Misleaders who imply causation in stories of true events where none exists.

• Misinformers who treat individual anecdotes as evidence of a more general claim.

PART TWO

SUBJECTIVE TRUTHS

6

Morality

It is forbidden to kill; therefore all murderers are punished unless they kill in large numbers and to the sound of trumpets.

VOLTAIRE

When in Athens . . .

Somewhere around the fourth or fifth century BCE, a remarkable document was written in Greece. 'To the Spartans it is seemly that young girls should do athletics and go about with bare arms and no tunics, but to the Ionians this is disgraceful,' the unknown author observes. 'To the Thracians it is an ornament for young girls to be tattooed, but with others tattoo-marks are a punishment for those who do wrong.' Well, cultures vary. No surprise there.

But the author goes on:

The Scythians think it seemly that whoever kills a man should scalp him and wear the scalp on his horse's bridle, and, having gilded the skull or lined it with silver, should drink from it and

131

make a libation to the gods. Among the Greeks, no one would be willing to enter the same house as a man who had behaved like that.

The Massagetes cut up their parents and eat them, and they think that to be buried in their children is the most beautiful grave imaginable, but in Greece, if anyone did such a thing, he would be driven out of the country and would die an ignominious death for having committed such disgraceful and terrible deeds.

And that's not all. In Persia, reports the author, men are free to have sex with their mothers, sisters and daughters, while in Lydia young girls are expected to earn money through prostitution before getting married. Such things in Greece would be anathema.

The *Dissoi Logoi* is not an anthropological survey of the ancient world's cultural quirks. It is an exercise in rhetoric, intended to teach students how to explore both sides of an argument. The author takes the view that good and bad are not absolutes, but that what is good for one person may be bad for another. The evidence for this view lies in the divergent moral values found in different cultures. We may think that filial cannibalism is a horror, but the Massagetes didn't; prostitution may carry a stigma in many societies, but it was the done thing in Lydia.

As the author writes, 'If someone should order all men to make a single heap of everything that each of them regards as disgraceful and then again to take from the collection what each of them regards as seemly, not a thing would be left.'

Philosophers, theologians and politicians have long talked of *moral truths*. 'America will remain a beacon of freedom for the world as long as it stands by those moral truths which are at the very heart of its historical experience,'[1] declared Pope John Paul II. 'The Christian religion,' said British prime minister Margaret

Thatcher, 'embodies many of the great spiritual and moral truths of Judaism.'[2] 'Moral truths that should govern a just society are accessible to all,' said would-be Republican presidential nominee Rick Santorum.[3]

The rest of us may not often use that rather grand term, yet we are inclined to think that certain moral views are self-evidently true:

It's wrong to steal.

Giving to charity is good.

We should help people in distress.

But as the *Dissoi Logoi* nicely illustrates, one person's moral truth may be another's cultural aberration. We see this most starkly today in the different moral values held by different cultures. Societies around the world take strongly opposed views on issues like assisted suicide, sex and abortion, what women should wear, what we can eat, how resources should be distributed, and how criminals can be treated. And moral truths change over time: in recent decades, we've seen a huge shift in opinion on homosexuality and atheism. Good and bad are not set in stone.

The social psychologist Jonathan Haidt identifies six moral 'foundations' which different groups or cultures emphasize to different degrees. Liberals, he observes, are more concerned with *fairness*, *care* and *liberty*, while conservatives balance those values with *authority*, *loyalty* and *sanctity*. According to Haidt, we are all born with the same moral foundations, but our societies encourage us to develop them in different combinations. If there are common moral ideas, we apply them in markedly different ways.

We can view a moral idea that is subject to evolution or cultural variation as a competing truth. Like other competing truths, moral truths can be manipulated. Skilled communicators – especially those entrusted with the moral guidance of a society – can reshape reality for the rest of us by casting things, events or even people in a different moral light.

Evil plant extracts

Ada Lovelace is a hero of mathematics and a feminist icon. Her work on Charles Babbage's Analytical Engine has led some to call her the first computer programmer. She was also a drug addict. Following bouts of asthma and digestive problems, her doctors prescribed opium and laudanum as painkillers, and Lovelace developed a habit that would last the rest of her short life. She was not alone. Laudanum, a form of opium, was widely used in the nineteenth century as an analgesic. Mary Todd Lincoln, wife of the US president, was an addict. So was Samuel Taylor Coleridge. Regular users of laudanum included Charles Dickens, Lewis Carroll, George Eliot and Bram Stoker. Slave-trade abolitionist William Wilberforce preferred opium as a palliative for his gastro-intestinal pains. Opium-based products such as Mother Bailey's Quieting Syrup were even given to babies. Meanwhile, Queen Victoria and Pope Leo XIII were both said to be keen drinkers of Vin Mariani, which contained 6mg of cocaine per fluid ounce of wine. A non-alcoholic cocaine-based drink was launched in 1886 and given the catchy name of Coca-Cola. Sears Roebuck marketed a cocaine kit for $1.50 in the 1890s, complete with a vial of cocaine and a hypodermic syringe.

Opium and cocaine were simply not considered in any way morally problematic. Intoxicating and hallucinatory substances derived from plants had been habitually used in almost every culture on the planet for thousands of years.

Fast forward to the second half of the twentieth century, and there was no blacker villain for a Hollywood movie than a drug dealer. Even Don Vito Corleone, a Mafia boss happy enough to extort, blackmail, terrorize, torture and murder, drew the line at selling drugs. Users were little better: Los Angeles police chief Daryl F. Gates told a Senate hearing in 1990 that casual drug users 'ought to be taken out and shot', adding later that drug use was 'treason'.[4] In a few decades, these traditional plant extracts had gone from being morally neutral substances of significant pharmacological and recreational value to the embodiment of pure evil.

Why did this happen? *How* did this happen?

Early legislation in Britain recognized the very real health risks associated with these substances and required opiates and cocaine to be labelled as poisons, although none were prohibited. High rates of addiction in the US towards the end of the nineteenth century led to increased understanding of the potential for drug abuse. Nevertheless, in 1906 the American Medical Association still felt able to approve the recently invented substance known as heroin for medical use. In society at large, it was considered merely unwise, rather than immoral, to use opiates or cocaine.

Then everything changed.

Through the early decades of the twentieth century, international treaties and legislation were introduced to control drug production, trade and use. 'Concurrent with this,' writes Julia Buxton, a professor of comparative politics at Central European University, 'governments engaged in a concerted campaign to demonise drugs and drug users and this was strongly supported by the print and broadcast media . . . As in the United States, the European anti-drug propaganda emphasized the relationship between a dangerous substance, threatening "out groups" and criminality.'[5]

This association of narcotics with 'out groups' – ethnic minorities, homosexuals, artists and, later, anti-war protestors – is a particularly nasty theme in the history of drug prohibition. 'Negro Cocaine "Fiends" Are a New Southern Menace' ran the headline of a 1914 *New York Times* article, which detailed the 'Murder and Insanity' taking hold among 'Lower Class Blacks'.[6] 'Most of the attacks upon the white women of the South are the direct result of the cocaine-crazed Negro brain,' declared Christopher Koch, head of the State Pharmacy Board of Pennsylvania.[7] The US opium commissioner claimed that cocaine was 'used by those concerned in the white slave traffic to corrupt young girls'.[8] *Good Housekeeping* terrified its readers by declaring that 'old coloured men' were 'selling cocain [sic] under the name of "flake" or "coke" to school children at recess time'.[9]

During the 1920s and 1930s, writes Susan Speaker in the *Journal of Social History*, 'Authors routinely described drugs, users, and sellers as "evil" and often asserted or implied that there was a large sinister conspiracy at work to undermine American society and values through drug addiction.'[10] A similar connection was made with Marxists in Europe.

The United States has continued to lead the propaganda offensive against drugs, with notable spikes of paranoia under the Nixon and Reagan presidencies. 'Drug criminals are ingenious . . . They work every day to plot a new and better way to steal our children's lives,' asserted Nancy Reagan during her 'Just Say No' campaign.[11] In a 2016 article for *Harper's Magazine*, Dan Baum quoted Richard Nixon's domestic policy adviser John Ehrlichman making an extraordinary admission:

> The Nixon White House . . . had two enemies: the antiwar left and black people. You understand what I'm saying? We knew we couldn't make it illegal to be either against the war or black, but by getting the public to associate the hippies with marijuana and blacks with heroin, and then criminalizing both heavily, we could disrupt those communities. We could arrest their leaders, raid their homes, break up their meetings, and vilify them night after night on the evening news. Did we know we were lying about the drugs? Of course we did.[12]

A great deal of effort has been expended by politicians, law-enforcement officers and journalists to transform narcotics into evil substances. In 2017, as a mounting opioid crisis gripped the United States, attorney general Jeff Sessions declared that his new, tougher sentencing regime for drug users was 'moral and just'.[13] Over the decades, millions of people have been locked up, with terrible consequences for their employment prospects, their families and their mental health. A large proportion of these people, particularly in the United States, were jailed for nothing more than possession.

> **Morality tactic #1**
> *Demonization*

Notwithstanding the Trump administration's attitude to drugs, there is something of a reversal underway in our wider society. Advocates of drug legalization are campaigning to reframe drug addiction as a health issue requiring treatment rather than a moral failure deserving of punishment. The more than two million Americans currently addicted to opioids need help, not condemnation. This message was taken up by President Obama's drug czar, Gil Kerlikowske, in 2013: 'I've spent my entire career in law enforcement. For most of those 37 years, like most people, I believed that a person addicted to drugs had a moral problem – a failing, a lack of will. I was wrong. Addiction is not a moral failing.'[14]

In response, defenders of prohibition are experimenting with new and very modern ways to cast drug users as morally bad. By buying drugs, they say, users are perpetuating a trade that causes great social and ecological damage in supplier and transit nations. Consumer responsibility for a harmful global supply chain is just the latest battleground on which the moral war on drugs is waged.

Good or evil?

It's hard to imagine that anyone ever thought cannibalism was morally acceptable, but they did. It's hard to imagine people could be sentenced to death for homosexuality (and in some places still can), but they were (and are). Our ancestors would have been baffled by our moral panic over drugs, and quite possibly our descendants will feel the same way. Different moral truths apply at different times and in different societies.

At this point you may be feeling sorely tested by my moral relativism. 'We know now that homosexuality is not morally wrong and never has been!' you may be saying. Or, if you live in certain societies, you may be saying exactly the opposite. In either case, you may object strongly to the idea of an alternative moral view being 'true'. But that's the trouble with morality: whether we believe it to be a psychological adaptation, a social construct or a universal law set down by God, the fact is we are living in a world where people hold very different moral truths to us; and for them, their moral truths are just as valid as ours are for us.

It can be difficult even to contemplate alternative moral truths on long-standing issues. If you have a firmly established mindset that drugs are evil, there's probably not much anyone can do to persuade you otherwise. We can see the potential flexibility of moral truths more easily in an issue about which we don't yet have fixed opinions.

Living organ donation, particularly altruistic donation to a stranger, seems like a morally admirable act. But how about organ donation via social media? Traditionally, individuals who have made the deeply generous decision to give a kidney or part of their liver to a stranger have not been able to choose who gets it. Now, with Facebook and specialist platforms like MatchingDonors.com, it is possible to search online for compatible patients in need of the organ and select a preferred candidate. Donors might choose a recipient because of their family situation, their background story, their profession, their race, their creed or just their looks. And why not? If you're going to sacrifice a kidney, why shouldn't you be able to give it to the pretty white Christian girl who's just won a scholarship to Harvard?

Perhaps because it's unfair to less photogenic patients, or those with less imaginative storytelling skills or a fainter social media presence, or those who aren't comfortable promoting themselves on the Internet. Perhaps because the beauty-pageant format is deeply inappropriate to matters of life and death. Perhaps because an emotive YouTube video could stir someone to do something they might later regret. Perhaps because it undermines a well-established transplant system that has efficiently matched recipients and donors for decades.

Health professionals certainly seem to think it's morally problematic. Various clinical teams have refused to conduct transplants between compatible donors and recipients who have connected via social media. Is their refusal morally justifiable? What if such a principled stand costs a would-be recipient their life?

This is a new moral conundrum for us to work out. It's likely that each society will settle on a moral truth with regard to social-media organ donation and most people will abide by it. What that truth is remains to be seen, but there is a good chance it will be shaped by competing truths put forward in media or social media campaigns.

My group, right or wrong

Most of us belong to groups such as political parties, businesses, academic institutions, sports clubs, residential communities or faith organizations, and we tend to adapt to the prevailing moral truths of our groups. When a moral controversy arises, we take our lead from the majority group reaction. If others of our political affiliation tweet in support of Muslims who have been turned away at the airport, we will probably do the same. If we grow up in a community that views abortion as murder, we are likely to join the pro-life protests. Moral truths bind a group together – indeed, evolutionary biologists tend to see morality as a set of psychological adaptations that have evolved to encourage co-operation within groups. If different members of a group start to adopt different moral truths, then the cooperative function of morality evaporates and the group is undermined. Consequently, peer pressure to conform to group moral truths is strong in every culture.

When our group's position on a moral issue is challenged, we will defend the position – even if we are starting to have doubts about it – as a way of defending the group and justifying our membership of the group. We may even come to define our group in opposition to other groups according to our conflicting moral truths. Such *Us v. Them* moral distinctions drive different societies further apart, particularly if we see other groups as 'immoral' and therefore somehow deserving of attack.

Individual groups can come to hold very different moral truths to the rest of the society in which they live. This moral dislocation may happen by gradual drift in relatively isolated groups, but more commonly it is engineered deliberately by leaders or influencers who, for whatever reason, want to take the group in a particular moral direction. Christianity is built on a set of stories in which Jesus persuaded his followers to see things differently to the rest of Jewish society. 'An eye for an eye' had seemed a very fair approach before Jesus put forgiveness ahead of justice by turning the other cheek. Strong communicators can encourage whole groups to adopt new moral truths.

Morality tactic #2
Shaping group moralities

One moral truth that has a good claim to being a universal moral law is that we ought not to kill each other. Yet most societies depend on a group of their peers being willing to kill to order. We call these people soldiers, and we try to instil in them the moral truth that it is right to kill in certain circumstances. This is not easy. Research conducted by Brigadier General S. L. A. Marshall during the Second World War suggested that less than a quarter of US soldiers fired their weapons in combat. 'Fear of killing,' he wrote, 'rather than fear of being killed, was the most common cause of battle failure.'[15]

Today, soldiers are conditioned to kill in a number of ways. In training, they repeatedly bayonet and shoot images of likely enemies. They are put through aggressive exercises and exposed to brutalizing conditions. But the moral reframing of killing is done through words. They use different vocabulary: killing on the battlefield is not murder – in fact, it is often not even 'killing'; soldiers are more likely to talk about 'engaging' or 'dropping' the enemy. Killing an enemy soldier who has the capacity to kill you is framed as self-defence. And the act is above all a public duty: 'Not only is it morally permissible for soldiers to kill enemy soldiers in combat,' writes Pete Kilner, a philosophy instructor at the US Military Academy, West Point, 'but also it is morally obligatory for them to use the force necessary to defend the rights of those who depend on them.'[16]

Public health officials hold different moral truths to most doctors and nurses. Those civil servants who have to think about disease epidemics and widespread health challenges must make risk and resourcing decisions in the interest of a whole population, whereas clinical healthcare professionals are focused on individual health and well-being. Consequently, a public health official may opt to ration expensive drugs, withhold antibiotics, limit personal freedoms and forcibly quarantine those exposed to infectious diseases, even if some patients suffer as a result. A hospital doctor, by contrast, will do everything possible to avoid causing harm or distress to an individual patient, even if at some cost or risk to their community. Antibiotic resistance would not have become such a problem if prescribing physicians prioritized community over patient.

Many thousands of people are employed by the World Health Organization, the Centers for Disease Control and Prevention, and equivalent public health bodies around the world. To do the job well, they need to hold – or develop – moral truths that put the interests of the population above the interests of any one individual. In extreme circumstances – an Ebola outbreak, for example – this might mean letting some die to protect the majority. Most of us would steer clear of a family doctor who subscribed to such utilitarian moral truths.

A Harvard research team led by psychologist Joshua Greene tested the responses of public health professionals to a range of ethical dilemmas and found that they typically take a more utilitarian approach than doctors, or indeed the rest of us. The public health professionals were more willing, in the hypothetical scenarios presented, to harm or kill one person to save several others.

Even within the public health community, competing moral truths coexist. Amongst the greatest threats to public health in the developed world are smoking and bad diets. Some public health officials believe it is morally right to enforce measures to curb these ills, including taxation and the denial of public resources to smokers or the obese. Others follow the moral guidance of liberal philosopher John Stuart Mill, who argued that 'The only purpose for which power can be rightfully exercised over any member of a civilised community, against his will, is to prevent harm to others. His own good, either physical or moral, is not a sufficient warrant.'[17] This group advocate smoking bans to reduce passive smoking but not to save people from their own bad habits; they would not support any compulsory measure to change adult diets, whereas their more authoritarian colleagues might call for a sugar tax or minimum alcohol pricing. Further moral differences arise over the social justice question of whether public health policies should seek to reduce health inequalities or simply optimize overall public health.

We can understand why soldiers and public health officials need to subscribe to different moral truths to the rest of us. In fact, we require it of them. In other cases, group moral truths develop that our wider society abhors.

South Yorkshire Police has been roundly criticized for a group morality that seems to be prevalent in many police forces around the world. Following the Hillsborough Stadium disaster, when 96 people died during a 1989 football match, South Yorkshire Police repeatedly covered up the failures of its officers during the event and attempted to place the blame for the 'human crush' on drunken, unruly fans. The police force appeared to value loyalty to fellow officers above truth and justice. In the United States, this police moral code of loyalty over truth is known as the 'Blue Wall of Silence'.

Perhaps it is naive to ascribe any morality at all to police officers who lie. But I don't believe people take on this dangerous and vital job in order to be evil. A more likely explanation is that some officers come to see protecting their colleagues as their primary moral obligation – as doing the right thing – whatever moral sacrifice it may entail.

Lying, even under oath, also seems to have become morally acceptable for some police officers if it allows them to take down those they believe to be criminals. 'Police officer perjury in court to justify illegal dope searches is commonplace . . . it is the routine way of doing business in courtrooms everywhere in America,' said former San Francisco Police commissioner Peter Keane.[18] A moral culture that probably originated with the sincere ambition to ensure villains were locked up and to protect fellow officers in a difficult and dangerous job has degenerated to the point where, for some police officers, the moral truth is that truth just doesn't matter.

Morality tactic #3
Making morality irrelevant

Equally worrying group moralities take root in business. Here, it is not so much a question of whether one moral virtue trumps another but whether morality need apply at all. Some companies, it seems, encourage employees to believe that actions most of society would condemn are simply morally neutral. There is nothing morally good about them, but there is equally nothing morally wrong.

'We all knew that what we were doing was illegal,' said Reinhard Siekaczek, a Siemens manager found guilty of corruption after admitting to creating slush funds to pay bribes. 'I didn't really look at it from an ethical standpoint. We did it for the company.'[19]

Enron executives deceived shareholders and tax authorities, and disrupted essential power supplies. Volkswagen engineers sabotaged emissions tests intended to protect our health. Odebrecht executives bribed politicians. Rolls-Royce staff indulged in corrupt sales practices over more than two decades. Wells Fargo employees created more than three million unauthorized accounts. Kobe Steel managers falsified quality-control data relating to metal products used in aircraft, trains, cars and even a space rocket. The people working for these illustrious companies presumably did not set out to do evil, yet somehow they came to believe that their actions were permissible within their corporate context.

While investment bankers generally seek to obey the law and follow the myriad complicated rules set down by financial regulators, many of them do not believe they have any moral obligation beyond that. If they can legally make money at the expense of their own clients, plenty will do it. 'It makes me ill how callously people talk about ripping their clients off,' wrote senior banker Greg Smith of his own colleagues in a 2012 *New York Times* article entitled 'Why I Am Leaving Goldman Sachs'.[20] Joris Luyendijk interviewed hundreds of employees from different banks in the City of London: 'Banking staff working in risk and compliance, the legal department and internal audit told me the question is always: how can we game the system within the rules? . . . The bankers wanted to know if what they did was legal and, if so, then that was the end of the discussion.'[21]

Each of these groups has developed a set of moral truths far removed from the rest of society. So moral truths are subjective and changeable, and groups that change their moral truths will act in very different ways. We need our soldiers to be willing to kill and our public health officials to prioritize community interests, but we are naturally concerned when other groups we depend on diverge significantly from our own moral truths.

Business leaders should also be concerned: whatever short-term gains may be made by encouraging alternative moral truths among employees, if a company is perceived to be drifting away from the moral truths held by the rest of society it will ultimately pay a big price in brand value, recruitment and government relations. Even more so in the social media age, where an organization's reputation can be so quickly trashed if its employees are seen to be disregarding society's preferred moral truths.

Where harmful group moral truths arise, we need to work hard to change them.

Moulding morality

The Los Angeles LGBT Center has pioneered a campaigning tactic that consists of engaging people in conversation and encouraging them to take the perspective of those not like them. The efficacy of this approach has now been scientifically validated. In one study, 56 canvassers spoke to 501 householders for around ten minutes each, using the time to discuss how transgender people are treated unfairly and comparing this to the householders' own experiences of being treated unfairly. Following the interviews, researchers found a significant and enduring change in householders' attitudes towards transgender people.

By encouraging empathy in those they visit, Advocates from the Los Angeles LGBT Center are changing moral truths. This technique is far older than the LGBT movement. Philosophers and clerics have long sought to change their own moral truths by putting themselves in the shoes of others. Twentieth-century philosopher John Rawls argued that the only fair way to establish principles of justice was from behind a 'veil of ignorance': if we do not know what role we will occupy in society – man or woman, black or white, convict or jailer, wealthy or poor – we will be better placed to decide the rules that should govern us all. The 'veil of ignorance' thought experiment forces us to imagine what it would be like to be different. As theatre director Richard Eyre wrote, 'Change begins with understanding and understanding begins by identifying oneself with another person: in a word, empathy.'[22]

Empathy is an essential tool for any leader wanting to change the moral culture of their organization. A police chief determined to shift the balance between loyalty and truthfulness would do well to get his officers reflecting on the consequences of their lying for the very people they are supposed to protect. An officer forced to think and talk for an extended period about what it must be like to be wrongly imprisoned or unfairly ostracized because of police falsehoods will be less likely to lie in future, even in support of a fellow officer. It's not a silver bullet; there will be officers who cannot or will not empathize with their victims, or who genuinely don't care enough to change their behaviour. But even a minority changing their views can make a difference and can start to shift the moral truths of their colleagues. Movies like *Pride*, *Kinky Boots* and *Guess Who's Coming to Dinner* illustrate how just one or two early movers can change the prejudices – or moral truths – of a larger group.

Another approach is to redefine what is considered admirable within a group. Investment bankers, asset managers and traders tend to admire performance above everything. This may be manifested in simple metrics: the size of a deal, the value of a fund, the ratio of return to risk. But performance can also be defined as winning – against competitors or, worryingly, against regulators. When bankers admire peers who get one over the regulator, the institution is headed for trouble. If a diagnosis of a bank's culture reveals this tendency, leaders have to work hard to reset the values of the organization. Performance needs to be redefined in terms of the ethical qualities the bank wants to promote. Employees need to be persuaded to celebrate the big deal won in an ethical manner, rather than the profit made by taking reckless risks with clients' capital. We will look at how truths around what is desirable and admirable can be changed in the next chapter.

Sometimes it is possible to make an evidential case for a new moral truth. We can persuade people to behave differently by demonstrating how current ways of working are harming their own interests. This is often the most effective approach with analytically minded people, who may be less susceptible to empathy-led interventions. At one manufacturing business going through a major culture-change programme, I collected dozens of stories detailing how employees who already subscribed to the new moral truths were achieving better results. The stories became the data that convinced analytically minded sceptics to adopt the new moral truths.

Finally, for those who will not empathize, or accept new definitions or intellectual arguments, there is a last technique with a strong grounding in classical ethics. 'Moral virtue comes about as a result of habit,' wrote Aristotle. 'None of the moral virtues arises in us by nature . . . we become just by doing just acts, temperate by doing temperate acts, brave by doing brave acts.' In other words, by going through the motions we may actually become the thing we pretend to be. This won't happen straight away, but if we force ourselves to be collaborative or generous day after day, the habit will eventually become internalized as a moral truth.

What does this mean for leaders of morally troubled organizations? If Aristotle was correct, incentives to act the right way will eventually lead employees to think the right way. Promotions and bonuses offered to those who act in accordance with a desired moral truth will start to embed that moral truth across the organization, however cynically employees may comply at first. So, if all else fails, incentivize your people to act as if they subscribed to the moral truth you want to encourage. Pretend virtue may well turn into real virtue.

From Ancient Greece to Ancient Greece

It shouldn't surprise us that we've circled back from the *Dissoi Logoi* to Aristotle in this discussion of moral truths. The Greeks devoted a great deal of time to considering what it meant to live a good life. Virtue was understood to be integral to human happiness. But, as we've seen, there has never been clear agreement as to what is virtuous, what is good.

It is up to us as a society to define and agree our moral truths.

As ideas and technologies develop, as difficult cases arise or minority interests become more apparent, moral truths are bound to shift and evolve. With an increasingly connected society and a proliferation of communications tools at our disposal, we each have an unprecedented opportunity to help shape the moral truths our society lives by. We can suggest new ways of looking at old moral dilemmas, or we can lend our support to movements dedicated to shifting long-held moral truths. When leaders try to take us back to moral truths we have written off as old prejudices, we can resist them loudly and firmly.

The truths we choose to propagate will determine how those around us act. To avoid the senseless waste of prisons filled with drug users, the injustices perpetrated by lying police officers, the financial inequity caused by mercenary bankers, and a host of other damaging outcomes for society, it is imperative we pick our moral truths carefully and communicate them well.

In practice

• Recognize that morality is subjective and that damaging group moralities can be changed.

• Use empathy, new definitions of what is admirable, logical argument and incentives to instil new moral truths.

But watch out for . . .

• Misleaders who demonize morally neutral things and people.

• Groups that favour one moral truth over another to the detriment of society.

7

Desirability

What is food to one is to another bitter poison.
LUCRETIUS, *De Rerum Natura*

A rainbow of tastes

While we may try to act according to what we think is morally good or bad, many of us are much more motivated by what we like or dislike. We crave delicious food and the latest fashions, work long hours to enjoy a foreign holiday, cross the street to avoid certain people and leave the room to escape unpleasant odours. We are drawn towards things that evoke pleasure, interest or excitement, and repelled from things that evoke hate, fear or disgust. The power of such emotions to motivate us far exceeds most other psychological forces. Hatred can drive us to terrorize and murder. Excitement can persuade us to take extraordinary risks. Fear can paralyse us, while passion can make us strive beyond imaginable limits.

Each emotion motivates us in different ways, but for the sake of simplicity we can group together the positive emotions that draw us towards a stimulus and describe such a stimulus as *desirable*. Stimuli that evoke negative emotions we can call *undesirable*.

*

Once upon a time, men wore long shoes. Very long shoes. Poulaines, as they were called, had long beaks that extended the toe by as much as 50 per cent of the length of the foot. Some had to be held up by silk threads or silver chains tied to the knee. The shoes made walking difficult and climbing stairs almost impossible. Yet medieval nobles and merchants across Europe were willing to endure these handicaps because, to them, the shoes were so desirable.

On the other hand, some of their contemporaries considered poulaines to be extremely undesirable. Some saw them as evidence of gross extravagance and decadence, others as phallic symbols that had no place in a godly society. Consequently, they were banned, with laws limiting toe length to two inches. Today, we would regard any retailer offering such shoes as insane: who would ever want footwear that limited their ability to walk? Yet, we have our own strange fondness for high heels; in 200 years, what will our descendants make of the 6-inch stiletto?

Fashion is just the most conspicuous manifestation of the subjectiveness and changeability of desire. Tastes differ between people and over time for all kinds of things, from balsamic vinegar and potbellied pigs to boy bands and whitewall tyres. Some people love 4X4 vehicles, lawns, wolves, guns, Snapchat, aeroplanes, amusing ringtones, working breakfasts, Anonymous, jogging, celebrities and microwave ovens; others hate them. What you consider desirable, others see as undesirable. As a result, you will be motivated to buy, to support, to campaign or to build, while others will act quite differently.

But surely there are some things we can all agree on, some absolutes in the spectrum of desirability? No one likes the Zika virus, after all, and who could resist a newborn kitten?

Perhaps so, but it turns out that desirability is far more mutable than even an ardent fashionista might imagine.

Failure is now an option

Cass Phillipps understands the market for corporate events better than most. She has claimed that of all the conferences she has organized, not one ever lost money. In 2009, she launched a one-day conference in San Francisco that would have been unimaginable in previous decades. FailCon was dedicated to celebrating – or at least studying – failure.

Silicon Valley was awash with Internet start-ups, many of which were failing, and Phillipps recognized that there were lessons to learn from those failures that might benefit other entrepreneurs. The first FailCon attracted more than 400 attendees, and the annual conference has become yet another Northern California success story, exported to cities around the world. People everywhere are increasingly drawn to failure.

This has to be one of the most unlikely shifts in desirability in our lifetime. Failure, for millennia, was a bad thing. Even people who went on to recover and succeed would rather not have failed in the first place. Yet in many organizations and industries, failure is now celebrated for the experience and character it develops in those who have failed.

Recruiters single out entrepreneurs who have failed, viewing them as 'risk-takers' and 'innovators' who will bring a different perspective and attitude to staid businesses in need of a bit of disruption. Those who have failed now find themselves members of a popular club; the more spectacular and painful their failure, the higher their ranking within that club. They talk of 'failing upward', meaning that their career has actually *improved* as a result of their failure.

Bookshelves and newspapers that previously overflowed with titles like *Driven: How to Succeed in Business and in Life* now include a whole range of articles and books called, for example, *The Gift of Failure* and 'What if the Secret to Success is Failure?'

Failure is acknowledged to lead, in many instances, to better practices, clearer thinking and more imaginative solutions. Encouraging employees to own up to failures can avoid greater problems down the line and usher in more effective processes and ways of working. People who have failed once may be less afraid of failing again and so more willing to try something unproven.

This is not a new idea. Lilly, a pharmaceutical company, has been throwing 'failure parties' to celebrate research work well done that nevertheless led nowhere since the 1990s. Management guru Tom Peters started urging business leaders to 'embrace failure' around the same time. Winston Churchill remarked that 'Success is stumbling from failure to failure with no loss of enthusiasm.'

But never before has failure been painted in such beguiling colours. Many technologists and entrepreneurs now welcome failure as a rite of passage that will open doors and hasten success. 'Post-mortem' blog posts become calling cards. The Silicon Valley mantra 'Fail fast, fail often' is spreading to other industries and regions. A new corporate culture has developed around failure: companies that pursue an unsuccessful business model now 'pivot' to something else; products are 'tweaked', ways of working 'reinvented'. Design consultancy IDEO adopted the slogan 'Fail often to succeed sooner'. Bankruptcy, for some, is a badge of honour.

This new truth about the desirability of failure has in many quarters out-competed the older, harsher truth that failure often imposes enormous costs on multiple parties. For every soul-baring entrepreneur applauded at FailCon, there is typically a string of investors who have lost thousands or even millions of dollars in their failed venture. There are employees out of work, there are customers who will never receive the products they've paid for and partners who will never be compensated for broken contracts.

As John Browne, the former boss of BP, caustically observed, for some companies 'failure is just a slightly different form of success'.[1] It was BP, after Browne's time, whose management failures contributed to one of the worst environmental disasters of our age in the Gulf of Mexico. Failure can mean destruction, suffering and death. 'Fail often' is not good advice in the air traffic control or heart surgery professions.

Is failure desirable? Like so much else, it depends on the context. But it would have astonished our forebears that we would even ask the question.

Life on the farm

If we were challenged to list the great innovations that have made modern life possible, far ahead of electricity and the Internet we would surely have to acknowledge the vital importance of agriculture to humanity. Though most city dwellers rarely bother to think about the fields of corn, wheat and rice that feed them, none of our other achievements would have been possible without the task specialization and social structures that agriculture enabled. Before we started planting crops, most humans had to devote part of each day to foraging or hunting for food. Only with the food surpluses achieved through agriculture did it become possible for our species to multiply and for a large proportion of humans to dedicate themselves to building, trading, fighting, inventing, preaching or ruling.

Agriculture is surely very desirable indeed.

Not for most of its practitioners, suggests Yuval Noah Harari in his book *Sapiens*. He has provocatively called the Neolithic agricultural revolution 'History's biggest fraud' because it 'left farmers with lives generally more difficult and less satisfying than those of foragers'.[2] Farmers, he argues, worked longer hours than their ancestors and had a much worse diet. Where hunter-gatherers had enjoyed a diverse menu of berries, nuts, meat, fish, fruit, roots and honey, farmers often subsisted primarily on a single crop. That made them more vulnerable to disease, climatic variation and hostile tribes, any of which might destroy a vital harvest. The hunter-gatherer way of life suited the human body and mind; we are built to climb trees and explore, to chase things and discover. We are not well suited mentally or physically to digging fields, clearing rocks, carting manure, and all the other repetitive, boring, back-breaking tasks of manual agriculture. Yet that is precisely what many humans had to do for most of the last 10,000 years.

Looked at from their perspective, agriculture has been a thoroughly undesirable thing.

On the other hand, agriculture allowed elites to develop, freeing a minority of humans from the drudgery of feeding themselves and letting them concentrate on building armies, developing religions and sponsoring artists. For the elites, who did not need to get too close to it, agriculture was always a wonderful invention.

Those of us who live middle-class lives can be grateful that our ancestors went through such misery for millennia, because their efforts ultimately made possible all the comforts and pleasures we now take for granted. With mechanized agriculture and modern plant genetics and agrochemicals, we can have all the nutrition we need at remarkably little cost. But there are still many people working in manual agriculture around the world who might indeed have been better off as hunter-gatherers.

Acting on our desires

The cases of farming and failure demonstrate that even things that seem at face value universally desirable or undesirable can be painted in quite different colours. And they are not alone. Many a Victorian gentleman celebrated the chivalry of war, dreaming of mythical medieval knights doing battle according to a strict code of honour, even as the horrors of the Crimean War unfolded. Piero Manzoni managed to make his own excrement highly desirable in certain circles by labelling ninety cans of it 'Artist's Shit' and declaring them works of art. Today, some have suggested that knowledge may become a bad thing if, for example, it gives us too much insight into our future diseases and death, or it reveals to us how much better off other people are elsewhere; both forms of knowledge are liable to make us unhappy. Some scientists suggest that excessive domestic cleanliness may be responsible for a rise in autoimmune and allergic diseases like asthma. If agriculture, hygiene and knowledge can be seen as undesirable, while war, faeces and failure can be seen as desirable, there does not seem to be any limit to the subjectivity of desire.

As Shakespeare's Hamlet has it, 'There is nothing either good or bad, but thinking makes it so.'

Or, to put it another way, there are competing truths about the desirability of just about anything.

Of course a sunny vacation is more desirable than a car crash, but the vacation can be made more or less desirable by your perspective, and so can the car crash. Maybe the vacation is taking you away from work you love at a critical time. Maybe the car crash helps you get your priorities straight and make more of life. Desirability is never set in stone.

Because desirability is subjective, it can be changed with the right competing truth. The toiletries brand Dove challenged conventional ideas of physical desirability with its Campaign for Real Beauty. In a series of billboard advertisements, an image of a woman was displayed next to two tick boxes with descriptors such as *grey?/gorgeous?* for an older woman, or *flawed?/flawless?* for a heavily freckled woman. We can change what we think of as beautiful, the campaign suggested, in others and in ourselves.

As our view of what is desirable and undesirable drives so much of our behaviour, the right competing truth can substantially influence what we do. This can be very helpful if we are trying to make changes in our lives. In theory, we can choose to want what's good for us – and nudge others in the same direction.

Who wants a cookie?

Obesity is killing us.

Around the world, people are eating too much of the wrong stuff, and it is laying the fatty foundations for a global health catastrophe. More than two billion people are overweight or obese. Over 340 million children and adolescents aged 5–19 are overweight or obese, or 18 per cent of the global population for that age group, up from just 4 per cent in 1975. It is no longer solely a rich-world problem: over ten million children in Africa are overweight or obese. Up to 20 per cent of global healthcare spending is attributable to obesity, whether through measures to prevent or treat the condition, or related conditions such as heart disease and type 2 diabetes. Government budgets are being stretched as dangerously as waistlines.

We are bringing this avoidable problem upon ourselves by eating high-fat, high-sugar foods. One reason is that these foods are often cheaper than more nutritious, less fattening alternatives. But the other driver is taste: we find such foods more desirable than lentils, kale and celery. In fact, research suggests that not only do we expect unhealthy food to taste better, we actually enjoy eating food more if we believe it to be unhealthy.[3]

The most common strategy for fighting obesity is to bribe or bully ourselves into avoiding desirable foods. Governments in a number of countries are considering sugar taxes and regulations to persuade food manufacturers to use less fat and sugar. Diet plans built on self-denial have proliferated over the decades. Parents try to persuade their kids to eat broccoli by hiding it in pasta sauce or promising high-sugar rewards for compliance. None of these tactics seem to work well. Rates of obesity keep on rising, despite the billions of dollars spent each year on diet plans, food substitutes and laxatives.

A more successful approach would be to change the way we see nutritious, low-sugar, low-fat foods. We need to make the good stuff desirable.

> **Desirability tactic #1**
> *Persuading people to like what's good for them*

A fascinating series of experiments shows how readily the human brain can change its tastes when prompted in the right way. Researchers gave subjects two glasses of the same wine to taste but told them that each glass contained a differently priced product. When drinking wine they believed to be more expensive, subjects reported greater pleasure than for the wine they were told was cheaper. This was no trick of the imagination. When the same experiment was carried out in an fMRI scanner, subjects drinking what they believed to be more expensive wine showed greater neural activity in the brain region associated with experiencing pleasure: as in the case of the 'real' works of art, they genuinely were enjoying the taste more. The same results have been obtained with chocolate.

It seems that when we expect to enjoy something, we are more likely to enjoy it, a phenomenon observed in a range of consumer products from movies to beer and referred to as 'marketing placebo effects'. This happens because pleasure is not, biologically speaking, an end in itself but is a mechanism to persuade us to pursue certain evolutionarily useful objectives such as food and sex – a mechanism which can be recalibrated.

'The brain encodes pleasure because it is useful for learning which activities to repeat and which ones to avoid, and good decision-making requires good measures of the quality of an experience,' said Antonio Rangel, one of the researchers behind the wine study. 'As a way of improving its measurements, it makes sense to add up other sources of information about the experience.

In particular, if you are very sure cognitively that an experience is good (perhaps because of previous experiences), it makes sense to incorporate that into your current measurements of pleasure.[4] In this case, a high price tag made people believe they were going to find the wine delicious – and so they did.

This suggests that if you can convince yourself you are going to enjoy broccoli, you may actually enjoy it, with real pleasure-associated neural activity in your ventromedial prefrontal cortex. It's a difficult trick to pull off in an adult with fixed ideas about broccoli, but we might have a better chance of encouraging children to eat healthily if we accept the implications of the research. We aren't born knowing what we like to eat; we learn it from our parents and those around us. The standard technique of bribing or browbeating kids to eat their greens, or smuggling vegetables into sauces and cakes, only reinforces the expectation that healthy food will taste bad, which becomes a self-fulfilling prophecy. If, instead, parents and other healthy-eating Advocates can communicate a competing truth – that healthy foods taste delicious – then, the wine experiment suggests, children may indeed find they taste good and develop lifelong healthy eating habits.

I fully admit this is easier said than done. But studies have shown that schoolchildren will voluntarily eat more vegetables if they are served next to imagery of vegetable cartoon characters[5] or given fun and attractive names like 'X-ray Vision Carrots'.[6] Parents can set an example for their kids, enthusing over their spinach and brown rice, associating favourite dolls or toys with cauliflower, positioning mushrooms and walnuts as a reward.

And there may be a way we can work a little of the same magic on our own brains.

Researchers from Stanford's Department of Psychology have investigated the impact of names and labels on our food choices. They assigned 'indulgent' labels to randomly selected vegetables served in a university cafeteria, such as 'Twisted citrus-glazed carrots', 'Dynamite chili and tangy lime-seasoned beets' and 'Sweet sizzlin' green beans'. On other days the same vegetables, prepared in exactly the same way, were given standard or healthy-sounding labels, such as 'Green beans' or 'Light 'n' low-carb green beans'.

They observed a significant increase in the number of people choosing vegetables (25 per cent more) and the total mass of vegetables consumed (23 per cent more) when the 'indulgent' labels were used. Vegetables with labels highlighting their healthy properties were no more popular than those with standard labels, a finding that poses a critical challenge to conventional public health strategies. If cerebral Stanford students can't be persuaded to choose vegetables for their health benefits, it is unlikely that approach will work on the wider population. Making vegetables sound desirable, the study demonstrates, is a much more effective approach.

Despite what you may have read about humans' age-old desire for sugar and fat, there is no neurological reason why the brain can't be trained to crave cabbage rather than cake. We are omnivores: we are supposed to be up for eating all kinds of things. 'We try to eat more vegetables, but we do not try to make ourselves enjoy vegetables more,' reflects food journalist Bee Wilson, 'maybe because there's a near-universal conviction that it is not possible to learn new tastes and shed old ones. Yet nothing could be further from the truth.'[7]

The meaning of life

Most of us have to work to earn a living. But beyond the money it generates, is work desirable?

Train driver Amy Carpenter says, 'I enjoy interacting with customers, using my knowledge to help make someone's journey easier or giving an excited child a wave as I pull into the platform.

But at the most basic level, I just really, really love driving trains.'[8] 'Wouldn't want to work anywhere else!' writes one nurse at the Aspen Valley Hospital on anonymous company review website Glassdoor.[9] 'Best Job Ever!' declares an NBCUniversal employee on the same site.[10] 'Every day I get up excited and ready for work which to me is the most rewarding experience in the world,' raves tech entrepreneur Michael Sliwinski.[11]

These are the kind of lucky people who might say, 'I love my job so much I'd do it for nothing.' So work, for some people, is desirable.

Sadly, for many others, a different truth prevails. In 2013, Gallup published the results of a monumental study, conducted across 142 countries, which found that only 13 per cent of the global workforce are 'engaged at work'.[12] 63 per cent of employees are 'not engaged', meaning they 'lack motivation and are less likely to invest discretionary effort in organizational goals or outcomes'. The remaining 24 per cent are 'actively disengaged'. That means almost a quarter of all employees essentially hate their jobs. They are 'unhappy and unproductive at work and liable to spread negativity to coworkers'. That's an estimated 340 million people who are made miserable by the way they spend a large part of their waking hours. Almost a billion more people are getting little beyond pay from their primary activity in life. Even in the United States and Canada, where the most positive attitudes to work are found, more than 70 per cent of employees are 'not engaged' or are 'actively disengaged'.

This is a pretty poor state of affairs. In fact, given the huge psychological and economic cost to humanity of all that disengagement, it is a scandal.

How can we make work more desirable? Many factors, from a pleasant working environment to increased autonomy, can help, but perhaps most important is a clear and worthwhile purpose. People need to feel that what they do matters. As the economist

John Kay puts it, 'Making a profit is no more the purpose of business than breathing is the purpose of living.'[13] People want to have a goal beyond making their employer rich.

If you ask executives to describe the purpose of their company beyond making money, the result is often a blank look or a stock platitude about 'serving our customers'. In fact, some leaders get quite irritated by the idea that a commercial organization needs any kind of purpose beyond growing shareholder value. It's no wonder that so many employees are disengaged.

You might think there either is or isn't a worthy purpose for an employee to contribute to. But purpose, important as it is, may be considered to some extent a figment of our imagination. You might say that your primary purpose in life is to raise your kids well. You might say it is to spread joy among those you meet. You might say it is to build an enduring company, or win an Olympic medal, or be the best drummer in your city, or find a cure for lung cancer. In fact, you might pursue more than one. Your reason for getting out of bed every morning is up to you. So purpose can be constructed – that doesn't make it any less valuable.

I have helped clarify and communicate the purpose of dozens of organizations. Some purpose statements were competitive: people love to feel they are doing better than the competition, and the unending struggle to surpass rivals may be sufficient motivation for some employees. For Pepsi, the underdog in the cola wars, the simple ambition to 'Beat Coke' was incredibly motivating. Other companies powerfully engage their employees with a determination to achieve some goal or innovation before anyone else. But the majority of effective purpose statements are about helping, protecting or making life better for others.

When the Bank of England asked me to craft a purpose statement for the UK's new Prudential Regulation Authority, we cut through all the complexity of microprudential policy and forward-looking, judgement-based supervision, the EU's Capital Requirements

Directive, compliance costs and resolvability assessments, proactive intervention and counterparty risk, to come up with a simple but crucial purpose: *We protect the UK financial system*. In the wake of the catastrophic global financial crisis and the near-collapse of two major British banks, that was purpose enough to motivate any financial regulator.

An altruistic purpose does not need to be grand and world-changing. One company I advised over several years sold the seeds and seedlings of ornamental plants like geraniums, pansies and cyclamens. They were not vital to public health or world peace, yet we were able to show the real contribution they made to the happiness of millions of people who love cultivating flowers. The company had a strong Research and Development function developing new breeds that were more resilient, able to withstand nutrient imbalances and too much or too little watering. This addressed a big pain point for buyers of ornamental plants: they hated seeing plants die through their own error. So the purpose we were able to offer employees was to enrich lives by making flowering plants not only enjoyable to look at but also easier to look after – a small but real contribution to global happiness that was enough to energize a whole workforce.

Anyone who feels an ideological dislike for business may be surprised to hear that many employees tend to enjoy their work more, and perform it more diligently, if they feel they are helping others in some way. Companies may be set up to make money, but their people often long to make a difference, and this tendency seems to be growing. If we want to make work more desirable, we need to understand and answer that longing.

Lead us not into temptation . . . or revulsion

Like so much else in the world of competing truths, manipulating desirability has a dark side. We've looked at how we can increase the desirability of healthy food or useful work. But it is also possible to make us desire things that harm us or our society. The advertising industry has been doing it for decades. Cigarette commercials are still being produced that glamorize smoking, creating a desire in young people for a product that may kill them. By making us crave grease-laden fries and sugary drinks, fast-food marketing has contributed significantly to our obesity problem.

Even more insidious is the tactic of turning us against something or someone by persuading us that a particular organization, individual, object or group is undesirable. Newspapers and politicians have exercised this unsavoury form of mass influence against targets as diverse as sports fans, welfare claimants, pit bulls, tourists, single mothers, socialists, GM food, vegetarians, Muslims and obese people. But the most pernicious case of this phenomenon today is the campaign being waged against immigrants.

> **Desirability tactic #2**
> *Turning people against entire groups*

We've seen Donald Trump denounce Mexican immigrants and Syrian refugees, while Britain's UKIP, France's Front National, Germany's AfD, the Netherlands' Party for Freedom and the Freedom Party of Austria have all made great advances in political power by demonizing immigrants. Media organs like Breitbart News, the *Daily Mail* and *Daily Express* have lent their considerable support to the campaign, along with celebrity commentators like Rush Limbaugh, Ann Coulter and Katie Hopkins. Hopkins went so far as to compare migrants to 'cockroaches' in one inflammatory *Sun* newspaper article.

What effect has this verbal offensive had on the average citizen's view of the desirability of immigrants? A substantial one it would seem from opinion polls and events such as the Brexit referendum and the 2016 Austrian presidential election. To get a clearer picture of the effect of political and media influence on public opinion, we can look at Hungary, a country that – with the exception of the Roma – has an especially homogenous white population and little experience of other cultures within its borders.

The TÁRKI Social Research Institute has been gathering data on Hungarian attitudes to immigrants for decades. They divide survey respondents into 'xenophiles', 'xenophobes' and an intermediate group. Between 2002 and 2011, the proportion of Hungarians they classified as xenophobes fluctuated between 24 per cent and 34 per cent. Since then, it has risen substantially, reaching an all-time high of 53 per cent in 2016. Over the same baseline period, 6–12 per cent of Hungarians were classified as xenophiles; that figure dropped to just 1 per cent in 2016.[14]

What caused this dramatic rise in dislike and distrust of foreigners? In 2015, hundreds of thousands of people from Syria, Afghanistan and Iraq entered Hungary. But the vast majority passed through the country as quickly as they could, on their way to Germany and Austria. Hungary received 177,135 asylum applications that year – the highest rate per head of local population in Europe – yet it approved only 502 of them. Over 90 per cent of asylum applicants left Hungary before their cases had been decided. Most Hungarians never saw a migrant in the flesh. Almost none experienced any threat, reduction of living standards or inconvenience as a result of this historic movement of people. The xenophobes 'have probably seen more aliens from other planets in their lives than immigrants,' noted one Hungarian sympathetic to the plight of the migrants.[15]

But what Hungarians may lack in terms of direct experience of migrants, they have been amply compensated for in government propaganda. 'Did you know that the Paris terror attacks were carried out by immigrants?' read one government-funded advertisement. 'Did you know that since the start of the immigration crisis, harassment of women has increased in Europe?' read another.

Prime minister Viktor Orbán initiated the anti-immigrant campaign in early 2015, and TÁRKI registered an immediate upsurge in xenophobia. His propaganda had very effectively disseminated a new competing truth about the desirability of immigrants. Tellingly, during the summer of 2015, while the mass migration was taking place across Hungary, the number of xenophobes recorded by TÁRKI actually went *down*: it seems that, confronted by daily TV images of immense suffering, Hungarians briefly became more nuanced in their opinions. But the anti-immigrant rhetoric continued after the mass migration had ended, and the proportion of Hungarians registering as xenophobes went up again, rising to an all-time high even though there were very few migrants or asylum seekers left in Hungary.

Right across the Western world, demagogues and anti-immigrant media have managed to forge a new competing truth: where previous generations have seen immigrants as a source of new ideas, enterprise, energy and culture, they are now widely seen as undesirable. The long-term consequences for politics and society in North America and Europe may be profound.

Change what people want and you change the world

It is not easy to change tastes, but it can be done. In fact, it has probably been done to you. We all need to get better at recognizing when marketers, politicians and journalists try to redefine what is desirable in ways that may hurt us or others. At the same time, we have an immense opportunity to change our lives for the better by acknowledging and exploiting the plasticity of our desires. Where existing desires are destructive or problematic, using competing truths to change the desirability of things for ourselves and for others may be both effective and ethical. We really can want what's good for us if we try.

In practice

• Learn to like the things that are good for you – it *is* possible!

• Use names, purpose statements and other competing truths to help those around you do the same.

But watch out for . . .

• Demagogues and other Misleaders who try to make you dislike whole groups of people.

8

Financial Value

Price is what you pay; value is what you get.
WARREN BUFFETT

Fungal fortune

How much would you pay for a piece of mould?

Perhaps you would like some more information before placing your bid. The size? The colour? The condition?

Well, it's about one inch in diameter. The colour is a greeny grey. It sits between two glass discs, sealed with clear packing tape. It is old and dead. It has no possible practical use.

How much is it worth to you?

Most likely your valuation is close to zero. You might even pay money *not* to have the mould in your home.

On 7 December 2016, this scrap of inedible fungus was sold at auction by Bonhams in New York for $46,250. It was marketed as 'Original Penicillin Mold culture'.

In 1928, medical researcher Alexander Fleming was studying *Staphylococcus*, a type of bacteria that causes sore throats, boils and blood poisoning. On his return from holiday, he noticed that one petri dish containing the bacteria had become mouldy – an accidental contamination. Remarkably, around the mould spot was a bacteria-free circle. Fleming realized that the fungus must be producing some kind of substance that was killing or inhibiting the bacteria. The fungus was *Penicillium chrysogenum*, the source of the first scientifically understood antibiotic.

Fleming was made famous by his accidental discovery and was jointly awarded the Nobel Prize in Physiology or Medicine in 1945. He seems to have enjoyed his fame, sending samples of the miracle mould to other celebrities of the day, including the Pope and Marlene Dietrich. The lot auctioned at Bonhams was given by Fleming to a neighbour in 1955, in gratitude for scaring off some burglars. The sample is signed by Fleming and is accompanied by letters from him and his housekeeper addressed to the neighbour. The housekeeper's letter ends, 'P.S. As though you didn't know – but just in case – this round affair is a blob of the original Mould of Penicillin, not to be confused with Gorgonzola cheese!!!'

So, now that you know the context, how much would this small patch of mould be worth to you?

Perhaps a bit more than your first valuation. You might be willing to pay a few hundred dollars to own a piece of medical history. Perhaps, if you are a canny investor, you might even pay a few thousand. It is unlikely that you would pay $46,250. In fact, if Bonhams has done its job properly, there should be only one person (or organization) in the world who values it that highly – the buyer who won the auction.

That buyer was bidding on the same item as everyone else. They knew the same context of the mould as everyone else. So why did they put a different financial value on it?

Price does not equal value

In the last chapter, we saw how we can be persuaded to like or dislike just about anything. But if we come to like something, just *how much* do we like it? Or, to put it bluntly, how much would we be willing to pay for it? What is its financial value?

Auctions show why this is not an easy question to answer: different bidders place different values on the same lot. We can think of these subjective valuations as competing truths. No one is 'wrong' in their own valuation just because someone else bids higher.

Outside the auction room, we tend to think a good or service has a set price and that is its value. But how is the price decided? Many people feel instinctively that the price of a car, say, should be closely related to the cost of the materials that went into the car and the labour required to assemble it. We would expect a mark-up for administrative and marketing costs, and a further mark-up for a reasonable profit margin. The result would be the fair price for that car.

But this idea falls apart when we think about some simple examples:

> *Why does a Picasso painting, which took one man only a few days to create, cost more than an aeroplane that required many thousands of man hours to build?*

> *Would you pay more for an emerald that had been mined at great effort by a team of 200 engineers than for an identical emerald that I stumbled upon while hiking in Zambia?*

> *If a thousand people work for a year to build a machine that glues ice cubes together, does their labour make that machine valuable?*

As each of these examples suggests, pricing cannot be based on the effort of production alone. Instead, the price of a thing is determined by what we collectively think it is worth. Like the selling price of Fleming's mould, it depends on our subjective valuations.

Take a standard 50mm brass padlock with a stainless-steel shackle. If I need to secure a storage unit containing all my worldly possessions, I might be willing to pay a great deal for that padlock. But the manufacturer wouldn't sell many padlocks if she priced them according to my circumstances alone. She also needs to take into account people buying padlocks for their gym locker, or that old bike in the backyard, or as a memento to attach to a Parisian bridge. She needs to consider rich people and poor people, people in a hurry and those who have time to shop around. Each person looking for a padlock may be willing to pay a slightly different amount.

From all these different subjective valuations, economists derive a 'demand curve': when the price is low, lots of us will buy; as the price rises, the number of potential buyers falls. Economists pair this with a 'supply curve', which plots the equivalent willingness of manufacturers to produce and sell the same type of good at different prices. Where the supply curve and the demand curve meet, in theory you have the perfect price to match supply and demand.

So our subjective valuations – our competing truths about the value of that padlock – help to set the market price.

Competing truths about financial value are essential to trade. The main reason we exchange or trade things is because we value them differently. If an apple farmer valued the apples in his store as much as his customers do, he would never sell any of them. But because an individual apple is worth less to the farmer than it is to a nearby chef, they are able to find a price that works for both of them.

Imagine you make rocking chairs, and you value each finished item at $50. Below that price you would rather keep a chair than sell it. I want one chair and would pay up to $400 for it. A transaction at any price between those two figures would leave us both better off. Let's say we agree a price of $200. You have pocketed

$150 more than your valuation of the chair, and I have acquired $400 worth of rocking chair at a saving of $200. Between us, we are $350 better off as a result of the trade.

Most of the wealth in the world has been created in this way. Crude oil isn't directly useful to a landowner in California, but he can sell it to an oil refiner for far more than his own subjective valuation. Three hundred million iPads aren't much use to Apple's shareholders, but they can sell them to us for less than our individual subjective valuations of the devices, leaving us all better off. Competing truths about financial value have made our species rich.

How we value

How do people arrive at different valuations? We value a good or service in a number of ways, each of which can vary for different individuals:

1. What is the benefit to me?

The benefit we will derive from something depends on our tastes and our circumstances. A music-streaming service may be worth a lot to you if you love music, but not if you are too busy to log in more than once a month. A ladder may be just what you need for those essential roof repairs . . . unless you already own one. A car may be worth a lot to you . . . until petrol becomes too expensive to buy or a new train line makes public transport more convenient. A cinema ticket may seem less valuable to you once other options for spending your time present themselves.

The benefit we gain from buying something is not necessarily limited to its immediate function. Would a holiday package be worth as much to you without the pictures to post on Instagram? Do the bragging rights of owning a limited-edition phone increase its value for you? Will there be a cost to maintaining and storing that sailing boat, and if so how does that impact its net value?

2. What is the benefit to someone else?

We may not see any benefit from something to ourselves yet still value it highly if we think we can sell it to someone else. That is why tradable assets like gold, fine wines and art are worth so much.

Stock-market traders often value securities according to how much they think someone else will value them. In theory, the value of a share in a company is determined by the expected future income stream from that share. In practice, shares can trade far above that level if traders believe other traders will value them foolishly highly. This happens in stock-market bubbles: 'wise' traders know that shares are over-priced but reckon there are 'foolish' traders out there who will buy later at an even higher price, allowing the 'wise' trader to make a gain. This is delightfully known as the 'greater fool theory'. Of course, the other trader may not be all that foolish but may reckon there is a further 'foolish' trader out there to justify the investment.

3. How rare is it?

If we buy something solely because of the value we think someone else will put on it, we had better make sure it is unique or in short supply. Other people might need water, but they won't buy it from you if they can get it free from a tap. Rarity is critical to both investible assets and luxury goods. Sometimes such rarity is based on a real constraint, but often it is artificially imposed to keep valuations high.

Rarity also influences our valuation of tickets for popular theatre shows or sporting events. The American musical *Hamilton* became such a hit that official ticket prices for the best seats were raised in 2016 to $849, a Broadway record. These were still much cheaper than many of the tickets sold in the secondary market, revealing the immense value some theatregoers placed on these scarce assets.

Some people derive pleasure from owning something rare or unique and will pay high sums even for objects of no obvious value. Actor William Shatner sold a kidney stone for $25,000. His *Star Trek* costumes have sold for more than $100,000, although in Hollywood that's none too impressive; Marilyn Monroe's levitating white dress from *The Seven Year Itch* sold for $4.6 million.

4. *What are the risks of buying it?*

You can pick up great electrical goods on eBay for a fraction of their retail prices. They've been pre-owned, but often you'll barely notice any signs of wear. Why is that immaculate TV so cheap? Because we don't know if the seller has dropped it, or exposed it to the wrong voltage, or done some other unknowable but damaging thing to it. We are taking a risk buying it, and that risk diminishes its value. Similarly, a developer buying land may be unsure whether she will be granted planning permission to build on it; that risk will reduce the value of the land for her until the planning authority rules on the matter.

Risk and uncertainty are difficult to quantify objectively, so they are important sources of competing truths. You may estimate the probability of that eBay TV breaking down after a year is one chance in ten, while I might think it is one chance in two. My pessimism will lead me to a lower valuation of the TV.

5. *What does the future hold?*

So many of our judgements depend on our predictions for the future, and financial valuation is no exception. Reckon electric vehicles will proliferate? Those lithium-battery stocks might be worth more than everyone thinks. Will climate change bring more volatile weather? Comprehensive house insurance sounds a bargain.

Fear of future scarcity leads people to put a higher current value on things. When Hostess Brands Inc. announced its impending bankruptcy in 2012, panic spread among fans of the company's most famous product, the Twinkie. Normally priced at a few dollars a box, Twinkies saw a surge in valuations on eBay following the bankruptcy announcement.

Our subjective valuations depend on our wealth: the richer we are, the more we may be willing to pay for something. It follows that the richer we *think we will be*, the more we may be willing to pay. It could be three months before you start your new job, but you will probably be willing to spend more on that new fridge now than before you secured the job offer.

> **Financial Value tactic #1**
> *Including all relevant factors in*
> *subjective valuations*

We can be strongly influenced by others on each of these dimensions. This matters because our financial valuations of the goods and services on offer drive our consumer behaviour. We buy things only when we value them more highly than their price. Yet partial truths about the benefits, popularity, rarity, risks and future circumstances of any product or service can be deployed to make us change our valuations.

That opens the door to a whole industry of advertising agencies, marketing executives and salespeople whose job it is to raise our valuations above the threshold of their prices. By shifting the competing truths we hold about financial value, businesses drive our actions in malls and online.

Learning to love stones

There is precious little that most of us can do with a small rock, however sparkly it is. Perhaps that's why diamonds were not widely valued for most of human history. A well-cut diamond is a beautiful thing, so they have long had a place in the jewellery boxes of the very wealthy. But until the twentieth century, almost no one else ever saw one.

When diamonds were rare, it didn't matter that few people valued them. That changed after a teenage boy found a shiny pebble by South Africa's Orange River in 1867 and took it home for his sisters' entertainment. His discovery turned out to be a 22-carat diamond, and it set off an extraordinary diamond rush. Prospectors began scouring alluvial deposits in the area, and within a few years miners were digging large numbers of diamonds out of the earth and rock around Kimberley. Previously, most of the world's diamonds had come from India, and the mines there were largely depleted. In a little over a decade, South Africa produced more diamonds than India had in centuries.

The immediate effect of this flood of new diamonds was to bring down prices. Diamonds were no longer rare, and buyers could negotiate more keenly. Moreover, the relative abundance of diamonds reduced their appeal to the aristocracy, who turned to 'less common' stones like rubies and emeralds. The diamond entrepreneurs, who had invested so much in their new South African mines, risked destroying the value of their assets through over-production.

This supply problem was quickly resolved when one of the entrepreneurs, a young Englishman named Cecil Rhodes, obtained sufficient financial backing to buy up or combine with all the other diamond-mining operations in South Africa. The resulting company, De Beers, was able to use its monopolistic power to restrict the supply of diamonds, create an illusion of scarcity and dictate market prices for decades. As other diamond finds emerged around the world, De Beers was quick to gain control of them, preventing any further bursts of excess supply. But that created a second problem: De Beers was left with a mountain of unsold diamonds.

How to offload them profitably without destroying their apparent rarity value? The obvious solution was to get more people to buy the pretty stones, and that meant persuading millions of us to value the things more highly. Before the Second World War, the average man on a good wage did not view a diamond as a useful savings vehicle or have any practical need for glittery lumps of carbon. Most people's subjective valuations of diamonds were low. De Beers somehow needed to raise those valuations above a price point that would offer them a healthy profit. And it needed to discourage buyers from reselling their stones in a secondary market that would depress prices.

In 1938, De Beers turned to New York advertising agency N. W. Ayer & Son to enquire whether 'the use of propaganda in various forms' might help boost demand in the United States. Their partnership would go on to create a vast market for diamonds – a market centred on the engagement ring.

Rings have been used as symbols of love and nuptial commitment for millennia. Copper, gold and even braided hair have been used to form betrothal rings in numerous cultures throughout history. A small fraction were adorned with jewels. But the dominance of the diamond engagement ring as a man's most sincere proof of his love for a woman is a modern invention.

An invention manufactured by De Beers and N. W. Ayer.

Between the two world wars, diamond consumption in the United States had halved. N. W. Ayer reckoned that the way to reverse this decline was to develop a connection between diamonds and romance. Women should be persuaded to view the quality and size of a diamond as representative of their suitor's love. The agency's stated goal was 'to create a situation where almost every person pledging marriage feels compelled to acquire a diamond engagement ring'.

The advertising agency used magazine stories, product placement in movies and full-colour advertisements to build an indelible link between large diamonds and true love. 'A diamond is forever' the advertisements declared in 1948 and in most years since, cleverly implying that selling a diamond would be pretty despicable behaviour, if not an outright betrayal of love. Portraits were commissioned of well-born fiancées with impressive rocks on their fingers, and diamonds were lent to socialites attending the Kentucky Derby. When television arrived, the campaign carried the romance/diamond message into American living rooms.

'We are dealing with a problem in mass psychology,' explained N. W. Ayer in a 1947 strategy plan. Their ambition was to make buying a diamond ring 'a psychological necessity'. Astonishingly, the advertising agency even organized an indoctrination programme for American high schools: 'All of these lectures revolve around the diamond engagement ring, and are reaching thousands of girls in their assemblies, classes and informal meetings in our leading educational institutions.' Moreover, there must be no room for substitute goods: the agency was determined that 'only the diamond is everywhere accepted and recognized as the symbol of betrothal'. The focus on shifting men's subjective valuations of diamonds was made explicit when later advertisements arbitrarily asked, 'Isn't two months' salary a small price to pay for something that lasts forever?'

The campaign, as we all know, was spectacularly successful. By the late 1950s, N. W. Ayer was able to report that 'To this new generation a diamond ring is considered a necessity to engagements by virtually everyone.' In 2015, De Beers valued the US diamond jewellery market at $39 billion dollars per year. Today, three quarters of American brides wear a diamond ring. Few women ever sell their engagement ring, which helps keep prices high; their subjective valuations of their diamonds are well above the prices they would get on the secondary market.

With mission accomplished in the United States, De Beers turned its attention to other markets, notably the rising economic power of Japan. Before the 1960s, diamond engagement rings were almost unheard of in this strongly traditional country. But young Japanese were increasingly open to Western influences, and De Beers commissioned an advertising campaign that showed beautiful Western women sporting diamond rings while engaged in fun modern activities like yachting or camping. Less than two decades later, 60 per cent of Japanese brides wore diamond rings. A similar mindset shift has been achieved in China, where more than 30 per cent of brides now wear diamond rings – up from almost none thirty years ago.

De Beers faced a further over-supply problem in the 1960s, when the Soviet Union discovered new diamond deposits in Siberia. These stones were tiny, but there were a lot of them, and released on to world markets they could have seriously challenged the industry's precious scarcity illusion. So De Beers struck a deal to market these diamonds on behalf of the Soviet Union. At first, it wasn't clear what anyone could do with all those tiny stones. Then De Beers came up with the concept of the eternity ring, a variation on an ancient tradition: modern eternity rings would be studded with tiny diamonds, helpfully soaking up the Siberian supply. As investigative journalist Edward Jay Epstein put it, 'Sentiments were born out of necessity: older American women received a ring of miniature diamonds because of the needs of a South African corporation to accommodate the Soviet Union.'[1] Subjective valuations of tiny diamonds had been correspondingly tiny until the De Beers marketing machine helped us reassess their worth.

This story of sensational marketing achievement over decades is particularly interesting because the product being marketed was not branded. No company logo featured in the campaign.* N. W. Ayer changed our subjective valuations of diamonds, not of De Beers. Many other famous campaigns have radically shifted our subjective valuations of branded goods, but successful campaigns promoting an unbranded commodity are as rare as De Beers would like you to believe its products are.

Getting it wrong

Time for a reality check. I have talked about subjective financial valuations as if we each have a clear sense of a thing's worth to us. But a series of experiments by behavioural economists and psychologists like Daniel Kahneman, Amos Tversky, Richard Thaler and Dan Ariely has now shown how very poor our valuation skills can be. Marketers take full advantage of this human weakness.

Ask a keen fisherman how much he would pay for a good-quality fishing rod, and he will probably give an answer close to the average market price. But a novice who knows nothing about the fishing-rod market might give a subjective valuation far above or below it. With no points of reference, he just doesn't know what a fishing rod *should* be worth. An economist might say he should be able to deduce what a fishing rod is worth to him by comparing it with all the other things he could buy with whatever money he has. In practice, few people think like that. Instead, we take steers when forming our subjective valuations from whatever guides we can find. More often than not, those guides are salespeople and their marketing material.

How much is a one-hour helicopter ride over your city worth to you? You've probably never thought about it, but let's say you value it at $100. On your way to work, you see just such a ride

---

* De Beers was until recently banned from operating in the United States on antitrust grounds.

advertised at $800. You decide it's not worth the money to you, but would your subjective valuation still be $100? If you walked round the corner and found another operator offering an identical flight for just $200, might you now be tempted? If so, you've allowed a lone price signal to double your subjective valuation.

You visit a new restaurant and your eye is caught by the scallops with risotto nero and smoked paprika. The price is $37. Next to the scallops on the menu is a Wagyu beef steak priced at $89. When you spot that, the scallops start to look very good value. It's obviously a high-quality establishment, and you're getting a bargain!

If you stopped to think hard about it, you might question whether you really wanted a few scallops and a bit of fancy rice more than all the other things you could buy with $37 (plus service and taxes). But in the context of that menu, such extraneous considerations melt away. Compared to that expensive steak, your scallops look like a good choice. There is a strong chance the restaurant sells very few $89 steaks, and moreover *expects* to sell very few. It may be that the steak is only on the menu in order to influence your valuation of the less extortionate dishes.

We are much better at making relative valuations than absolute valuations. Without previous pricing knowledge, we don't really know what anything should cost, but we can usually say whether one thing is worth more or less to us than some other thing. Marketers exploit this contrast effect by planting 'anchors', prices that steer our valuations of their products upwards. The expensive menu item is one form of anchor. Another is the original retail price on a 'sale' item; next to the first price, the actual price the retailer wants you to pay looks cheap.

> **Financial Value tactic #2**
> *Using price anchors and other tricks to
> influence other people's valuations*

Another psychological weakness is our attitude to risk. In general, we don't like it, even when a probability expert assures us the potential upside outweighs the downside. This means we will pay more for certainty – of transport schedule, of grocery delivery time, of insurance payout – than is strictly rational. Marketers can play on this bias by using language like *guaranteed*, *certain* or *commitment* to raise our subjective valuations.

We also react irrationally to perceived unfairness. We may turn down the chance to buy something we value highly if we think the seller is profiting too much or taking advantage, even if the price is below our subjective valuation. When retailers put up the price of umbrellas during rainstorms, we may refuse to buy one – not because we can't afford the new price or don't value the umbrella that highly but because we resent the store for taking advantage of our temporary meteorological difficulties.

We may value something less if we believe it has cost little to produce, even if it offers considerable benefit to us. Keen readers get great pleasure from novels, sometimes losing themselves in a single book for several happy weeks. One might think that a reader's valuation of such a book would be sky high. Yet if the book is an e-book and the reader thinks that his copy cost nothing to produce, he may refuse to pay more than a couple of dollars for it, while being willing to spend five times as much on a cocktail that promises only a few minutes' pleasure. Many people now object to paying anything at all for digital goods for this reason.

These are just some of the ways in which we think oddly, perversely or irrationally about the financial value of things. Our valuations are not wrong, just because the thinking that has produced them is flawed; they are our truths, and it is as pointless to tell a millennial that she should value music tracks more as it is to criticize a diner for paying $37 for a few scallops. In the end, we make our choices in a market economy, and we live with the consequences.

Valuing ourselves

We've focused on how subjective truths about financial value affect our buying behaviour. For anyone posting stuff on eBay, holding a garage sale or putting their house on the market, the same principles hold true for selling: we sell when our subjective valuation of an item is less than the price someone else is willing to pay for it. Whether or not we sell something therefore may depend on how the buyer influences our subjective valuation of the item.

Selling stuff is an infrequent activity for many people. However, there is one thing that most of us sell routinely: our time. The labour market is changing fast, with more and more work being offered piecemeal in the so-called 'gig economy'. The fragment-ation of work will require us to think harder about how we price ourselves in different situations. Developing smart subjective valuations of our own time is going to be critical.

A few years ago, I set up a small business that required some dis-tinctive icons for the website. I needed a graphic designer, but my budget was extremely limited, so I consulted Google and was soon led to DesignCrowd.

This Australian company offered an interesting proposition they called a 'Design Contest'. For a modest fee, I could post a description of what I needed on their site, and then freelance designers around the world would create icons to meet my brief. I could pick my favourite, and that designer would be paid most of the fee, with the remainder going to DesignCrowd. If none of the designs were to my liking, I would get my money back.

For a customer, it's an appealing proposition. But what is this crowdsourcing model like for the designers? I received dozens of fully executed designs, each of which was customized to my requirements and must have taken at least a few minutes – and in some cases hours – to create. Almost all of that effort went unrewarded. So how are those designers valuing their time?

Some might be hobbyists, doing it for fun and counting the occasional winning design as a bonus. Others are presumably making a risk–reward judgement, assessing their chances of winning the contest against the cost in time of competing. Designers from countries with low living costs will be able to put lower valuations on their time than those from Western countries. Designers with families to feed and other financial obligations will also make different calculations. In theory, there is nothing wrong with this. Rational designers will only give up their time for these projects if the potential pay-off is worth it to them. But, as we have seen, humans are often far from rational when it comes to valuation.

DesignCrowd is one of many players in the rapidly expanding 'labour on demand' industry. Amazon's Mechanical Turk allows employers to post 'Human Intelligence Tasks', which freelancers can complete for a designated fee. Upwork connects companies with professional freelancers all over the world. Fiverr does the same for micro-jobs starting at $5. CrowdFlower pairs an army of remote freelancers with artificial intelligence technology to offer clients 'human in the loop' data services. TaskRabbit offers scraps of paid work to anyone willing to walk dogs, clean, carry, assemble furniture or do a spot of DIY. Brands can use Gigwalk to commission people in distant cities to check up on retail displays, photograph stores or gather location data. Client Partners lets lonely Japanese rent a 'friend' for a chat, for company at a wedding or to populate a selfie.

For people who can't – or don't want to – commute, or commit to a single role, or work rigid hours, such gig-economy champions are a godsend. Some industrious freelancers can make a lot of money; one DesignCrowd designer earned a million dollars in five years. Platforms for digital and desk-based services also allow workers from poorer countries to tap into the global economy, reducing inequality and aiding development. The flexibility and efficiency of on-demand labour can be good for both worker and employer – so long as we get the pricing right.

The problem is that most of us aren't very good at making sensible valuations of our time. We don't know what we're really worth, and we don't think through the hidden costs and risks of undertaking particular work. Writers like me can spend years working on a book that will never sell. Personal trainers who have to pay fees and offer free introductory sessions just to operate in a gym may find their net earnings from private clients are a poor return on all the time and money invested. TaskRabbit and Gigwalk workers may sign up for a micro-job without fully accounting for the time or expense of travelling to it. Workers who are paid for on-spec work or for piecework delivered, rather than an hourly wage, may underestimate the real time cost of that work.

Freelancers tend to underestimate how much they need to earn per hour to cover tax, pension and maternity provision, health and long-term disability insurance, along with all the other costs they face. Consequently, they put a lower subjective valuation on their time than they should, and so accept work at lower rates than they need. This is bad for them, but it is also bad for all the other workers they are competing with, as market rates are driven down below sustainable levels. Minimum-wage legislation, if it exists at all, seldom applies to the self-employed and is meaningless for on-spec work models like the Design Contest. Sadly, there is nothing stopping freelancers undervaluing themselves to the detriment of the entire self-employed workforce. We are in danger of seeing a race to the bottom in on-demand labour pricing, resulting in a kind of virtual global sweatshop.

As more and more people transition into the gig economy, those of us who work for ourselves have got to get better at valuing ourselves – for everyone's sake.

The value of everything

As a direct consequence of our valuation-based choices, companies flourish or fail and economies boom or collapse. Some of the most powerful and sophisticated organizations on Earth have an almighty incentive to play on our psychological weaknesses and shape our consumer behaviour by influencing the truths we hold about financial value. It is not illegal in most jurisdictions for marketers to frame things in a particular way, to use price anchors or to encourage us to believe that goods like diamonds are more valuable than we might otherwise have concluded. So it's important that we make ourselves aware of the sales tricks and psychological pitfalls, and keep asking ourselves whether that tasty, shiny, intriguing thing we are thinking of buying is *really* worth more to us than its price. And when we come to sell ourselves, we need to think very hard about all the different things that should influence the value we place on our time.

A little extra reflection on value is almost always worth it.

In practice

• Work out what things are really worth to you, rather than being driven by the price others put on them.

• Factor in risk, future expectations and scarcity to your valuations, as well as the benefit you or others will derive from something.

But watch out for . . .

• Misleaders who use anchors and other psychological tricks to influence your valuations.

• Business models, platforms or environments that encourage you to undervalue your time and labour.

PART THREE

ARTIFICIAL TRUTHS

9

Definitions

When I use a word it means just what I choose it to mean – neither more nor less.

HUMPTY DUMPTY in *Through the Looking-Glass* by Lewis Carroll

The f-word

'It is a very strong word, with a strong impact.'

What comes to mind? A swear word? Something religious or spiritual? A holy name?

The speaker was Brendan Paddy, Head of Communications for the Disasters Emergency Committee, the organization that brings together 13 major UK charities in times of crisis. He went on: 'We have to be precise about how we use it. We have to raise the alarm before it's too late, but we also don't want to be accused of crying wolf.'[1]

The word Brendan Paddy is treating with such cautious respect is known as the 'f-word' amongst aid workers and international development professionals. It is *famine*.

So important is this word that various UN agencies and NGOs

have come together to give it a precise definition. The 'Integrated Food Security Phase Classification' (IPC) states that a famine can only be declared when 'at least 20 per cent of households in an area face extreme food shortages with a limited ability to cope; acute malnutrition rates exceed 30 per cent; and the death rate exceeds two persons per day per 10,000 persons'.

Why the fuss over the meaning of a word any child can learn about in history class? The declaration of a famine carries no binding obligations on the international community to act. It is purely the power of the word to shape public opinion that matters.

'Using the f-word gives a very strong message to donors and politicians. It brings in publicity and puts it on the news agenda – without it, the public doesn't know it is happening,' says Ian Bray of Oxfam.[2]

Many will remember the famine of 1984 that killed hundreds of thousands of people in Ethiopia. Thanks to appeals by aid agencies, powerful reporting by journalists like Michael Buerk and the fundraising efforts of Bob Geldof and friends, over $200 million was donated for emergency relief. The mobilization of goodwill around the world was extraordinary.

Relief workers know that such a mobilization can only rarely be achieved. Therefore, the word *famine* must be reserved for those occasions when international action is absolutely essential to prevent mass starvation. To use it more often is to risk 'crying wolf'. This leads to the perverse situation where a continuous variable, the level of food insecurity (or, bluntly, starvation) in a region, is converted into a discrete variable with only two possible values: famine or no famine.

In 2014, a team of food security experts travelled to Juba in South Sudan to assess whether the desperate situation there qualified as a famine. The stakes were very high: 'A declaration [of famine] can have a significant impact on the level of support that goes toward the crisis,' said Chris Hillbruner of FEWS NET, a famine early-warning system created by USAID.[3] The group reviewed the malnutrition rates, the ravaged crops and diminished livestock of South Sudan and concluded that the situation met the conditions of IPC Phase 4 (Emergency) but not IPC Phase 5 (Famine).

'This means that it will be much harder for humanitarian actors to raise the funds necessary to help people who are already faced with terrible conditions, and to prevent the situation from deteriorating further,' wrote Davina Jeffery of Save the Children, who was part of the Juba team. 'Although IPC Phase 4 still denotes an emergency, there will now be little media interest, almost certainly no Disaster Emergency Committee appeal, and probably no sharp rise in funding.'[4]

Without such donor mobilization, the situation in South Sudan continued to deteriorate, until a famine was finally declared in 2017. It was the first time the word had been officially deployed in six years, and it had an immediate impact. The UK famine appeal alone raised £50 million ($65 million) in just three weeks.

Such is the effect of one word. It has no legal power, yet its use can mean the difference between life or death for thousands.

Imagine, then, the impact of a word that does have legal consequence . . .

When is a genocide not a genocide?

In the space of a few weeks in 1994, an estimated 800,000 people were murdered in Rwanda. Following the assassination of the president, the majority ethnic Hutu group waged a vicious campaign to eliminate the minority Tutsi group. UN and media reports of the ongoing massacres were quickly circulated. The Hutu killers were armed with machetes and basic firearms – they would have been no match for a Western military intervention. Yet none came.

According to declassified government documents, US officials were using the word *genocide* in private to describe events in

193

Rwanda within 16 days of the outbreak of violence. But President Bill Clinton's administration would not publicly use the word until 49 days of killing had passed, and even then they would speak only of 'acts of genocide'. As Reuters correspondent Alan Elsner asked of a flustered State Department spokesperson, 'How many acts of genocide does it take to make genocide?'[5] The Clinton administration seemed entirely unwilling to admit the reality of the horror taking place in East Africa.

Here's why:

Issues for Discussion:
1. <u>Genocide Investigation:</u> Language that calls for an international investigation of human rights abuses and possible violations of the genocide convention.

Be careful. Legal at State was worried about this yesterday – Genocide finding could commit USG to actually 'do something'.[6]

The text is from a US Department of Defense discussion paper dated 1 May 1994, less than a month after the killing began. Declassified in 1998, the paper shows exactly why the administration would not use the word *genocide* when talking about Rwanda: legal counsel at the State Department was worried that labelling the killings as genocide would commit the US government to intervening, something they were loath to do following a disastrous military–humanitarian intervention in Somalia just a few months earlier.

The concept of genocide is a relatively recent legal innovation that originated with the Nuremberg trials of Nazi war criminals following the Second World War. The word was coined by a Jewish lawyer, Raphael Lemkin, who had seen most of his family murdered in the Holocaust. Article 1 of the 1948 Convention on the Prevention and Punishment of Genocide states that contracting parties (including the United States) 'confirm that genocide, whether committed in time of peace or in time of war, is a crime under international law *which they undertake to prevent* and to punish' (my emphasis). So, if it was genocide in Rwanda, the United States and other countries would indeed have to 'do something'.

But the definition of genocide, as set out in the 1948 Convention, comprised not only the physical act of killing multiple members of a defined group but also the *intent* to destroy part or all of that group.

While it was undeniable that large numbers of Tutsis were being killed, the intent to eliminate the Tutsis 'in whole or in part' could not easily be proven in the first weeks of the killing. Hutu-controlled radio stations were urging their listeners to go out and kill Tutsis, but was that proof of intent to destroy a population? According to the Hutus, they were fighting a civil war following the murder of their president. If it was indeed a civil war, then other countries would be expected to stay out of it.

So although we know it to be true that a genocide was taking place in Rwanda in 1994, it may also have been true that there was – for a time – insufficient proof of intent to declare it a genocide. The United States and other countries were able to dodge their responsibilities on a point of definition. Bill Clinton has since acknowledged that the United States could have saved at least 300,000 lives by intervening sooner.

> **Definitions tactic #1**
> *Interpreting circumstances to fit a definition*

'Thousands risk dying of starvation' and 'Thousands risk dying in a famine' are two competing truths that describe more or less the same situation yet produce two very different outcomes.

'Thousands are being murdered' and 'Thousands are being murdered in a genocide' similarly lead to completely different results.

When powerful words are so precisely defined, there is a temptation to try to shape circumstances to fit the word. For the Clinton administration, this meant interpreting events in Rwanda in a way that avoided acknowledging a systematic genocidal intent. For a well-intentioned aid worker, it might mean massaging malnutrition data in order to alert the world to a genuine humanitarian disaster.

But most words are not so precisely defined. There is wiggle room. And for those words, the temptation – or opportunity – is to shape the word to fit the circumstances.

It's pure, it's natural, it's clinically proven!

A popular phrase among marketers of haircare, skincare and hygiene products is *scientifically proven* or *clinically proven*. For uncertain consumers, scientific validation is an irresistible product attribute. For example, Unilever's Sure Maximum Protection is 'scientifically proven to help with excessive sweating when you need it most'.[7]

But what does 'scientifically proven' mean? Suppose that, on average, 10 per cent of a population contracts a virus in any one year. You give an experimental drug to 100 people and only nine of them get the virus (rather than the expected ten) – does that *prove* it is effective against the virus? How about if only seven people get the virus? Scientists use statistics to calculate the likelihood of all these outcomes, and from those likelihoods they determine levels of confidence that the drug works given each outcome. If seven people in a hundred contract the virus, they may have moderate confidence the drug has some effect; if only four people contract the virus, confidence levels will be greater. But scientists will be reluctant to talk about *proof*.

Determining the presence or absence of a virus may be straightforward with the right diagnostic test. Objectively measuring whether skin is smoother or breath fresher is much harder. Proving that a particular chemical formulation leaves hair significantly silkier – whatever that means – is not a job many reputable scientists would want. Yet statistical nuances and the complexities of measuring desirable hygiene and beauty outcomes are generally lost on marketers and consumers alike. Parse the line 'scientifically proven to help with excessive sweating when you need it most' and you may wonder what exactly is being promised. Will this deodorant *not* be effective except in extreme circumstances? What does 'help with' mean exactly, anyway?

Scientifically proven sounds weighty, clear, indisputable. Unfortunately for marketers who use the phrase, it has nevertheless been strongly disputed in a number of cases. Dannon (a subsidiary of French food company Danone) settled a multi-million-dollar US class-action lawsuit over its claims that Activia yogurt was scientifically proven to regulate the digestive system.[8] Under the terms of the settlement, Dannon had to remove the words 'clinically proven' and 'scientifically proven' from its products and advertising, and replace them with phrases such as 'clinical studies show'. Even that is a dubious claim, as the phrase 'regulate the digestive system' has no real medical or scientific meaning. Nevertheless, the company maintained it was telling the truth: 'Dannon stands by its advertising and denies it did anything wrong,' according to its statement.

Bottled water manufacturers frequently stretch definitions to breaking point. What does *pure* mean, for example? Mineral water is not pure water by definition, as it contains minerals. Mineral water could be more accurately described as contaminated H_2O. But somehow we accept that 'pure' in this context means something else: 'from an unpolluted natural source' perhaps. The trouble is that such a working definition grants a lot of freedom to unscrupulous marketers. An unpolluted natural source might be the groundwater under your city.

Nestlé faced a class-action lawsuit in 2003 over Poland Spring Water, marketed as natural spring water found 'deep in the woods of Maine'. Nestlé does not actually draw its water from the original Poland Spring, but from a variety of wells in the vicinity. The company's definitional response: 'Poland Spring is exactly what we say it is – natural spring water – and there are many criteria for that.'[9] Nestlé settled the suit without admitting to false advertising.

In 2004, Coca-Cola launched Dasani water in the UK. Already successfully established in America, the brand was marketed as 'one of the purest waters around'. It was quickly revealed, however, that the UK product was nothing more than treated tap water from Sidcup, a London suburb. The launch failed, in part because the British public did not accept Coca-Cola's truth that a 'highly sophisticated purification process' that removed 'bacteria, viruses, salts, minerals, sugars, proteins and toxin particles' made London tap water 'pure'.[10]

Contains essential minerals is another misleading bottled water phrase. It may be true that trace quantities of nutritionally important minerals are present, but the concentrations are far too low to make any contribution to your health. You would have to drink a lake of mineral water to get your daily dose of minerals. Premium sea salt, too, frequently boasts of its essential minerals. It is certainly true that those appealing flakes contain a great deal of one essential mineral – sodium chloride – but other minerals are rarely present in nutritionally significant quantities.

But then sea salt is *natural*, isn't it? This is a very odd idea. Sodium chloride is sodium chloride, regardless of whether it has been sourced by evaporating seawater, mining rock or combining sodium and chlorine in the lab. There is no material difference. So what do marketers mean by *natural*? It has no legal or scientific meaning. Marketers want us to assume 'natural' products come directly from Nature, implying they are uncontaminated and free from industrial manipulation, and that they are just like the kind of thing our savannah-dwelling ancestors would have consumed. None of this is likely to be true.

In 2010, PepsiCo rebranded its lemon-lime soft drink Sierra Mist as 'Sierra Mist Natural', on the grounds that they had replaced the corn syrup in it with regular sugar (corn is, of course, just as 'natural' as sugar cane). If even a canned soda can be marketed as 'natural', then the accepted definition of the word must be truly vague. Three years later, PepsiCo dropped the 'natural' label 'due to the lack of detailed regulatory guidance on the use of the term'.[11]

You know your marketers have lost touch with reality when they need 'detailed regulatory guidance' on how to use a word like *natural*.

> **Definitions tactic #2**
> *Warping a definition to fit circumstances*

'Words of this kind,' wrote George Orwell of *democracy, socialism* and *freedom*, 'are often used in a consciously dishonest way. That is, the person who uses them has his own private definition, but allows his hearer to think he means something quite different.'[12] Today, we might add to his list *artisan, gourmet, premium, iconic, next generation, finest, sustainable, curated, state of the art, value, designer, sophisticated, bespoke, authentic* and many more once-innocent words. Orwell was concerned with politics and tyranny, but the practice he observed of conscious dishonesty with definitions has bloomed beyond all imagination in the marketing profession.

Think of the children

It's not only businesses that push the boundaries. In 2013, Shelter, a major UK housing charity, issued a press release with this emotive headline: '80,000 children facing homelessness this Christmas'.[13]

How would you interpret that? When we talk of 'homeless people', we generally think of men and women living and sleeping rough on the streets. Our minds conjure up cardboard boxes, sleeping bags in doorways, shopping trolleys laden with dismal possessions, unkempt beards and begging bowls. Type the term into Google Images and that's exactly what you'll see in all the pictures.

The thought of thousands of British children sleeping rough in winter was appalling. Unsurprisingly, Shelter's headline got widespread coverage. Less well publicized was its definition of *homelessness* below the headline: Shelter did not mean rough-sleeping at all. It was referring to the children of families without their own home and therefore dependent on temporary accommodation arranged by their local government authority. Many of these families were lodged in bed & breakfast accommodation, paid for by the local council. Although some such accommodation is pretty squalid, almost no family with children would be denied a roof over their heads in the UK at any time of the year, let alone in winter. A B&B may not be the ideal place for a child to spend Christmas, but this reality is a long way from the freezing park bench readers might have imagined from Shelter's headline.

Was the campaign wording justified? Many of those who read the headline and reached into their pockets to help the 'homeless children' might not have suspected they were already in accommodation. Yet a B&B is not a home and therefore, technically, those kids were 'homeless'. Shelter was being truthful in its assertion, even if some may have misunderstood its headline.

To be fair to Shelter, its website made clear that the charity was concerned primarily with people who lack their own private housing:

Homeless families are all around you. But you won't see them, because they're hidden – sometimes sleeping in different places from one night to the next. And although they have a roof over their heads, it's not a place to call home. Nowhere to eat dinner, or do homework. Sharing a bathroom with countless others. Worst of all, no door to lock at the end of the day.

You should be considered homeless if you have no home in the UK or anywhere else in the world available for you to occupy. You don't have to be sleeping on the streets to be considered homeless.[14]

Shelter was essentially trying to re-establish the literal meaning of *home-less* – lacking a 'place where one lives permanently' – over the more popular definition we see manifested by Google Images.

'I did not have sexual relations with that woman'

When President Bill Clinton was accused of having sex with a White House intern, he concluded a televised speech on education with these words:

> I want to say one thing to the American people. I want you to listen to me. I'm going to say this again. I did not have sexual relations with that woman, Miss Lewinsky.

Clinton had previously denied having sexual relations with Monica Lewinsky during a deposition for a civil case brought by Paula Jones, a former employee. Yet it soon emerged that Clinton had enjoyed a number of 'sexual encounters' with Lewinsky, most notably oral sex and some fun with a cigar. The president of the United States of America appeared to have lied under oath in court. Perjury would be grounds for impeachment, so the charge could not be more serious.

But had he lied?

Clinton is a lawyer and understands the importance of definitions, so it's no surprise he appears twice in this chapter. At the Jones deposition, his legal team had successfully argued to have the court's definition of *sex* narrowed to:

> Contact with the genitalia, anus, groin, breast, inner thigh, or buttocks of any person with an intent to arouse or gratify the sexual desire of any person.

As the *mouth* was not listed among all those body parts, Clinton later argued before a grand jury that fellatio performed on him by 'any person' (Lewinsky) did not count as him having sex under this definition. 'If the deponent is the person who has oral sex performed on him, then the contact is with – not with anything on that list, but with the lips of another person,' he testified. Bizarrely, this would mean that Lewinsky was having sex while he was not. His argument depended on the interpretation of 'any person' as meaning 'any *other* person', thus excluding himself. Whether this was a reasonable interpretation has since been hotly debated. It would imply, for example, that the court's definition of sex did not cover rape unless the rapist intended to arouse his victim.

Part of the definition of sex that the Clinton team had removed was this: 'Contact between the genitals or anus of the person and any part of another person's body' – which would have covered oral sex performed on Clinton. The fact that Clinton wanted this line removed suggests he was already planning how to shape reality by tweaking his definitions.

Not content with scrambling the meaning of *sex*, Clinton even took apart the meaning of the word *is*. He was asked before the grand jury to defend his earlier assertion, with regard to Monica Lewinsky, that 'There's nothing going on between us.' His response was pure definitional gold:

It depends on what the meaning of the word 'is' is. If the – if he – if 'is' means is and never has been, that is not – that is one thing. If it means there is none, that was a completely true statement . . . Now, if someone had asked me on that day, are you having any kind of sexual relations with Ms. Lewinsky, that is, asked me a question in the present tense, I would have said no. And it would have been completely true.[15]

Although Clinton was impeached by the House of Representatives, he was acquitted by the Senate. A majority of senators voted that he was not guilty of perjury. They accepted his convoluted truth, and he got to keep his job.

Define this

Definitions are not set in stone. They evolve with time, adding to the complexity of the world we are trying to describe and navigate. Take the subject of this book. I've coined the term 'competing truths' to define my subject, but when the book comes to be categorized for the retailers and search engines, keywords such as *spin* and *propaganda* will inevitably be used. Both are pejorative, suggesting half-lies or outright dishonesty. It was not always so.

The word *propaganda* comes from the Office for the Propagation of the Faith (*Congregatio de propaganda fide*), set up by Pope Gregory XV in 1622 to oversee missionary work and combat the spread of Protestantism. Propaganda, for centuries, implied nothing more insidious than broadcasting the truth, at least as the Church saw it. Its Catholic origins put the word in bad odour in some Protestant countries, but it was only with the work of Joseph Goebbels, minister of propaganda in Nazi Germany, that propaganda became a noxious concept. The first definition in my dictionary reads, 'information, especially of a biased or misleading nature, used to promote a political cause or point of view'. No one today would want the job of minister of propaganda.

More recently, 'spin doctors' have become important players in the political teams of our elected leaders. 'Spinning the truth' used to mean putting things in a good light and perhaps leaving out a few inconvenient facts – the same thing people do with their Facebook and LinkedIn profiles. My dictionary defines *spin* as, 'the presentation of information in a particular way, especially a favourable one'. Put like that, spin is how most of us communicate much of the time.

While no spin doctor ever claimed their output was the whole truth, they saw their selective truth-telling as the sensible, tactical and morally neutral way to achieve their masters' goals. 'I was obviously quite proud to be a spin doctor,' recalls Lance Price, who before working for Tony Blair had been a respected BBC political correspondent.[16] Price was very clear about the difference between spin and mendacity: 'Lies aren't spin, they are just lies.' If that was the common view now, I would have used the word *spin* a lot more in this book. But thanks in part to the work of Price and his boss, Alastair Campbell, in Blair's Downing Street operation, *spin* too is now a dirty word.

The popular definitions of *propaganda* and *spin* have shifted from positive or neutral ideas towards something much more nefarious. And so, in order to shape your perception of this book, I'm not using either word much. This book is about truth-telling.

This book is about *selective* truth-telling.

'I'm not a feminist, but I believe in equality . . .'

While definitions may evolve naturally, we can also usefully nudge some of them in a constructive direction. One word that needs a little help, in a world where gender equality is still a distant dream, is *feminism*.

A 2005 poll by CBS News found that only 24 per cent of US women surveyed considered themselves to be feminists;[17] 17 per cent considered the term an insult (against only 12 per cent who considered it a compliment). When Susan Sarandon, star of female empowerment movie *Thelma and Louise*, was asked in 2013, 'Would you call yourself a feminist?' she replied, 'I think of myself as a humanist because I think it's less alienating to people who think of feminism as being a load of strident bitches.'[18] Over 45,000 people have liked the 'Women Against Feminism' Facebook page, which describes itself thus: 'Women's voices against modern feminism and its toxic culture. We're judging feminism by its actions, not by dictionary definitions.'[19] One of the most powerful women in Silicon Valley, Yahoo CEO Marissa Mayer, declared, 'I don't think that I would consider myself a feminist . . . I don't, I think, have, sort of, the militant drive and the sort of, the chip on the shoulder that sometimes comes with that.'[20]

So the word *feminism* has an image problem. Yet that same CBS News poll found that when given a definition of a feminist as 'someone who believes in social, political, and economic equality of the sexes', the proportion of women who considered themselves a feminist rose from 24 per cent to 65 per cent. Provided with the same definition, 58 per cent of men considered themselves a feminist, up from 14 per cent without the definition. However little respect 'Women Against Feminism' may have for dictionary definitions, the poll numbers show that definitions do matter.

We can shift the definition of words through association with specific actions, and perhaps that is what 'Women Against Feminism' is on about: if you witness multiple women identifying as feminists and then spitting hatred against men, you might well conclude that the de facto definition of feminism veers to the toxic. A much more positive definition emerged in 2014, when leading British politicians – female and male – posed in T-shirts produced by the Fawcett Society that bore the message 'This is what a feminist looks like'. The leader of the Labour Party and the deputy prime minister – both men – were photographed for *ELLE*'s Feminism Issue wearing the shirts. Prime minister David Cameron declined *ELLE*'s invitation to don the tee, although he did say, 'If that means equal rights for women, then yes. If that is what you mean by feminist, then yes, I am a feminist.'[21]

It was surely something of a triumph for the movement to have a male prime minister of the United Kingdom declare himself a feminist. Not even Margaret Thatcher did that; indeed, she is reported to have said, 'The feminists hate me, don't they? And I don't blame them. For I hate feminism. It is poison.'[22] How could two Conservative Party leaders hold such different points of view? The answer lies in Cameron's words: *If that means . . .*

It all comes down to how you define the word.

> **Definitions tactic #3**
> *Modifying definitions to transform a debate*

Just as we try to establish a more positive definition of *feminism*, so our very understanding of what it means to be a woman – or a man for that matter – is coming into question. The underlying genetics haven't changed, but our understanding of the limitations of gender has. Gender fluidity used to be the exception – David Bowie, Joan of Arc, Grace Jones – but is increasingly a mainstream choice. Some assert a non-binary gender identity. In 2016, Jamie Shupe became the first person in the United States to be legally recognized as non-binary, raising the prospect of third-gender options on passports, driving licences and job applications. India, Germany, Pakistan and Australia have already introduced third-gender options.

People who identify as non-binary often prefer the pronoun *they* over *he* or *she*. 'Singular *they*' was the American Dialect

Society's word of the year in 2015. Some reject 'labels' or adopt such bespoke identifications that categorization becomes near impossible. This trend suggests the definitions traditionally used around gender and sexuality are frequently seen as unhelpful or even oppressive.

The power of definitions to shape reality is nowhere more clearly asserted than in a refusal to accept those very definitions. But then the denial of definitions is in itself a form of competing truth that shapes the reality of those who prefer to go through life uncategorized. In the #insta words of singer Miley Cyrus, 'NOTHING can/will define me! Free to be EVERYTHING!!!'[23]

\<redefine.everything\>

If gender and sexuality are increasingly fluid, the definition of sex itself may soon be stretched far beyond even Bill Clinton's tortured formulations. The development of remotely controlled sex toys, depressingly known as teledildonics, means that partners with Bluetooth and a good Internet connection can offer each other tactile stimulation while on different continents. Virtual reality may soon take us even further. Remote sex is now a thing (to use the recently evolved definition of *thing*). But is it really sex? That's something we'll need to work out. Can you, by definition, have sex with someone who's not in the same room as you? If that's not sex, then is it cheating to use these devices remotely with someone other than your partner (or with an operating system)? If it *is* sex, what happens when a third party hacks your connection without you knowing? How should we define *that*?

Technology is challenging definitions in a lot of fields. The meanings of work, money, friendship, education, war and language are all shifting just as vertiginously as sex. Is a cyberattack by one nation on the infrastructure of another a hostile act that justifies a 'kinetic' (lethal military) response? If state-sponsored hackers drain the accounts in a foreign bank of systemic importance, is that robbery or war? Are Facebook 'friends' really *friends*? What does *like* mean these days, given its proliferation as a social media nod and a linguistic filler? As Massive Open Online Courses (MOOCs) and online information resources proliferate, should we redefine *learn* and *educate*? Does a *job* or *career* still mean what we think it means? Will *death* always be so final and irreversible?

This tech-driven definitional flux is a golden opportunity for marketers, social innovators and tech visionaries to shape reality. But it is also, for many others, an unnerving time to be alive. Navigating a world of changeable definitions may soon become an essential skill for humans everywhere.

In practice

• Be upfront about your definitions but don't hesitate to modify them if it helps clarify or advance a debate.

• Move with the times, accepting that definitions will change along with everything else.

But watch out for . . .

• Misleaders interpreting circumstances differently so as to fit a vital definition.

• Misleaders using their own questionable definitions for words in common use.

10

Social Constructs

The imaginary is what tends to become real.
And␣é Breton

Human creations

Strange things are happening on the northwestern tip of Africa.

Some years ago, a five-mile fence was built across a peninsula, cordoning off the historic port of Ceuta. A short while later, another fence was built alongside the first. The fences are equipped with movement sensors, lined with anti-climbing mesh and topped with razor wire. Every day, a select group of people are allowed to pass through gates in the fences, carrying extremely bulky packages. Occasionally, a different group of people will attempt to climb over the fences, while a third group try to repel them. The climbers persist in their attempts despite incurring lacerations from the razor wire and risking fractures and concussions if they fall. Several have died in the process. Others have drowned while trying to swim around the fences.

Why are these things happening?

To understand the strange and dangerous behaviours exhibited around Ceuta, we first need to know that this African city is technically part of Spain. Which makes it part of the European Union. Which means that anyone in the city can travel without hindrance to almost anywhere in Europe. It also means that any EU good can be bought tariff-free in the city and carried into neighbouring Morocco. The same applies to another Spanish-African port, Melilla.

Spain began building the fences around its North African enclaves in 1998. The EU has contributed millions of euros to the project. Since then, African migrants have repeatedly tested the EU's southern defences. In 2016, around a thousand migrants are thought to have made it past the fences. Not all were so lucky. In 2014, 15 people died while trying to swim round Ceuta's fence. Spanish border guards fired rubber bullets at the swimmers; they later claimed they could not go to their rescue because they could not cross into Moroccan waters. Migrants caught by the Guardia Civil are returned to Morocco immediately, without being given the chance to claim asylum – a violation of international law, according to the UN.

Meanwhile, 'porteadores' – Moroccan men and women authorized to cross the Ceuta and Melilla borders – are paid $5 a time to carry great packages weighing as much as 80kg into Morocco. Their employers are taking advantage of a legal quirk that sees anything carried by an individual across the border as 'personal luggage', not subject to import tariffs. So European-made clothes, tyres, electronics, fridges and tools that would otherwise be transported by ship or truck are borne into Morocco on the backs of the poor.

The strange behaviours observed around Ceuta and Melilla are not the result of any physical phenomena. True, there are two cities, some fences, some sea and some men with guns. But the back-breaking portering and the perilous fence-climbing are driven by other factors: national borders, the EU, international agreements, immigration laws, policing protocols, euro investments and trade tariffs. And these factors all have one thing in common: they only exist because we have collectively agreed they exist. They are not 'real', like goldfish or oxygen. They are all products of human imagination.

We call such imaginary yet true things *social constructs*. They may have physical manifestations – fences, documentation, buildings or symbolic representations – but they can exist perfectly well in our minds without them. The social construct we refer to as Spain will endure long after the fences around Ceuta and Melilla are taken down. The European Union could survive even if all its buildings in Brussels and Strasbourg were demolished. The porteadores could still be paid in euros or dirhams, even if the European Central Bank and the Bank Al-Maghrib withdrew all notes and coins from circulation and gave everyone a digital account. The Michelin tyres they carry over the border might disintegrate, but the brand and company will be around for years to come. Spain, the EU, euros, dirhams and Michelin are truths not because of any physical entity; they are truths because we collectively agree they are. And they only have meaning and power because we collectively agree they do.

The writer Yuval Noah Harari has described social constructs as 'figments of our collective imagination'.[1] They become true only when enough of us believe in them. This is not to downplay their importance or impact. Social constructs like the US dollar, India and Facebook shape countless lives. It would be foolish to say the dollar is 'not true', or to suppose that any one person could wish away Facebook by no longer believing in it.

But because social constructs are the product of our collective imagination, with countless people contributing slightly or substantially different ideas and aspirations to their formation, they often end up as much more flexible truths than real-world entities like goldfish and oxygen. They can be described in an even greater variety of truthful ways than that egg on the table or the view from your window. Such flexibility is a gift to communicators who want to argue for or against a social construct.

We're leaving the EU . . . whatever that is

In the hours following the historic UK referendum vote to leave the European Union, it was said that one of the top British searches on Google was 'What is the EU?'[2] Much mockery and scorn ensued, but in fact the question is not a stupid one. As a vast and highly complex social construct, the EU can truthfully be described in a multitude of ways. This is one of the reasons why the Brexit debate was so acrimonious: both sides described the EU in terms that favoured their side of the argument, so that at times Remainers and Brexiteers seemed to be speaking different languages.

The precursor to the EU was the European Economic Community (EEC), a common market and customs union that facilitated free trade and economic integration for its member countries. Many Remainers looked back to this history and saw the EU largely in trade terms. They noted that Britain had enjoyed a long period of economic recovery and growth in the decades after it joined the EEC. They saw a direct connection between British economic prosperity and membership of the largest single market in the world. For this group, the most important truths about the EU were all about trade: leaving the single market would hurt us financially.

Brexiteers, one might say, had a more up-to-date conception of the rapidly evolving social construct headquartered in Brussels. They understood that the EU's interests and activities had progressed far beyond trade. By 2016, the EU had introduced laws and regulations on a plethora of issues from pollution limits to workplace safety and electrical appliance specifications. EU rules dictated who could fish in UK waters, how powerful UK vacuum cleaners could be and how UK goods should be packaged. British citizens and companies felt themselves bound by rules made by people they hadn't voted for, most of whom came from other countries. And when disputes arose, they were arbitrated by foreign judges in the European Court of Justice. The EU they saw when they gazed across the Channel was well on the way to becoming a super-state in which the democratic voice of one nation's citizenry would count for little. Their resistance to this conception of the social construct was expressed in their favourite campaign slogan: 'Take back control'.

Plenty of Remainers also understood that the social construct had moved on since the days of the Common Market, and they liked its direction of travel. For them, the EU was an important political and economic counterbalance to the world's two superpowers, China and the United States. It was a champion of precious European values such as freedom of expression, democracy, scientific progress and the rule of law. It was the perfect forum for cooperation on transnational issues such as terrorism, climate change, migration and corporate taxation. And it could play a vital role in maintaining peace in the face of a resurgent Russian threat and destabilizing forces all around the continent's southern perimeter.

Social Constructs tactic #1
Selective description of social constructs

As an evolving social construct, the EU offered Remainers and Brexiteers the opportunity to describe it in widely contrasting ways. Free-trade area, unelected rule-maker, political superpower, moral champion or defensive bulwark: the EU could be any or all of these things. Ultimately, the truth of the EU will depend on what its members want it to be. The UK, however, will have no further say in the matter.

The business of make-believe

Perceptions of social constructs like the EU can be easily influenced by competing truths. But because they are imaginary entities, the *reality* of social constructs can also be changed, sometimes with just a few words. Indeed, the truth about some social constructs can be modified simply by certain people saying so.

From time to time, I help business leaders redefine the companies they run by choosing different words to describe what they do, which customers they serve, what they value, what makes them special and where they are going. The new words are no less true than previous formulations – usually they emphasize a different aspect of the business and downplay activities that had previously been central. The company's offices, factories and warehouses haven't changed (although they might as a result of the re-definition), yet the ideas employees, customers and regulators hold about the company are transformed. The corporation, an endlessly flexible social construct, has been reshaped by a competing truth.

> **Social Constructs tactic #2**
> *Redefining social constructs*

Listed among the critical assets of many companies are their brands. These imaginary truths are everywhere: brands for products; brands for charities; brands for government initiatives; even brands for branches of the military. None of them really exist, however solid the products, services and people they represent may be. They are conceptual creations, conjured up by a combination of imagery, words, music, experience, association and belief.

Like any social construct, they can evolve naturally or they can be deliberately modified.

The Nokia brand has been on a remarkable journey. To early Finnish consumers, the brand first meant wood pulp for paper, then rubber boots. To my generation, it meant sleek little mobile phones. Following Microsoft's acquisition and demolition of its devices business, the company has had to adapt the Nokia brand again. The name has no underlying meaning – Nokia is a town in Finland – so perhaps it is innately flexible. But what about the Microsoft brand? *Soft*ware for *Micro*computers? Until the Nokia acquisition, Microsoft had remained reasonably true to its software roots, building on its two great monopolies of Windows and Office, although it had made exploratory forays into the hardware field with the Xbox and the Surface tablet. Now, the old brand identity has gone out of the window; Microsoft is presenting itself as an integrated hardware/software brand to rival Apple.

Apple has been on its own brand-stretching adventure, from desktop computers via music retail to smartphones, mapping, TV, publishing and much else besides. The brand was once all about computing; now the Svengalis in Cupertino have modified it to represent an abstract combination of design, quality, usability and individuality, which, one suspects, could be comfortably extended to solar panels, space travel or kitchenware.

This is all fairly remarkable when we consider what a brand is meant to be. Every expert will offer a different definition, but a core feature of the brand is a *promise to the customer*. We buy XYZ brand rather than a cheaper rival because we trust the promise implicit in its name, logo, colour scheme or mascot that the XYZ product or service will benefit us in a particular (often unexpressed, even inexpressible) way. And for that promise to be credible, to hold its value over repeated transactions, it has to be – at least to some extent – true.

So what is the truth of a brand that can change as much as

Nokia, Microsoft or Apple? Can a brand bear competing truths? Can it mean different things to different people, in different places, at different times, and still maintain its integrity? This is a subject of great debate among branding gurus, and for every successful brand transformation story like Virgin or Samsung there is a cautionary tale about *the brand that stretched too far* (Zippo perfume or Colgate food, anyone?). Consumer brands that represent luxury in one geographical market yet target the value consumer in another come unstuck as globalization and the Internet reveal all. Banking brands that mean financial prudence and safety to one consumer segment are playing with fire if they promise high-risk super-profits to another.

Nevertheless, the general trend has been away from the disciplined consistency that marked early brand management and towards fluidity across all the many media and social media platforms now available to marketers. And where brand identity used to be closely tied to core products and services (BMW meant cars; Gillette meant razors), now brand-shapers concern themselves more with core principles, values or emotions. These are intended to be fundamental, almost primeval in their longevity and deep meaning. But of course they also have the benefit of being endlessly flexible in terms of the products and services that can be tacked on to them. If you can mould your brand to represent 'Environmental responsibility, Playfulness and Family unity', you are far less restricted in your future business activities than if it spells out 'Safe air travel'. Such flexibility is helpful in a world where companies everywhere are radically rethinking the business they are in.

But this can be problematic. If a brand no longer promises anything directly related to the product or service you are actually buying, does it still convey a truth of any practical consequence? What truth about our clothing are we supposed to derive from the fact that it bears the Marlboro or Harley-Davidson brand? What about Sainsbury's and Tesco supermarket logos on our mortgages and current accounts?

Ultimately, brands have to offer some truth more than 'We're a successful company you've heard of so you can trust our product to work'. They have to confer an extra layer of value on products and services, be it technical mastery, environmental responsibility, glamour or meaning. And they have to do this in a business environment where rapid, radical innovation is increasingly the norm. Multiple truths are therefore inevitable, and some of these truths will seem contradictory, even when they are well supported by one or other facet of the evolving business offering. Where competing brand truths arise, it is essential to have a good story – consistently expressed by all members of the organization – to explain how they all fit together.

An imaginary shield against oppression

Just as social constructs can be changed, so they can also be created or eliminated. Like magical incantations, the right words can bring a social construct into existence. What was not true becomes true.

> **Social Constructs tactic #3**
> *Creating or eliminating social constructs*

One of our most important invented truths is the notion of human rights. If you believe human rights are somehow inherent to humanity, consider our history. People were starved, enslaved and slaughtered in vast numbers across all inhabited continents without much thought for their rights. It is a challenge to see rights that were not known of or discussed throughout most of the historical record as natural or intrinsic.

There is even something contradictory about human rights:

individual freedom lies at the heart of human rights, yet most human rights constrain someone's freedom, even if only the freedom to hurt others. Renowned philosopher Jeremy Bentham mocked the concept of natural rights – precursor to human rights – as 'nonsense upon stilts'.

Yet through words alone, some exceptional communicators were able to bring human rights into legal force across the world.

The campaign to assert the natural, universal and inalienable character of rights like life and liberty originated with Enlightenment philosophers such as John Locke, Immanuel Kant, Thomas Paine and Jean-Jacques Rousseau. The Virginia Declaration of Rights (1776) states that 'All men are by nature equally free and independent, and have certain inherent rights.' Drafted by George Mason, this document inspired Thomas Jefferson's more famous claim in the US Declaration of Independence, 'That all men are created equal, that they are endowed by their Creator with certain unalienable Rights, that among these are Life, Liberty and the pursuit of Happiness.' The French Revolution followed just a few years later, built on the Declaration of the Rights of Man and of the Citizen (1789): 'These rights are Liberty, Property, Safety and Resistance to Oppression.'

But it was not until after the Second World War that human rights took on the worldwide significance they hold today. Horrified by the atrocities of the Holocaust, political leaders from around the world came together under the auspices of a newly created social construct, the United Nations, to proclaim the Universal Declaration of Human Rights (1948). For the first time ever, a comprehensive set of fundamental human rights were named, and the world collectively agreed to protect them. In the words of the preamble, 'Recognition of the inherent dignity and of the equal and inalienable rights of all members of the human family is the foundation of freedom, justice and peace in the world.'

The 30 articles of the declaration cover uncontroversial

expectations like life, liberty, equal treatment before the law, and freedom from slavery and torture. They also include less obvious ideas, such as the right to a nationality, the right to protection of material interests for writers, the right to leisure, and the right to enjoy the arts. It would be hard to argue that such apparently arbitrary claims might be encoded in our DNA or bestowed on us all by God. Laudable as they are, surely we must agree that at least some of these so-called rights are the product of human thinking and experiences rather than anything more intrinsic to our species. Social constructs, in other words. In 2016, the UN even passed a resolution stating that 'measures to intentionally prevent or disrupt access to or dissemination of information online' was a violation of human rights law.[3] Again, it's hard for anyone over the age of 40 to see Internet access as something essential to the human condition.

But however artificial human rights may be, the idea, so strongly taken up and reinforced by the global community, has done immense good. Human rights have become very real checks on the power of states over the things that matter most to us. The harshest tyrants have been chastened into more moderate behaviour following public documentation of their human rights abuses. Even governments that continue to pursue repressive and cruel policies bend over backwards to give an impression of respect for human rights.

Of course, as social constructs, human rights laws have come in for all kinds of interpretation. The European Court of Human Rights (ECHR) has made itself deeply unpopular in the UK by barring the deportation of some foreign criminals and demanding that prisoners be given the vote. In the opinion of one British tabloid, recent judgements by the ECHR mean the European Convention on Human Rights (1951) 'has become little more than a charter for criminals and a bonanza for Left-wing lawyers'.[4] All laws are social constructs that can evolve through precedent and interpretation; international human rights law, being rather more vague, political and utopian than other legislative codes, is perhaps more vulnerable to applications that were never intended by its drafters.

Nevertheless, the idea of human rights – this wonderful imaginary truth – remains the best defence many people have against the brutal treatment suffered by our ancestors. It is a fiction to treasure.

Spinning gold

Few social constructs have contributed as much to human progress as money. The many stores of value that we have collectively agreed on, from cowry shells and gold to euros and bitcoins, have enabled us to trade, to plan economic activity and to invest in others' enterprises. Without agreed stores of value, we would still be living a precarious Stone Age existence. Yet all such stores of value are imaginary. Most of the money we use is called 'fiat money', meaning it has been established by government decree rather than representing any asset of fundamental value; *fiat* is a Latin word meaning 'let it become', the kind of something-out-of-nothing command we would normally expect from an all-powerful deity or a lunatic. To value such currencies, we must believe and trust in the governments and central banks – themselves social constructs – that created them.

It is only through our collective imagination and the mass suspension of disbelief that money works at all.

We see this painfully clearly when people lose faith in a particular store of value. The meaning of the Argentinean peso, the Zimbabwean dollar and the Weimar mark all changed radically as people lost confidence in both the issuing governments and the currencies. The truth of each currency was transformed over a matter of weeks.

Nevertheless, stores of value work extremely well most of the time. They are worth making up. The euro, created out of thin air in the 1990s through sheer political will, is now one of the strongest and most widely accepted currencies in the world. Its formation perfectly illustrates the imaginary nature of social constructs: the euro came into being on 1 January 1999, but no notes or coins were made available until the end of 2001. You could take out loans and buy all kinds of things in euros long before you had anything physical to put in your wallet.

Inhabitants of Eurozone countries currently have little choice but to receive their salaries and make their purchases in euros. But various forward-looking technologists are seeking to change that. Cryptocurrencies such as Bitcoin are just the latest innovation in the long history of stores of value. They are as imaginary as any other currency, and no less 'real'. The main difference between a fiat currency and a cryptocurrency is that the former is backed by a national government. But as we've seen from the cases of Brazil, Argentina, Zimbabwe and Weimar Germany, that backing may not be worth very much. Indeed, national governments have been known to deliberately devalue their own currencies – and so diminish the wealth of anyone who holds them – in order to reduce the burden of national debt denominated in those currencies.

Thus proponents of cryptocurrencies see their independence from nation states as a good thing. Bitcoin and its rivals are entirely dependent on our collective faith for their value; no government or central bank will underwrite them, but then none can unilaterally decide to devalue them. The blockchain technology on which cryptocurrencies like Bitcoin are built brings other benefits: it's effectively impossible to forge bitcoins and they cannot be seized by a third party; transactions cannot be traced or intercepted, and there are negligible transaction costs. But the main advantage, in the eyes of many, is their independence from those other social constructs we call nation states. Only the users of bitcoins can decide what a bitcoin is worth. It is a highly democratic store of value. Whether or not it endures as a figment of enough people's collective imagination remains to be seen.

Into the artificial future

Where will social constructs take us next? What new truth will we dream up to empower or ensnare ourselves? One likely candidate is the personal rating, as popularized by tech platforms such as Uber and Airbnb. This entirely imaginary concept is already having a significant impact on the incomes of taxi drivers, nannies, builders and other freelance workers. What if the concept was extended to other areas of our lives? What if we rated our friends and lovers in the same way?

The ingenious dystopian TV series *Black Mirror* took on the idea in one episode: everyone was assigned a public rating that could be nudged up or down by anyone they encountered. High ratings brought sought-after invitations, employment opportunities and better housing; low ratings brought embarrassed looks and distrust. The show rendered a world in which people went out of their way to be nice even to strangers, but where a string of bad luck could leave you ostracized and excluded.

One country that may be heading this way is China. Its government is currently developing a system that will combine financial credit scores with assessments of legal, social and political standing to generate a single trustworthiness rating for every citizen. This 'social credit' score will be used to determine the citizen's access to services and state resources. Just as a history of not paying bills makes it hard for Westerners to get a mortgage or buy a fridge on credit, so Chinese people could soon find that a few poor moral choices or parking tickets lead to exclusion from more comfortable train carriages, popular housing projects or high-performing schools. Fail to visit your elderly parents and you could be barred from travelling abroad. 'If trust is broken in one place, restrictions are imposed everywhere,' say the architects of the scheme. With disturbing echoes of Orwell's *Nineteen Eighty-Four*, this instrument of social control 'will reward those who report acts of breach of trust,' according to a state planning document.

The government's scheme is likely to be modelled on the social credit systems already used by various Chinese companies, including e-commerce group Alibaba, to rate the trustworthiness of their customers. These scores are made available to partner companies, such as matchmaking services that pair individuals of good standing (in the company's eyes). Customers with high scores proudly post them on social media and in dating profiles, reinforcing the truth of the social construct.

Exactly how these scores are calculated is not disclosed, and the national scheme is likely to be similarly opaque. But one Alibaba executive revealed the kinds of variables that count: 'Someone who plays video games for ten hours a day, for example, would be considered an idle person, and someone who frequently buys diapers would be considered as probably a parent, who on balance is more likely to have a sense of responsibility.'[5] So we know that such scores are influenced by what consumers buy and do online. Will they also be affected by comments posted or pages 'liked'? Will every digital trace an individual leaves potentially count against them? Will scores be vulnerable to bureaucratic error or malicious hacking?

China's social credit system could substantially alter life experiences for millions of people. It has been made possible by the increasing digitization and storage of every trivial piece of information about people, combined with new big-data analysis techniques. With so much information now being collected, we should not be surprised if states and other powerful organizations use it to create further social constructs that impact our lives in ways we may not welcome.

If this happens, we need to remember that social constructs, being artificial truths, are changeable: if we don't like them, we can always band together to alter or eliminate them. We can't change the boiling point of water, but we can change 'the EU', 'Bitcoin' or 'social rating systems' if we want to. Such truths only have meaning and power if we collectively agree they do.

In practice

• Recognize that social constructs are products of our imagination and we can change them if necessary.

• Define social constructs in whatever helpful way their flexibility allows.

• Modify social constructs, if you have the requisite influence, by describing them differently.

But watch out for . . .

• Misleaders who present highly skewed impressions of important social constructs.

• People, institutions and states that create malign social constructs.

11

Names

I don't believe a rose *would* be as nice if it was called a thistle or a skunk cabbage.

ANNE SHIRLEY in *Anne of Green Gables* by L. M. Montgomery

Man-made Earth

We were born in the Holocene, the geologic epoch that dates from the last ice age, around 11,700 years ago. By the time we die, it is likely that my first sentence will no longer be true. There is a good chance that soon we will be able to say we were born in the Anthropocene.

Ask yourself this: if *Homo sapiens* disappears from Earth, what traces will remain? Most species leave precious little beyond petrified bones. Some preserved footprints perhaps, or a little DNA caught in amber. When we go extinct, by contrast, we will leave behind us ruined cities, highways, field systems, waterways, railways, sunken ships and uncountable pieces of plastic. Geologists have started to ask themselves how much of this man-made stuff will linger in the geologic record. What evidence of our existence could be detected by an alien geologist a million years after we're gone?

Concrete is one of the most likely human signatures to last, although it may not have the form it has now. Geologists of the future may become adept at identifying scatterings of concrete pebbles strewn around the sites of long-lost cities. Some plastics may last indefinitely in the right sedimentary environment. The chemistry of the Earth will be measurably different, reflecting our combustion of fossil fuels and widespread use of artificial fertilizers. Dams, mines and canals may leave lasting scars. Most tellingly, perhaps, the fossil record of other species will have changed drastically: elephants and tigers will have faded from the fossil record, while the chicken will have grown in size and extended its range across most of the current land mass.

Anticipating such human signatures in the future geologic record, atmospheric chemist Paul Crutzen has argued that we have entered a new geologic epoch, the Anthropocene (*anthropos* means *human* in Ancient Greek). His arguments have gained ground, and a group of geologists have proposed the adoption of the Anthropocene as a formal epoch. Various geologic organizations are now debating the issue, and many scientists have already begun using the term informally. A key question is the proposed epoch's start date: some suggest the industrial revolution, some the Neolithic revolution; the working group on the Anthropocene sees a stark chemical signature that could be used to define a precise geologic boundary in the radioactive elements dispersed around the world by the first nuclear weapons tests.

What does it matter if the geologic period in which most of us were born gets renamed? For climate Advocates like Crutzen, the new name is an important symbol of the lasting impact we are having on our planet. For environmental campaigners, it could be the wake-up call that forces us all to change the way we live. 'The Anthropocene tells us that we are playing with fire, a potentially reckless mode of behaviour which we are likely to come to regret,' says climate scientist Chris Rapley.[1]

Of course, what is really changing is our conception of ourselves and our role on Earth. But that conception is vividly encapsulated by the proposed name change. 'It is one of those moments where a scientific realization, like Copernicus grasping that the Earth goes round the sun, could fundamentally change people's view of things far beyond science,' declared *The Economist* in a 2011 edition entitled 'Welcome to the Anthropocene'.[2]

'It's become a political statement. That's what so many people want,' says Stan Finney, the former chair of the International Commission on Stratigraphy, the organization that will ultimately vote on formal recognition of the Anthropocene.[3]

Though most geologists would avoid placing a value judgement on the impact of humanity on Earth, if the new name can encourage us to think more deeply about the lasting consequences of our actions, then that can only be a good thing. 'This name change would stress the enormity of humanity's responsibility as stewards of the Earth,' wrote Paul Crutzen.[4] Imagine what a difference it might make to our mindsets and actions, and the consequences that might have for our planet's future.

Naming and shaming

Naming has at times been considered a magical act, because the name we give a person or a thing shapes the way the world sees them. We would struggle to take seriously a warlord named Cuthbert or a surgeon called Foxy. Consequently, names influence the way we respond to people and things. A research study found that fictitious job applications bearing 'white-sounding' names received 50 per cent more callbacks for interviews in Boston and Chicago than 'African-American-sounding' names.[5] Other studies have found that people with less common first names are less likely to be hired.[6]

Our own names can influence us in bizarre ways. Research by a team of marketing and psychology professors has found that we tend to favour brands or products that have the same initial letter as our name.[7] Individuals asked to rank candy bars according to their 'feelings' about each product ranked brands which had the same first letter as their name higher than average for the group.

But the power of naming to shape reality reaches a higher gear when it comes to the names we give new products, organizations, initiatives, ventures – and even laws.

> **Names tactic #1**
> *Persuading with an evocative name*

In general, we take the view that once a criminal has paid their debt to society they should be given a second chance and treated like anyone else. Not so with sex offenders in the United States. Following the rape and murder of seven-year-old Megan Kanka by a paroled sex offender in 1994, 'Megan's Law' was rapidly enacted in her home state of New Jersey, requiring the presence of high-risk sex offenders in a community to be made public. The federal government passed a 'Megan's Law' two years later, and all US states soon enacted some form of the law. Consequently, US sex offenders live with an unshakeable social stigma that makes it very hard for them to find housing and jobs or develop personal relationships. Some suffer verbal and physical abuse, and some become the victims of vigilantism.

It's a harsh measure against already troubled individuals – some of whom ended up on sex-offender registers while still children themselves – but it could perhaps be justified at the societal level if it was effective in reducing the incidence of sexual offences. Yet there is little evidence that Megan's Law has had the desired impact.

According to the respected children's charity the NSPCC,

'Although the law is popular with parents, there is no evidence that open access to sex offender registers actually enhances child safety. There is no evidence that Megan's Law reduces reoffending.'[8] A study by Rutgers University and the New Jersey Department of Corrections came to the same conclusion.[9] This is not surprising, given that the vast majority of sexual assaults on minors are committed by family members or acquaintances, with strangers responsible for only 7 per cent of US cases.[10] Moreover, there is evidence that some sexual abuse crimes are not being reported 'because of fears related to community notification'.[11] The law may also be driving sex offenders underground, making them more dangerous. Nevertheless, efforts to have Megan's Law modified, or to challenge the strong public support for it, have largely failed.

How much of this is down to the name of the law? It is very hard to hear those words without instantly thinking of that little girl and the fate she suffered. Does that affect our ability to assess the effectiveness and justness of the measure? Might there be a connection between the evocative name of the law and the continuing public support for its more extreme and punitive measures?

'Those who oppose a proposal such as Megan's Law are implicitly portrayed as indifferent to Megan, her family and/or others affected by the crime,' wrote Dr Brian Christopher Jones, a lecturer in Public Law, in his thesis, 'From the Innocuous to the Evocative: How Bill Naming Manipulates and Informs the Policy Process'. (He cites the US PATRIOT Act as another example of a law whose very name made it almost impossible to oppose.) He goes on:

> The measure becomes a remembrance for the person whose name appears in the title, and bears significant legal effects. Therefore an opposition legislator who feels sympathy for the individual but may not agree with the legislation proposed can be put in a very compromising position when they are voting on a public bill proposal.[12]

No wonder, then, that Megan's Law was passed in the US Senate by unanimous consent, after a 418–0 vote in favour by the House of Representatives. Such is the power of a name.

Improvised names can be deployed to denigrate and derail. One of Theresa May's flagship policies during the 2017 UK election was a change to the funding of adult social care. Under the proposed rules, people provided with care in their own homes by the state would have to pay for more of it than previously, if they owned assets – including their house – worth more than £100,000. They would not have to pay until after their deaths, when the cost of their care would be claimed from their estate. The policy was a sensible attempt to address the huge rise in social care costs that the UK is facing as a result of our greater longevity. It was also, in some eyes, an equitable proposal, as it shifted the burden of paying for social care away from young taxpayers struggling to buy their own homes and on to those older people who have benefited from massive appreciation in the value of their houses.

It was killed by a name. The opposition Labour Party dusted down an old but still virulent term, 'dementia tax', to describe the new proposal. According to the Alzheimer's Society, 'People with dementia face the highest costs of care of any group and have to pay the most towards their care. This is why charging for care is described as "The Dementia Tax".'[13]

Never mind that many of the people needing care at home do not have dementia, the name was powerful enough to render the policy toxic. Young voters, whom one might have expected to be glad of a policy that shifted the tax burden away from them, instead saw in Theresa May a monster who wanted to attack their grandparents in their infirmity. The Conservative Party lost a huge poll lead during the course of the election campaign, in large part due to this one policy. Whatever the merits of asking older people with valuable houses to pay for more of their own care, the 'dementia tax' name has ensured that few British politicians will be courageous enough to revive the idea.

> **Names tactic #2**
> *Denigrating with a negative nickname*

Google experienced a similar naming setback when it launched its head-mounted computer display, Google Glass. The display, positioned directly in front of one eye, offered users full Internet access while on the move. Users could look at a map while walking, read emails while doing the laundry, shoot video while clinging to a roller coaster, or receive Facebook notifications while out for a run. Technologists and science-fiction fans had long anticipated a wonder product like this.

But there was an unsavoury side to Google Glass. Users could take pictures simply by winking. People in the vicinity felt their privacy was being invaded by Glass-wearing technophiles winking at them. The Google support page on the Wink feature offered this guidance:

> Etiquette
> Use your best judgement when using Wink. Be careful who you're winking at and be conscious of your surroundings when you do it. You don't want to give the wrong impression. ;-)[14]

More generally, Google urged Glass users not to be 'creepy or rude'[15] and to respect others' privacy. The company's attempts to guide users on Glass etiquette did not placate the many people who objected to being photographed or videoed, often without their knowledge. Others resented Glass users' habit of checking their Twitter or Facebook feeds in the middle of a conversation. With Google Glass, you never knew what the user was actually doing, even when she was right in front of you. A darker fear also preyed on some minds: would Google's image-recognition software give Glass users the ability to identify strangers in the street? What would that mean for treasured urban anonymity?

The backlash came in the form of a name. Users were soon designated 'Glassholes'. It was devastatingly effective. However much you'd like to read your emails while gazing at the sunset, or nurture a cutting-edge tech image as you stride cyborg-like through town, could you honestly bear to be branded with that pithy neologism? After investing an undisclosed – but presumably vast – amount of money in Project Glass, Google withdrew the product in January 2015. Although it was re-released for industrial use in 2017, Google Glass is unlikely to reappear on consumer faces any time soon.

Inventing a name to pillory others doesn't always work. At a New York fundraiser two months before the 2016 US presidential election, Democrat candidate Hillary Clinton declared, 'To just be grossly generalistic, you can put half of Trump supporters into what I call the basket of deplorables. Right? Racist, sexist, homophobic, xenophobic, Islamophobic, you name it.'[16] Indeed, she did name it, or rather *them*. 'Deplorables', a plural noun previously unrecognized by lexicographers, became the progressive's label of choice for any Trump supporters suspected of illiberal attitudes and tendencies. But using the name backfired on Clinton, who was seen as elitist and snobbish, dismissing in one sentence a quarter of the electorate. Meanwhile, Trump fans embraced the vitriolic name, turning out to rallies in T-shirts and hats bearing the proud message 'I'm a Deplorable'. On the eve of Trump's inauguration, his keenest supporters celebrated at the black-tie *DeploraBall*.

Special, beautiful and unique

Among a number of great lines in Chuck Palahniuk's 1996 novel *Fight Club* is this marvellous put-down:

You are not special. You are not a beautiful and unique snowflake.

Two decades later, *snowflake* has emerged as a widespread term of
disdain for a generation of supposedly hypersensitive, entitled and
self-important young people. A snowflake is generally understood
to be a thin-skinned millennial who is self-absorbed and somewhat infantilized, more interested in taking offence than taking
responsibility. Snowflakes are caricatured as under-employed,
selfie-taking princelings who still live with their parents, expect
prizes for effort, and are easily distressed by vigorous debate and
points of view they don't share. The name is always derogatory,
as illustrated by novelist Bret Easton Ellis, who used his podcast
to denounce 'little snowflake justice warriors' as 'snivelling little
weak-ass narcissists'.[17]

Whether or not perceptions of the 'snowflake generation' are accurate or fair, the name has caught on across the political spectrum.
Conservatives of the Breitbart school mock snowflakes upset by
their attitude to immigrants' rights or climate change. Liberals
bemoan snowflakes on university campuses who demand 'safe
spaces' and trigger warnings, or refuse to tolerate visiting speakers expressing views they dislike. Somehow the name just seems
to fit many older people's impression of the youngest adults in our
societies; in 2016, 'snowflake generation' was named one of *Collins
Dictionary*'s ten words of the year, while the *Financial Times* chose
'snowflake' as one of the twelve words that shaped the year.

Why has such a derisive name taken root so quickly? What
makes us so ready to insult an entire generation? Many of the
people mocking snowflakes have colleagues and family members
who fit the profile. What has made us older folk so mean?

If we're honest, it's probably because we feel threatened. Highly
educated commentators of a certain age appear not only baffled by
expressions like 'check your privilege' but unnerved by the spate of

university no-platforming and censorship (although this is hardly new). In his podcast tirade, Ellis betrays his own anxiety: 'The little Nazis policing language have a new rulebook about how men and women should and should not express themselves.' He invokes the First Amendment, which protects freedom of speech, something he clearly believes to be under threat from the snowflakes he derides. 'We have entered into what is really an authoritarian cultural moment,' he claims. 'It's so regressive and so grim and so unreal, like in some dystopian sci-fi movie: there's only one way to express yourself.'

Anxieties about curbs to our freedom of speech are not unreasonable, given much of our history. The right to say and think what we like is precious, and it is vital to democratic society. There are also plenty of people who resent what they see as a youth-dominated media setting norms of acceptable expression on immigration, race, gender and sexuality. 'I'm not allowed to say what I think any more,' is a common complaint wherever progressive views prevail. It is natural to feel unsettled by a younger generation appearing to claim the moral high ground over issues on which we have always taken what we understood to be the mainstream view.

So fear and resentment are most likely behind the viral success of *snowflake*. This is dangerous because it implies the name is being used not as a joke, not as a light-hearted jibe, but as a weapon.

The consequences could be serious. Names have the power to heighten divisions between groups. Older generations run the risk of believing the caricature of the snowflake and applying it to all young people. They might dismiss reports of sexual harassment, as we have seen in Hollywood, the British Parliament and elsewhere, as just another manifestation of snowflake oversensitivity. Meanwhile, embattled millennials, already struggling to find a job, pay off student debt and afford a home, will have still one more grudge to hold against the rest of society. Admirable millennial traits, such as concern for the environment or social inclusion, risk being marginalized or crushed by inter-generational contempt. Unless we want to widen the gulf between the young and the less young, we should try to avoid using this expressive but ultimately destructive name.

Pulling teeth

Names can seem like permanent fixtures: once a name has been chosen, that's it – there is only one truth. But names are not carved in stone outside of the graveyard. The renaming of Jacob by an angel to 'Israel' is an important moment in Genesis. Women often take their husbands' names on marriage, a powerful statement about their changed circumstances and commitment. Loathed first names are discarded in adulthood, surnames are changed for reason of fear or fame. One disgruntled bank customer decided to protest an excessive charge by changing his name by deed poll to 'Yorkshire Bank plc are Fascist Bastards'; the bank had to write him a cheque in that name when they closed his account.

Country names get changed to mark independence or a new ideological leaning. City and street names are changed to celebrate famous people. The Russian city of St Petersburg saw its name changed twice before reverting to the original. Saigon, renamed for the North Vietnamese leader who had inspired its conquest, took on a very different character as Ho Chi Minh City. In 2015, the left-leaning municipal government of Madrid decided to re-name 30 streets and squares previously associated with the former dictator General Franco. Two years earlier, President Robert Mugabe of Zimbabwe declared that Victoria Falls was to be renamed Mosi-oa-Tunya (the smoke that thunders) to rid the land-mark of its colonial heritage. A more gradual evolution took place in Australia, where Ayers Rock was renamed Ayers Rock/Uluru in 1993, and then Uluru/Ayers Rock in 2002, to acknowledge the rights of the indigenous Anangu people.

Companies and other organizations get renamed to clarify or

change their missions, to appeal to new markets or to escape an unfortunate association. Tokyo Tsushin Kogyo would have been a mouthful for foreign shoppers, but Sony sold well. The Spastics Society changed its name to Scope when 'spastic' became a term of abuse. Old-fashioned His Master's Voice was abbreviated to the hip recording label HMV. British Petroleum, which had come into existence as the long-outdated Anglo-Persian Oil Company, changed its name to BP to reflect its global operations and ownership (a change that Barack Obama seemed to forget, in a moment of nationalistic posturing, when an oil rig leased to *British Petroleum* despoiled the United States' Gulf Coast).

We can change our names, we can change the names of countries, companies and cities, and we can certainly change the names of things. And, as we saw with the Stanford vegetables experiment, by changing the name of something we can change its meaning and the way people react to it.

> **Names tactic #3**
> *Changing perceptions by changing names*

The Patagonian toothfish is not a beautiful animal. If you were feeling uncharitable, you might say that this huge grey creature from the depths of the southern oceans has an almost monstrous appearance. The sharply pointed teeth set in a gaping, unbalanced mouth beneath bulging eyes make for a particularly ugly fish. Its unappetizing appearance is only underlined by its name: who wants to eat a *tooth*-fish?

Even the fishermen who hauled the Patagonian toothfish to the surface were largely uninterested in it. The flesh is bland and oily, and specimens caught on deep-water lines were often tossed back. What was the point of landing, gutting and cooking a fish with so little flavour?

In 1977, an American fish importer named Lee Lantz happened to see a specimen of *Dissostichus eleginoides* on a dock in the port city of Valparaíso, Chile. 'That is one amazing-looking fish,' he said. 'What the hell is it?' The answer he received was *bacalao de profundidad*, or 'cod of the deep'.

'Nobody knows what to do with it,' said his Chilean partner.

Several days later, Lantz was wandering through a fish market in Santiago, the capital of Chile, when he spotted another. Curious, he bought a fillet and fried it. True, it didn't taste of much, but the texture was moist, buttery and tender; the white flesh almost melted in the mouth. Americans, reckoned Lantz, might be more tolerant of the bland taste and more excited by the delicate oily texture than the local shoppers in Santiago. In fact, the lack of flavour might even be an advantage: the fish would be the perfect blank canvas on which US chefs could apply their own flavours, adding sauces, herbs and spices as they pleased.

But the name just wouldn't do. 'Cod of the deep' was hardly inspiring, and who would ever order a *tooth*-fish?

Lantz pondered his options as he transported his first cargo of Patagonian toothfish to the United States. American diners liked sea bass, he knew, so why not try that? More than 100 different species of fish share the name sea bass, so what harm was there in adding one more? The flesh of the Patagonian toothfish was white and flaky like sea bass, so diners would not be unpleasantly surprised. It didn't seem to bother Lantz that *Dissostichus eleginoides* was a cod icefish, not a bass at all.

He considered calling his discovery the 'South American Sea Bass' or the 'Pacific Sea Bass', but both sounded too generic. So, with a nod to the Valparaíso dock where he first stumbled across the fish, he dubbed it the 'Chilean Sea Bass'. The name was original, exotic and classy. It was perfect.

Another seventeen years would elapse before the US Food and Drug Administration would agree that Chilean Sea Bass was an acceptable 'alternative market name' for the Patagonian tooth-fish and its close relative, the Antarctic toothfish. But by then *Dissostichus eleginoides* had gone from being a little known deep-sea reject to one of the most sought-after items on the smartest menus. Initially welcomed as a cheap alternative to better known white fish such as black cod, Chilean Sea Bass went on to become a pricy favourite at restaurants like New York's Aquagrill (miso glazed) and London's Hakkasan (stir-fried in a truffle sauce). Changing the fish's name had worked wonders for its marketability.

The name change had less happy consequences for the fish it-self. Having been left in peace throughout most of its history, the Patagonian toothfish suddenly found itself targeted by fishing vessels equipped with lines that stretched for miles underwater, each bearing up to 15,000 baited hooks. A single boat could catch 20 tonnes of fish per day. Though attempts were made to regulate and control the activity, most Patagonian toothfish were caught in inter-national waters, far from view. Illegal fishing of the species was rife. By the turn of the millennium, conservationists were so concerned at the rapid decline in toothfish populations that they instituted a 'Take a Pass on Chilean Sea Bass' campaign, persuading hundreds of restaurant chefs to remove the fish from their menus.

The Patagonian toothfish is not the only piscine species to go through a dizzying cycle of consumer discovery, global popularity, population collapse and conservation boycott. Goosefish and slimehead have both experienced similar trajectories. Spiny dogfish used to be the most common shark on Earth, but their population has fallen by an estimated 95 per cent. What do the four have in common? All of them became newly popular with consumers following a name change. 'Monkfish' is a slight improvement on 'goosefish', while 'rock salmon' sounds a lot better than 'spiny dogfish' in the fish and chip shop, and 'orange roughy' is a million times more palatable than 'slimehead'. Now all four are on Green-peace's Red List of fish to avoid eating. As the *Washington Post* put it in 2009, 'If the slimehead were still a slimehead, it wouldn't be in this kind of trouble.'[18]

Not all piscine name changes have negative consequences. The foul-sounding mudbug, rebranded as 'crawfish', is sustainably farmed and makes a delicious Louisiana speciality. The dolphin-fish was given its Hawaiian name, mahi-mahi, to prevent confused diners worrying that they were eating a loveable mammal. Pilchards have undergone a renaissance as Cornish sardines. Now, attempts are underway to combat the spread of Asian carp in North America through a change of name.

These large freshwater fish are considered a major threat to the ecosystems of American rivers such as the Missouri and the Illinois. Hundreds of millions of dollars are being spent to keep Asian carp out of the Great Lakes. Deliberately introduced to the United States in the 1970s, Asian carp have multiplied to the point where, in several important waterways, they have pushed out most other species. Environmentalists and fishermen alike are desperate to get rid of them.

As we have seen from the unfortunate example of the Patagonian toothfish, a great way to destroy a population of fish is to get diners from Los Angeles to Dubai clamouring to eat them. Unfortunately, most Americans don't have a taste for Asian carp, although the fish is nutritious and is considered a delicacy in its native China. So a team led by Chef Philippe Parola have borrowed from the Chilean Sea Bass story and renamed Asian carp 'silverfin™'. This name, they hope, will hold greater appeal for American diners, encouraging more fishermen to target them.

While marketers may rename foods for commercial reasons, some-times the name of a food becomes a political battleground. During the First World War, Americans renamed sauerkraut 'liberty cabbage' to strip the popular food of its German connotations. The US Congress attempted something similar with 'freedom fries' when France fell out of favour for refusing to support the invasion of Iraq. When caricatures of the Prophet Muhammad were published in a Danish newspaper, Iranian bakers were instructed to rename their Danish pastries 'Roses of the Prophet Muhammad'.

Even the Asian carp underwent a second renaming for political reasons: in 2015, the Minnesota Senate approved a measure to rename the fish 'invasive carp', as calling the unwelcome arrivals 'Asian' was thought to be offensive.

The ravaging rabbit

Name changes can be critically important in politics. If an issue is contentious, then one effective tactic is to rename a key element of the debate. Anti-abortion campaigners have long understood the greater traction they achieve as 'pro-life' activists. Their opponents would much rather be called 'pro-choice' than 'pro-abortion'. Sometimes a well-chosen name can win the whole argument with the public. A former British defence secretary, Michael Heseltine, has claimed that the case for retaining nuclear weapons was finally made when his propaganda unit decided in 1983 to stop talking about 'unilateral disarmament' – 'a very nice benign sort of cosy thing'[19] – and have ministers argue instead against 'one-sided disarmament'. 'One-sided' implied the other side would take advantage. 'One-sided' meant being the dupe. 'That was absolutely the heart of the argument, encapsulated in just those two words,' Heseltine said.[20]

US political consultant Frank Luntz became notorious for his strategy of 'redefining labels' in support of Republican policy goals. Overweight and dishevelled, with an oddly boyish face and a penchant for combining designer sneakers with business suits, Luntz has become a highly successful pollster and communicator, in demand with both TV networks and business CEOs. He has a doctorate in politics from Oxford University yet claims, 'I don't know shit about anything, with the exception of what the American people think.'[21] That insight has made him very good at understanding what names and labels will resonate with the public.

To quote from the website of Luntz Global:

> In the political arena, our CEO, Dr. Frank Luntz, has helped re-define the discourse on countless issues . . . Luntz is known best for explaining how Americans call the 'estate tax' exactly what it is, 'a death tax.' He showed that parents don't debate 'school vouchers,' but they do discuss 'opportunity scholarships.' And he showed how Americans don't want 'drilling for oil,' but they do want 'American energy exploration.'*

The US estate tax was much less onerous than most European inheritance taxes. By 2017, it applied only to estates worth over $5 million, so a tiny fraction of Americans actually had to pay it. Even at the turn of the millennium, a couple with assets worth over a million dollars could go to their graves confident that the government couldn't touch a cent of it. Nevertheless, the tax had long been a Republican bugbear, and in 2017 it was slated for elimination as part of Donald Trump's tax reform plans.

At first, politicians campaigning to abolish the estate tax struggled to rouse much interest among voters. Understandably, few saw any great need to save the rich from contributing something further to society at the end of their lives. A campaigner named Jim Martin is thought to have coined the term 'death tax', but it was Frank Luntz who carried out the polling to show conclusively how much more voters resented the idea of a 'tax on death' than a commonplace 'estate tax'. The new name recast the tax in moral terms:

---

* Accessed January 2017; this text has since been removed.

how can it be right to add a tax demand to the tragedy of a death? The name also suggested a tax that could hit anyone, as everyone must die one day. 'It's all a matter of marketing,' said Martin, of what he ghoulishly referred to as 'the stiffest tax of all'.[22]

Luntz deployed the new name in the Republicans' 1994 'Contract with America'. He recommended that Republican senators and congressmen stage press conferences 'at your local mortuary' for added impact. Bill Clinton tried to counter Luntz's powerful terminology, offering up a catchy name of his own for the proposed repeal: 'a windfall for the wealthy'. Despite the president's best efforts, by 2001 nearly 80 per cent of Americans supported repeal of the 'death tax'.

'Language is like fire,' observes Luntz. 'Depending on how you use it, it can either heat your house or burn it to the ground.'[23]

Frank Luntz can work his fiendish name magic with just about anything: 'If I wanted to demonize a bunny, I would use a word like rabbit,' he says. 'The rabbit will ravage your garden. This is a language pivot. A bunny is cute; a rabbit that ravages your garden is a pest.'[24] Luntz not only made it easier for the oil majors to drill freely, under the bravely patriotic mantle of 'American energy exploration', but also played a critical role in retarding progress towards more sustainable forms of energy and transport. During the first George W. Bush administration, he advised Republicans to avoid the term 'global warming', which conjured up images of a melting planet superheated by burning fossil fuels, in favour of the more benign 'climate change'. A leaked 2003 memo from Luntz read:

> 'Climate change' is less frightening than 'global warming'. As one focus group participant noted, climate change 'sounds like you're going from Pittsburgh to Fort Lauderdale'. While global warming has catastrophic connotations attached to it, climate change suggests a more controllable and less emotional challenge.[25]

He was right. Eleven years later, researchers from the Yale Project on Climate Change Communications and the George Mason University Center for Climate Change Communications found that Americans were 13 per cent more likely to view 'global warming' as a threat than 'climate change'. 'The use of the term *climate change* appears to actually *reduce* issue engagement,' said the researchers.[26]

'My job is to look for the words that trigger the emotion,' says Luntz. 'Words alone can be found in a dictionary or a telephone book, but words with emotion can change destiny, can change life as we know it. We know it has changed history; we know it has changed behaviour; we know that it can start a war or stop it. We know that words and emotion together are the most powerful force known to mankind.'[27]

Naming right

Names matter. The names and labels we give people, laws, concepts and things shape the way the world sees them and so determine how we act towards them. The right name can get diners clamouring for an unknown fish; the wrong name can leave voters apathetic about an issue of global importance. Pick an emotive name for the issue under debate and you might win the argument before it has even begun. Names are not neutral. They have power and resonance; they can inspire action and they can do great damage. So if the current name of your product, movement or business isn't producing the desired outcome, change it. A new name is a new truth: if it leads to a new perception of reality, it might make all the difference.

In case you're wondering, the fact that this chapter features one story about a man named Lantz and another about a man named Luntz is pure coincidence.

I think.

In practice

• Choose names for projects and people carefully – they may affect their prospects.

• If a product or concept is not selling well, try renaming it.

But watch out for . . .

• People using evocative names to persuade you to buy, vote or act inappropriately.

• Opponents who confer a damaging nickname on you or your project.

• Misleaders who change the terms used in a debate to change the outcome.

PART FOUR

UNKNOWN
TRUTHS

12

Predictions

You don't make spending decisions, investment decisions, hiring decisions, or whether-you're-going-to-look-for-a-job decisions when you don't know what's going to happen.

MICHAEL BLOOMBERG

Pre-empting or preventing?

On the morning of 5 June 1967, almost every combat aircraft in the formidable Israeli Air Force (IAF) took off from their bases and flew low out over the Mediterranean. They continued west until they had passed Port Said, then turned south towards Egypt. They were not expected. An uneasy peace had held between Israel and Egypt since the Suez Crisis of 1956. Israel had made no formal declaration of war, nor had its politicians given any hint of their intentions. Although Egypt possessed an air defence system, the Israeli jets were flying too low to be detected by its radar. The IAF timed their attack shortly after the end of the habitual Egyptian dawn patrol, roaring into the Nile Valley while the Egyptian pilots were at breakfast.

Egypt's air bases lacked fortified aircraft shelters, and most of the planes were parked in the open beside the runways. The first wave of IAF aircraft targeted eleven Egyptian bases, cratering the runways with specially designed bombs and destroying 189 planes. The Israeli jets returned to base to refuel and rearm, and within minutes were back in the air and returning to Egypt. Two more waves of attacks saw 19 air bases disabled in all, and over 300 Egyptian aircraft destroyed. During the course of the morning, Syria, Jordan and Iraq responded to the attack on Egypt by deploying their own aircraft against targets in Israel. These had little strategic impact and led to IAF jets turning their attention to those countries' air bases. By the end of the day, Israel had eliminated around 400 Arab aircraft. It achieved total air supremacy across the region, ensuring its ground forces' dominance in the ensuing Six-Day War. The Israel Defense Forces took control of the Sinai Peninsula, the Gaza Strip, the West Bank, East Jerusalem and the Golan Heights, much of which Israel still occupies.

It was a stunning victory. But why did Israel do it? Why did this tiny country surrounded by hostile Arab nations choose to break the peace?

After the Suez Crisis, Israel had agreed to withdraw from occupied Egyptian territory in the Sinai Peninsula on condition that a UN Emergency Force (UNEF) be deployed as a buffer between the two nations. The UNEF remained in place for ten years, keeping the peace and guaranteeing freedom of movement for Israeli shipping through the vital Straits of Tiran, the narrow passage between the Sinai Peninsula and Saudi Arabia.

During this time, pressure on Israel from its neighbours continued to grow. The Soviet Union allied with several Arab states, supplying weapons and political support. The Palestinian Liberation Organization was formed. Irregular Arab militants staged attacks against Israel. In retaliation, Israel launched ground assaults against targets in Jordan and Syria. Tensions between the Jewish state and its Arab neighbours were high.

On 13 May 1967, Egypt – known at the time as the United

Arab Republic – moved a large number of troops into the Sinai Peninsula. Egyptian president Gamal Abdel Nasser was responding to an erroneous Soviet warning about Israeli troop activity on the Syrian border. Nasser ordered the UNEF peacekeepers on the Israel–Egypt border to withdraw, and on 22 May he closed the Straits of Tiran to Israeli shipping, cutting off vital oil supplies.

Israel concluded that it was about to be attacked. The Israeli government made a prediction and acted on it.

The IAF's strike against Egypt is still celebrated as perhaps the most successful example in modern times of pre-emptive war – the use of offensive military action as a form of defence in the event of an imminent military threat. Operation Focus, as it was called, had been a long time in the planning; it was founded on comprehensive intelligence-gathering and extensive training for the pilots. But it was only implemented once Egypt had made its belligerent moves in the Sinai.

Pre-emptive actions are always controversial, because they depend for moral justification on a competing truth about the future. For Israel not to be vilified as the aggressor in the court of world opinion, it had to make the case that Egypt and its allies were on the point of going to war themselves – that they were the real aggressors, even though Israel drew first blood.

It's impossible, after the fact, to say whether this prediction of an Arab attack would have come true if Israel hadn't acted. All we can do is look at the evidence of events prior to 5 June 1967 and conclude for ourselves whether Israel's competing truth about the future was credible and reasonable. It has, unsurprisingly, been contested in some quarters. There was indeed an Egyptian plan to invade Israel – known as 'The Dawn' – scheduled for 27 May, but it was cancelled at the last minute on Nasser's orders. Would Egypt have revisited this plan, or something similar, if Israel had not struck first? If not in 1967, then what about the following year, or the year after that?

A moral distinction is sometimes drawn between pre-emptive war and 'preventative war', of which the most notorious example is the 2003 Gulf War. When George W. Bush and Tony Blair led a coalition of nations in an ill-fated invasion of Iraq, their justification was Iraq's supposed intention, at some point in the future, to use weapons of mass destruction (WMD) against American or European targets. Many of the subsequent recriminations hinged on the misinformation provided by the Bush administration and the Blair government as to the existence of said WMD: after the invasion, no WMD were found in Iraq. But I would not be surprised if both George W. Bush and Tony Blair still cling to their 'truth' that Iraq under Saddam Hussein would eventually have attacked a target in the West, had they not removed him. That prediction cannot be as easily disproved as their claim that Saddam possessed WMD.

The practical difference between pre-emptive and preventative war is one of timing. In both cases, military action is taken to prevent a future attack by the other side; pre-emptive war counters an imminent threat, while preventative war anticipates a less well-defined attack at some point in the more distant future. It all comes down to how confident you are of your predictions and how soon you think they are going to come true. That leaves a lot of wiggle room for Misleaders to make the case for pre-emptive war, even when they may secretly doubt the imminence of enemy action. It's not necessarily a lie to declare that your country is going to be attacked; it might be grossly misleading, however, to imply it's likely to happen any time soon.

What the future holds

Is this a true statement?

The sun will rise tomorrow.

How about this one?

I am going to die one day.

My guess is you answered *yes* to both. They are truths that no one is likely to dispute. They are as true as truth gets.

This is interesting because neither statement is exactly a fact – it is conceivably possible that the sun will explode before tomorrow, or that some form of cryogenic preservation could keep you alive in perpetuity. We infer they are true because our experience tells us the sun rises every day and our education tells us everyone dies. They are predictions that we treat as absolute truths.

But how about these?

The train will leave at 20:45.

The school term will end on 15 December.

Millions of tourists will visit Paris next year.

The studio's next movie will be released in September.

We are getting married on 2 June.

These predictions seem very likely to be fulfilled. If things work out differently, we won't be too shocked: our predictions have been confounded before. But we are confident enough of such predictions to plan our lives around them, to invest, hire, relocate, vote, study, spend and build in accordance with what we expect to happen. If we don't, bad things are likely to occur: we miss the train; a child is left forlorn at the school gates; wedding caterers don't turn up.

We treat such predictions as actionable truths.

Farmers plant crops and spray pesticides; sports fans buy season tickets; happy couples book churches and marquees; hospitality companies build hotels; pregnant mothers purchase cots and strollers. They are all taking significant, costly actions on the basis of predictions that they confidently expect to be fulfilled.

But until such predictions come true, they are not absolute truths. It is always possible that something else might happen. And that means it is always possible *to predict* something else might happen – to offer a competing truth about the future.

We can use carefully selected predictions, just like other competing truths, to persuade, to influence, to motivate and to inspire.

Visionary leadership

Atkins is a global engineering consultancy that has designed, planned and project-managed the construction of skyscrapers, highways, tunnels, airports and much else besides. It was responsible for part of the 2012 London Olympics infrastructure and is currently working on the world's largest experimental nuclear fusion reactor and a pioneering array of floating wind turbines. These are huge endeavours that take years, or even decades, to complete. Unsurprisingly, Atkins' leaders spend a great deal of time thinking about the future.

The construction and engineering sector is arguably one of the few yet to be disrupted by the digital revolution, and the question keeping industry executives up at night is not *whether* that disruption will come but *when*. Atkins has been in business for over three quarters of a century and wants to remain competitive long into the future, so its leaders have been thinking hard about what's going to be different – where new opportunities might arise and what kinds of threats their business might face.

Rapid urbanization will require municipal and national governments to make bold plans for power, transport and water provision to expanding populations. Climate change may necessitate flood defences. New sources and uses of energy will mean different approaches to generation and distribution. Terrorism may force infrastructure owners to install security features across both buildings and networks. Perhaps most important of all, Atkins envisages a 'new wave of digital' converging with the built environment that will change the very nature of their industry.

I was invited to help Atkins' UK & Europe business prepare its 8,500 people for this brave new world. We set an ambition for the company to redefine the infrastructure design and planning industry, riding the new digital wave into a world of networks and big data. An organization that had built its reputation on combining steel, concrete and glass would have to become just as adept at incorporating bytes and algorithms. Automated design, reality capture with lasers and drones, predictive analytics, virtual reality and navigating the Internet of Things would all need to become core capabilities for Atkins. If the whole organization got behind this new vision of the future, we predicted that Atkins would become synonymous with world-class infrastructure. The firm is already highly respected by its clients; in the future, it would also be widely recognized and appreciated by the public.

This analysis of likely trends, coupled with a vision for the future and a plan for how to get there, proved highly motivating to Atkins' staff. Once their leaders had distilled all the various possibilities and uncertainties into a clear statement of expectations and intentions, they were far better able to direct their energies in a coordinated, constructive fashion. Their leaders' predictions made them more engaged, prepared and effective. When Atkins was acquired by SNC-Lavalin in 2017, that vision of the future remained constant – the light on the hill that would keep employees focused through the change of ownership and whatever else might be in store.

There is nothing unique about this corporate story. If you have ever worked in strategy consulting, policy development or business planning, you will recognize the main elements. It is a core requirement of good leadership to predict what's going to happen around your organization and offer a vision of the future that people can work towards.

But what's interesting about this process is how all that energy, investment and commitment is being applied on the basis of things that haven't happened yet and which, quite possibly, might never happen. I undertook a similar process with another client, the UK's Health Protection Agency, in 2008. We looked at the likely future threats to public health from epidemics, chemical spills, nuclear radiation and other major hazards, and we described how the agency would bring together the government experts in all these fields and build new nationwide response capabilities that would better safeguard the public. It was an inspiring vision that was already starting to pay dividends in staff engagement when David Cameron's newly elected government decided to abolish the agency.

Well, we hadn't predicted *that*.

Predictions in complex environments like banking, public services planning or infrastructure development are bound to be vulnerable to the unexpected. Nevertheless, we have to make predictions if we are going to achieve anything. Every organization needs a clear direction of travel, towards an anticipated goal, and it needs to know what to expect along the way. We view our predictions as qualified truths about the future that may be subject to revision at a later date. Without them, we would go nowhere.

Persuasive prediction

Let's imagine that you want to persuade a potential recruit named Christine to join your team at work. There will be a compensation package to discuss, and various roles and responsibilities to agree. But perhaps more than anything, Christine will want to know what lies ahead if she takes the job. What's it going to be like to work for you? How happy will she be in six months' time if she joins? What opportunities will she have and what new skills will she develop?

Her decision to accept the job is likely to hinge on such questions. So what might you say about the future?

Some options flash through your mind:

You will have to work late two or three nights a week.

You will be working with Jeff, who is a total nightmare but we can't get rid of him.

You will face unfair abuse from customers angry with our company's returns policies.

We won't be able to promote you for at least three years.

You know these things to be true. But you may prefer not to voice any of them. Instead, you focus on other, equally true predictions:

You will acquire valuable customer service experience.

You will receive two weeks of formal skills training each year.

You will get to travel to our offices in Paris and Singapore.

You will have the option to take on further responsibilities within a year.

Like the partial truths we discussed earlier, predictions can be judiciously selected to create a particular impression of reality. Communicators can omit and obfuscate with predictions in exactly the same way as with partial truths. That's why politicians talk about the spending they will authorize if elected rather than the debts they will run up or the taxes they will raise. We all do it. Parents trying to interest a child in an upcoming family holiday will preview the sunny beaches and fun activities, not the sleepless flight or the lack of Wi-Fi. It is even harder to paint a complete picture of the future than of the past, so of course we tend to focus on the elements that will further our agenda or win our argument.

If we come across a credible prediction that helps our case, we talk it up. Unhelpful predictions we may prefer not to mention at all. If we are faced with a choice of conflicting predictions by equally respected experts, it is only natural to select and share the one that most favours our position, ignoring the rest.

> **Predictions tactic #1**
> *Selective prediction*

During the Brexit referendum, one highly influential Vote Leave poster read, 'TURKEY (population 76 million) IS JOINING THE EU'. The citizens of any EU member state have the right to live and work in any other member state, so at a time of heightened concerns about Middle East instability and immigration that was all the Leave campaigners needed to say to scare a lot of British voters. But was their prediction true?

Turkey applied to join the EEC in 1987 and was given EU candidate status in 1999. It had long been British policy to promote Turkish membership of the EU. In 2010, prime minister David Cameron told a Turkish audience, 'Together I want us to pave the road from Ankara to Brussels.'[1] At the time of the referendum, the EU found itself in need of Turkish cooperation to control the flow of migrants into Europe, and many speculated that Turkish EU membership may have been the ultimate price of that coopera- tion. So if you were prepared to take a flexible interpretation of the timescale implied by the construction 'is joining', then it may well have been true that 'Turkey is joining the EU' at some point in the future.

On the other hand, like other member states the UK had a veto on new members; if the British government did not want Turkey in the club, then Turkey could never join (while the UK remained in the EU). Even if the UK did not use its veto, Cyprus certainly would until the long-standing Turkish occupation of northern Cyprus was resolved. Furthermore, a great many procedural hurdles stood in the way of Turkish membership, due to the corruption, lack of press freedom and human rights violations that had been documented. So it was equally true to say that Turkish accession was a very distant possibility. Indeed, David Cameron, a Remainer, declared during the Brexit debate, 'At the current rate of progress, [Turkey] will probably get around to joining in about the year 3000.'[2] On balance, the Vote Leave poster seems pretty misleading.

Much of the Brexit debate centred on competing predictions about what would happen if Britain left the EU. Remainers foresaw isolation, economic loss, insecurity, travel restrictions and perhaps even a breakdown in European order. Brexiteers predicted a new era of world trade and unfettered innovation, a fresh model of cooperation with our European allies and far greater control over our own destiny. Although both sides exaggerated the potential ups and downs of British fortunes, most of the claims made about the future were valid predictions based in some sort of fact.

Will water be the death of us?

Nowhere, perhaps, is the battle over competing predictions more keenly fought than in debates about global warming.

Carbon dioxide generated by humans is building up in our atmosphere, creating a greenhouse-like barrier that traps heat from the sun previously radiated back into space. This observable, measurable part of the global-warming story is now widely accepted. But the reason we are trying to make such major changes to the ways we travel, generate power and live comes in the next part of the story: the predictions about what might happen to our climate, and the harmful effects such changes might have.

The Intergovernmental Panel on Climate Change (IPCC) has estimated that global mean surface temperatures for 2081–2100 will be between 0.3°C and 4.8°C higher than in the period 1986–2005.[3] That's a very wide range, allowing for predictions of both benign and catastrophic futures. Why such uncertainty from the experts?

Carbon dioxide (CO_2) on its own is not predicted to cause more than a small amount of warming. Doubling atmospheric CO_2 concentrations would be expected to warm the planet by about 1.2°C, according to the IPCC. This is not considered particularly dangerous. Predictions of radical climate change depend on a secondary, amplifying factor – the warming effect of increased water vapour in the atmosphere.

Warmer air holds more water vapour, with the concentration increasing by about 7 per cent per degree Celsius. So a little CO_2-driven warming would lead to a significantly moister atmosphere. As water vapour is a potent greenhouse gas, this could more than double the future warming caused by increased CO_2 alone.

Water vapour also forms clouds, which both contribute to warming by trapping radiation from the Earth and reduce warming by reflecting sunlight back into space. Overall, clouds have a net cooling influence, but different types of cloud have different effects, with low stratocumulus clouds generally cooling the planet and high, thin cirrus clouds warming it. So if more water vapour were to lead to more low-altitude clouds, they could reduce or negate its amplification effect, while an increase in high-altitude clouds could exacerbate it.

However, more water vapour does not necessarily mean more clouds. In fact, research suggests that a moister, warmer atmosphere may result in fewer clouds at both low and high altitude (which would have worrying implications for rainfall and drought). The changing balance of high- and low-level clouds will determine whether the overall effect is warming or cooling.

Currently, climate scientists think that the net cloud effect of greenhouse gas-induced warming will be slightly positive, amplifying the effects of CO_2. But although scientists are doing their best to model future cloud behaviour, most would admit that they cannot yet do this with high confidence. The uncertainty around the effect that changing patterns of clouds will have on global temperatures makes long-term climate prediction very difficult.

Such uncertainty is a standard feature of scientific research. It doesn't mean the global-warming story is wrong; nor does it mean that we shouldn't take action now, in case our more pessimistic predictions prove correct. But it does mean that plenty of competing truths can be flung around at both extremes of the debate. Those scientists seeking to improve the quality of our climate predictions are frequently caught in the crossfire.

Even if temperatures do rise substantially, not everyone agrees that this will be bad for us. The disagreement is largely due to the unimaginable complexity of the planet-wide systems being modelled. Will hurricanes increase in frequency and intensity, as Harvey, Irma and Maria seemed to suggest? Will the thermohaline circulation that warms northern Europe be disrupted? Will melting permafrost release a large reservoir of trapped CO_2 into the atmosphere, accelerating global warming? Will droughts and crop failures lead to mass migration and war? Will sea-level rises threaten cities? No one can say for sure, so plenty of vaguely credible scenarios have been aired.

Partial truths presented in an appropriate context can be

useful to suggest what the future might hold. The 2017 Climate Science Special Report (part of the US National Climate Assessment) claimed 'relatively strong evidence' indicates that man-made factors contributed to the 2003 European heatwave and 2013 Australian heatwave. It also found that some storm types are 'exhibiting changes that have been linked to climate change', while acknowledging that such linkages are not sufficiently understood. But partial truths have also been stretched by both sides to justify fear or complacency about the future. Here's a 2016 Climatewire story published by *Scientific American*, written to show how climate change might drive future conflict:

> The ongoing Syrian conflict has killed 470,000 people and displaced millions. It, too, was preceded by an unusually severe drought between 2006 and 2010. Millions of farmers migrated to urban centers, the staging grounds for the civil conflict. The drought would have been highly unlikely without climate change, according to one study.[4]

The facts are largely true; the causal implication, most political experts would protest, is certainly not. Climate change was not responsible for the Syrian war.

Some climate sceptics have offered rosier predictions of a warm future. 'Fewer people will die from the cold,' wrote Myron Ebell, the lobbyist chosen by Donald Trump to lead the transition at the Environmental Protection Agency. He went on:

> Life in many places would become more pleasant. Instead of 20 below zero in January in Saskatoon, it might be only 10 below. And I don't think too many people would complain if winters in Minneapolis became more like winters in Kansas City . . . For the elderly and infirm, warmer weather is definitely healthier as well as more pleasant.[5]

All of which is probably true, even if it heartlessly ignores the fate of billions in hotter climes.

Science journalist Matt Ridley has pointed to the recent greening of the planet – an observed increase in plant matter across multiple ecosystems – as a major economic and environmental upside of higher CO_2 concentrations.[6] He notes that CO_2 is a vital raw material for plants: farmers routinely raise the concentration of CO_2 in greenhouses to stimulate crop growth. In the future, he suggests, farms and rainforests alike will benefit from the increased atmospheric CO_2. However, this optimistic outlook has to be weighed alongside the likelihood of disrupted weather patterns bringing droughts, storms and floods to agricultural regions and upsetting delicate natural ecosystems. Hurricane Maria, which may have been intensified by climate change, obliterated much of Puerto Rico's rainforest in September 2017 and destroyed up to 80 per cent of the island's crops.

All such predictions are based on a multitude of present-day variables that interact with other variables in complex ways that are not always fully understood. Adjust a variable or an inter-relationship by a small degree, and the predictions change radically. It's useful to think through what *might* happen, but few reputable scientists would be willing to say what *will* happen.

Transformative forecasts

Tomorrow's weather is independent of the predictions we make about it: the weather will do what it does, whatever the forecasters say. By contrast, if fears of dangerous global warming lead us to implement carbon reduction or geo-engineering measures which change the climate, the predictions themselves will have influenced the outcome.

The act of communicating a prediction can have an impact on the fulfilment of that prediction. Countries that loudly predict war are more likely to go to war. Central banks that target a particular inflation level steer markets to act accordingly, helping them reach it. Influential analysts who say a public company is going to fail may hasten its demise. Parents who talk down a child's chances of exam success may contribute to their failure. These are all *self-fulfilling* predictions.

By contrast, *self-defeating* predictions are those that, if acted upon, are *not* fulfilled. Timely warnings about the potential scale of the 2014 Ebola outbreak were frightening enough to galvanize the international community into action, thus avoiding most of the more than half a million cases forecast by the Centers for Disease Control and Prevention. Climate campaigners hope that their alarming predictions today will help prevent the worst warming scenarios actually occurring in the future.

> **Predictions tactic #2**
> *Predicting to prevent something*

Conditional predictions may be self-fulfilling or self-defeating. 'If you finish your homework on time, I will give you $20,' is likely to lead to a payout. 'If you send that memo, you will be fired,' ought to be sufficient warning to avoid dismissal.

Promises of action are a form of prediction that may be accepted as truths when coming from a sufficiently trustworthy individual or organization. 'I will meet you outside the theatre at 7 p.m.,' says your beloved, and from experience you know it is true. 'The ECB is ready to do whatever it takes to preserve the euro. And believe me, it will be enough,' declared Mario Draghi, the president of the European Central Bank, in 2012, and the credibility of both man and institution were enough to calm markets and bring down sovereign debt yields.[7] Four years later, the *Financial Times* described that self-fulfilling prediction as 'widely credited with bringing the eurozone back from the brink of possible disintegration'.[8]

> **Predictions tactic #3**
> *Predicting to make something happen*

So not only do predictions drive our actions and determine important decisions, communicating them can change the future by directly leading to their fulfilment or defeat. Predictions that are credible enough to be treated as truths are powerful motivators and shapers of reality. When more than one credible prediction is available, then the one we choose to listen to, act on and share may ultimately decide our future.

Utopia or dystopia?

The robots are coming.

Not just robots. Artificial intelligence (AI) coupled with big data, state-of-the-art sensors and unprecedented connectivity will soon render machines better at many physical and intellectual tasks than humans. Better – and much, much cheaper.

Numerous occupations will soon be obliterated as machines take over. We've already seen plenty of manufacturing tasks transferred to robots. Retail checkout staff, bank cashiers and telephone service agents are gradually being phased out. Next to go will be truck and taxi drivers, replaced by autonomous vehicles. There are 3.5 million truck drivers in the United States alone. Not far behind will be knowledge workers who perform routine tasks: accountants, property lawyers, financial reporters, administrative coordinators, medical laboratory assistants and so on. Even hands-on jobs like cooking, cleaning and hairdressing will be lost as robotic dexterity and spatial awareness improves.

Millions, perhaps billions, of people will be made redundant by the machines. Inequality will soar.

As machine learning inevitably enables computers to become

smarter than us, they may decide to take control. 'We should avoid strong assumptions regarding upper limits on future AI capabilities,' warned a group of AI and robotics experts in 2017:

> Risks posed by AI systems, especially catastrophic or existential risks, must be subject to planning and mitigation efforts commensurate with their expected impact . . . AI systems designed to recursively self-improve or self-replicate in a manner that could lead to rapidly increasing quality or quantity must be subject to strict safety and control measures.[9]

The experts' guidelines for future AI research are hardly reassuring to anyone who grew up with the *Terminator* and *Matrix* movies. Bear in mind that much of the most sophisticated AI and robotics research is currently directed towards military applications. Even if the machines don't decide to obliterate us, we may be reduced to the status of pets or slaves.

'The development of full artificial intelligence could spell the end of the human race,' warned Professor Stephen Hawking.[10]

'If greater-than-human artificial general intelligence is invented without due caution, it is all but certain that the human species will be extinct in very short order,' agreed Michael Vassar, the former president of the Machine Intelligence Research Institute.[11]

Clearly, we must do everything we can to prevent this catastrophe.

Tesla and SpaceX founder Elon Musk has called artificial intelligence 'our biggest existential threat'. 'With artificial intelligence we are summoning the demon,' he said.[12] He argues that AI must be regulated at the national or international level. But he has gone further than that. His terrifying vision of artificial intelligence is one of the drivers of his space programme: according to *Vanity Fair*, he wants to colonize Mars so that we'll have 'a bolthole if A.I. goes rogue and turns on humanity'.[13]

Aside from running away from the machines, which may soon

be impossible, he has suggested that another way we might survive is by joining forces with them – literally. He is already pursuing this cyborg option – 'having some sort of merger of biological intelligence and machine intelligence' – through his company Neuralink, which will develop a 'neural lace' of 'tiny brain electrodes that may one day upload and download thoughts'. [14] Musk is betting a huge amount of time, money and reputation on the effort to protect us from being replaced or exterminated by machines.

Microsoft founder Bill Gates has an alternative proposal to hinder the widespread adoption of robots: we should tax them. 'You ought to be willing to raise the tax level and even slow down the speed of that adoption,' he said.[15] Another way to achieve the same outcome would be to cut payroll taxes or provide wage subsidies for low-income workers, making them more competitive with machines and reducing the incentive for firms to invest in automation. Gates knows that tax won't keep the machines at bay for ever, but it might give humans time to adapt and develop the skills necessary to survive in an AI world.

We should demand that our governments regulate and tax anyone advancing artificial intelligence or developing new generations of robots. In fact, we should probably ban the blasted things altogether or take direct action if governments won't legislate to protect us from them. We need to act now to save ourselves.

Scaremongering nonsense! That view of the future is far too gloomy. Yes, machines will take over many of our more repetitive, degrading and boring jobs. What's wrong with that? Does anyone really want to sit hunched over an Excel spreadsheet all day or repair holes in the road all night? Is trucking, or flipping burgers, or staring at pathology samples a fulfilling way for complex brains to spend their time? Artificial intelligence will free us to do more interesting things and pursue more creative careers. As old jobs disappear, new jobs will be created in fields we can't even imagine yet. The industrial revolution did not cause mass unemployment and nor did the computer age. Now we need programmers and website designers, immunotherapy researchers, cyber security managers and data modellers – all jobs created by technology. For anyone willing to use technology to augment their own capabilities, the future will be bright.

Moreover, robots and artificial intelligence may prove to be our salvation. Some of the intractable problems we face, such as global warming and spiralling care costs for the elderly, may be solved by the machines. Robots capable of monitoring vital signs, supporting or gently carrying someone, or even holding an entertaining conversation, may improve the quality of life for millions of old people and allow them to live independently for far longer. Teams of autonomous robots could monitor and mend our crumbling roads and buildings. Swarms of drones may offer some kind of geo-engineering solution that helps keep Earth's surface temperatures in check.

Why should we fear machines that are smarter than us, so long as we programme them to serve our needs and tell them what we want? Maybe a superior intelligence will be able to figure out the Arab–Israeli conflict, or prevent nuclear war, or eliminate suffering. Smarter machines might take care of us as benevolently as we take care of our most pampered pets.

So let's do everything we can to speed the development of artificial intelligence. Let's give tax breaks to robotics companies and grants to university departments researching machine learning. Let's lift the regulatory barriers to autonomous vehicles and usher in a golden age of technology.

Which will it be? Are the doom-mongers Advocates or Misinformers? We know for sure the robots are coming and they will transform our world completely. We really have no idea what that transformation will look like. Yet we must choose soon how to respond to this remarkable new phenomenon. Even inaction is a form of response that will have consequences. How do we decide what to do? The only way to choose our response is to predict the future.

Or to accept someone else's prediction.

Future-proof

The future is coming at us faster and faster, thanks to the accelerating pace of technological development, global connectivity and political change. In an increasingly uncertain and volatile world, it is harder than ever to predict what's going to happen. Yet our need to plan, invest and prepare has never been greater. Prediction is an essential daily habit.

Companies that want to prepare for an uncertain future use scenario planning to analyse how they will cope in different situations. Large banks are now required to simulate extreme financial conditions to stress test their balance sheets. Institutions like hospitals and armies envision different futures to ensure they have the resources and plans in place to deal with a range of possible events. All of these organizations are essentially imagining competing futures in order to shape the decisions they make today.

We can learn from such organizations. In the future, it won't be sufficient to make one prediction: we will need to juggle a number of different competing truths about the future in order to be ready for whichever one is fulfilled. This is particularly true of the work we expect to do and the skills training we should therefore undertake. But it also applies to the number of years we might live, the kinds of environments we may live in, the machines we will need to accommodate, the cyber threats we will have to defend ourselves against, the activities we will be able to undertake, and even the desires we may have. Technology looks set to transform all of these things.

We can't know what the future holds, but by taking seriously a range of competing truths about the future we might just be able to survive it.

In practice

• Paint a positive and credible picture of the future to inspire people to act in the present.

• Consider a range of competing predictions to ensure you're ready for any likely scenario.

• If someone makes a prediction that calls for questionable action now, challenge the validity of that prediction and consider what alternative predictions would signify.

But watch out for . . .

• Misleaders who leave out relevant but off-putting predictions when convincing you to do something.

• People who share and promote only those predictions that support their side of an argument.

13

Beliefs

Who dares to say that he alone has found the truth?
HENRY WADSWORTH LONGFELLOW

A god among us

The first thing that drew people to James Warren Jones was his sincere and lifelong belief in racial equality. Growing up in 1940s Indiana, he was ahead of his time. The state still prohibited marriage between black and white people, and at one point Indiana was said to have the most powerful Ku Klux Klan in all of the United States. A combination of Christian bigotry and deep-seated racism had seen the people of Indiana elect Klansmen and pro-Klan candidates to all levels of state government in the 1920s. Jones's father was said to be a Klansman, and Jones would recount how he refused to speak to his father for years after he barred a black friend from their house. Jim Jones's beliefs were dangerously out of line with those of his community, and they made him an outsider.

Nevertheless, he stuck with them. Jones set up Indianapolis's

271

first biracial church in 1955, and he and his wife became the first white couple in Indiana to adopt a black child. He was invited to chair the Indianapolis Human Rights Commission in 1961, and he used the position to force desegregation in a range of municipal and private organizations. A highly charismatic speaker, his captivating preaching focused on healing the division between black and white. 'He was passionate about interracial integration,' according to former follower Teri Buford O'Shea.[1] His ambition, he declared, was to create a 'rainbow family'.

Racial equality was not the only belief that drove Jim Jones. He was also a communist, at a time when most Americans hated and feared the very idea of communism. Jones's conviction that everyone should be treated equally, and that those in need should be supported by those with means, led him to establish soup kitchens, nursing homes, an orphanage and an employment assistance service. 'The only ethic by which we can lift mankind today is some form of socialism,' he preached.[2]

Jim Jones's twin beliefs in racial equality and socialism made him an alien figure in his home state. But the admirable values he derived from those beliefs drew many followers to his church. When he relocated the 'People's Temple' to California in 1965, his calls for equality, socialism and political activism resonated with many young and altruistic liberal minds. They shared his beliefs, and they signed up to his church in droves.

What should have been an inspiring story of social progression started to go wrong when Jim Jones told his followers he was God.

Some of them believed him.

Jones began to 'heal' people, in faked rituals that were staged as elaborately as magic tricks. There were reports of intimidation and excessive control. Many of his followers signed all their worldly possessions over to Jones. Some even gave over custody of their children. Nevertheless, his fame grew, and the People's Temple pulled in thousands of new members through its churches in San

Francisco and Los Angeles, many of them poor and vulnerable, many of them African American. Jones's congregation became a political force that he could mobilize at will to support or take down Californian politicians.

But stories of abuse began to circulate, and Jones eventually abandoned California for a remote agricultural mission in Guyana. The hundreds of ordinary people that accompanied him to South America, inspired by his vision of a utopian jungle community free of racial or gender discrimination, found themselves isolated and entirely dependent on Jones for information and instruction. Jones took full advantage of his power, demanding sex from men and women alike, ordering public humiliations, and drugging and beating dissenters. Recordings of his voice played constantly through loudspeakers around the settlement. Bibles were torn up for toilet paper. Families were deliberately separated. Children were locked in sensory deprivation boxes. In this increasingly unreal environment, seated on a throne in sunglasses and safari suit, Jones grew more and more paranoid and deranged.

'Life is a fucking disease,' he told his followers. 'And there's only one cure for the sonofabitchin' disease. That's death.'[3]

And some of them believed him.

Jim Jones began rehearsing a mass suicide, persuading his followers to drink beverages he claimed were laced with poison. When many of them did so, he praised them for their loyalty. 'Now I know I can trust you,' he said. Such rehearsals were held every few weeks.

The end came in November 1978, when a US congressman visited Jonestown with an entourage of reporters and aides to investigate claims of abuse and intimidation. Congressman Leo Ryan was murdered by Jones's security guards, along with three journalists. Jones then summoned his followers to the centre of the camp and declared that it was time to die.

Cyanide was mixed with powdered fruit juice – which may or

may not have been Kool-Aid – and hundreds of his followers willingly drank it. Others – including over 200 children – were forced to drink the poison, were injected with a lethal dose, or were shot. Jones himself died from a bullet wound that may have been self-inflicted. In all, 918 people committed suicide or were murdered in Guyana in the name of the beliefs Jim Jones had fostered.

'There's a passage in the Bible where Jesus tells people to leave their families and follow him. Jim quoted that quite a lot,' recalled Teri Buford O'Shea. 'He said he was Gandhi, Buddha, Lenin – he said he was the coming back of anybody you'd ever want to come back. And we believed him.'[4]

True beliefs

We can be pretty sure that Jim Jones was not Gandhi, Buddha or Lenin. He was not God. So why, in this book about truth, should we concern ourselves with such lies?

Firstly, the thousands of followers of Jim Jones did not consider them lies. 'We believed him,' was O'Shea's simple testimony. For many members of the People's Temple, Jones was indeed a god. These were not stupid people. Plenty of them had college degrees and jobs that conferred significant responsibility. Plenty had thought long and hard about the ills of the world and concluded that the People's Temple offered a better way. That was their belief. That was their truth. And some of them were prepared to die for that truth.

Secondly, this story of extreme beliefs helps to throw a spotlight on some of our own beliefs. For many years, Jim Jones earned his following by proclaiming beliefs that many of us would consider true: that all races are equal; that those with means should support those in desperate need. We all have beliefs that feel like unqualified truths to us.

We can define a belief as an idea someone holds to be true that cannot be proved or disproved. We cannot disprove the belief that Jim Jones was God any more than we can prove that all races are equal. These are things we may feel very strongly to be true or false, but neither logic nor science can help us confirm or debunk them.

Here are some beliefs you may consider to be truths:

Men and women have equal value.

People should be loyal to their country.

Human life is more valuable than animal life.

We are real physical creatures, not computer-generated entities in a simulated universe.

People cannot be owned.

Such truths tend to take the form of metaphysical, religious, moral or ideological convictions. We can't prove them, but then the very concept of proof may seem entirely irrelevant for our most strongly held beliefs. Future generations may think our beliefs quaint or ridiculous, as we now consider belief in fairies or the divine right of kings, but for us these truths are often unshakeable.

It doesn't matter for practical purposes whether we actually call such beliefs *truths*, although many do. More than a billion people are members of the Catholic Church, which talks of 'the principal truths of the faith' and 'bearing witness to the truth'. The Archbishop of Kansas City has published a booklet entitled 'Fifty Truths Every Catholic Teen Should Know', covering matters of belief such as original sin, the resurrection and the Eucharist.[5] 'All men are bound to seek the truth, especially in what concerns God and His Church,' stated Pope Paul VI in *Dignitatis Humanae*. 'Thy law is the truth,' declared the author of Psalm 119, addressing God. 'And ye shall know the truth, and the truth shall make you free,' promised Jesus.

*

Belief is not limited to cults and religions. In an earlier chapter, I cast doubt on the scientific proof claimed for the efficacy of certain personal care and beauty products. But perhaps this is to miss the point. 'To advertise a product you must believe in it,' declared Marcel Bleustein-Blanchet, the founder of French advertising giant Publicis. 'To convince you must be convinced yourself.' Belief plays a big part in the marketing and enjoyment of those beauty products whose effects are not immediately obvious. Just as the placebo effect delivers a useful therapeutic dividend for some patients, so believing that your carrot seed oil facial will make you look younger may provide all the product satisfaction and inner glow you need to justify the purchase.

Nuclear deterrence also depends on belief. We are led to believe that the UK's nuclear weapons are active and ready to be fired on the prime minister's command. But not even he or she knows this to be true, whatever assurances the Ministry of Defence may have provided. No one has seen a British nuclear weapon detonate for over a quarter of a century, so we really have no idea if they still can. We believe they work, and more importantly our potential enemies believe they work, but for all we and the prime minister know those warheads might be stuffed with old newspapers. Fundamental military strategy, both in the UK and abroad, is premised on a belief in current British nuclear capability that almost no one can test.

Ideologies are beliefs about the best way to achieve the things we all want – peace, prosperity, security, food, shelter and dignity for ourselves and our fellow citizens. Some people believe that the best way to achieve these things is by letting everyone do their own thing, within a legal framework that protects property rights and enforces contracts. Others believe in a different route to the same goal, envisaging a collective structure which governs most activities and ensures assets are distributed appropriately. Others believe in privileging particular social or religious classes for the good of the whole society.

Capitalism has come closest to winning the ideology battle. Most countries have now embraced its primary elements: private property rights, competitive markets, freedom of choice, and private enterprise. But major doubts still linger, even among the faithful; the devastation caused by the global financial crisis, critical damage to our environment, widespread job losses in disrupted industries and increasing inequality all point to structural flaws in the capitalist model. Remarkably, in 2017 prime minister Theresa May judged it necessary to defend capitalism and free markets in the face of an upsurge of enthusiasm for Marxist alternatives, spearheaded by Labour's Jeremy Corbyn.

Our strongest beliefs form a rigid spine to our mindsets and drive our actions every day. Patriots show their loyalty to their country by flying flags, joining the armed forces and even sacrificing their lives. Our beliefs may push us to do things no other truth can inspire. We have no doubt of their truth and we act accordingly. We may smile at the idea of ancient farmers praying to Demeter for a good harvest, or modern Chinese igniting sheets of joss paper to provide cash for their ancestors, but we are just as yoked to our own beliefs as they are to theirs.

These are truths that shape our world.

Shared beliefs

Beliefs have the power to make individuals act in remarkable ways. And they have another critical function: beliefs unite groups.

It must be lonely to be a communist in Kansas. So if you happen to hold strong Marxist beliefs and you meet a fellow believer in Wichita, you are likely to band together. Your shared truth is not only comforting but is a source of meaning for any human relationship. It suggests your values and desires will be aligned, and your actions will be predictable. Beliefs serve as a kind of social glue, enabling strangers to connect and collaborate in large numbers to achieve extraordinary things. Less happily, beliefs can also aggravate partisan divides, where groups start to define themselves in opposition to other groups' beliefs. Republicans and Democrats in the United States appear to be on an increasingly divergent course, driven apart by ever more staunchly held and uncompromising beliefs.

But it also works the other way round. Should we want to join a particular group, we are likely to adapt our beliefs accordingly. To avoid the ill feeling or cognitive dissonance that may come from holding contrasting beliefs to those around us, we have a potent ability to shift our beliefs to align more closely with our peers. New beliefs that arise in groups can spread fast through the self-reinforcing process known as an 'availability cascade', whereby a particular idea gains plausibility as more and more members of the group express it, whether they believe it or simply want to fit in.

> **Beliefs tactic #1**
> *Encouraging conformity*

This was powerfully demonstrated by members of the People's Temple, many of whom came to the group out of need for support or concern for racial equality but ended up sharing the crazed beliefs propagated by Jim Jones. I once attended the evangelical Christian Alpha course, as a curious atheist, and I was fascinated to watch sensible participants begin to embrace some of Alpha's more unlikely claims – claims which at the start of the course they had easily dismissed – seemingly because they were eager to be part of a larger project that promised love, support and meaning.

A famous psychology experiment places a subject in a group of people that he believes to be subjects like him taking part in a 'vision test' but who are in fact confederates of the experimenter. The group is shown two cards. On one is a single black line. On the other are three black lines of different lengths. The experimenter asks the group to decide which of the three lines is the same length as the line on the first card. There is an obvious right answer, yet inexplicably the rest of the group choose a different line. What will the subject do? Will he state the obviously right answer or go along with the group view?

On average about one third of subjects disregard their own common sense and conform to the group view. When subjected to multiple trials, three quarters of subjects conform at least once. Afterwards, the subjects tend to give different explanations for their choices: some say they didn't really believe their own choice but wanted to fit in; others say they reckoned the group must know better.

If we are so ready to conform even when we can clearly see we are choosing the 'wrong answer', how much easier is it to adapt our beliefs about things we can't see or know for sure? Your extended family all agree that Jesus is the son of God, so on what grounds are you going to dissent? The learned scholars who lead your prayer group assure you that the holy book demands violent action against non-believers, so why would you seek out a different interpretation? Your whole village believes that collective property ownership is the best route to collective happiness, so how are you going to defend your selfish desire to keep all the food you've grown?

We may not instinctively believe something unknowable to be true, but make us live in a convinced group for long enough and their truth will become our truth.

If we show signs of resisting group beliefs, there are ways to overcome our scepticism. In popular culture, this process has come to be known as brainwashing. Neuroscientist Kathleen Taylor has identified the main techniques shared by cults like the People's

Temple, modern extremist groups and the communist ideologues of twentieth-century China and Vietnam.

The subject is isolated, so that the only sources of information and human warmth are believers. Jim Jones took his followers to a remote jungle in Guyana; religious and ideological groups use summer camps, convents, madrassas and gulags to achieve the same detachment. Isolation allows the believers to control the competing truths heard by the subject. They set the context, choose the stories and determine the moral truths. They say what is desirable, they set the definitions and they make the predictions. Through their choice of competing truths, they shape the subject's mindset.

> **Beliefs tactic #2**
> *Isolation and control*

The believers challenge the subject's pre-existing beliefs, casting doubt on loyalties or assurances he has always held dear. They question the cause-and-effect narratives that he has long taken for granted and offer their own alternatives when he starts to waver in his certainty. The believers offer absolute authority and expertise when the subject's comfortable mental picture of reality starts to crumble; they provide a rock to cling to – an apparently simple yet complete belief system ready to adopt.

> **Beliefs tactic #3**
> *Repetition*

The believers will repeat their core messages over and over. Repetition lodges new beliefs deep in the subject's mind. The subject is encouraged or forced to repeat the core messages as well, until their own words take root in their brains. The whole process is steeped in emotion; love and hate, fear and anger are much stronger evangelists than rational argument. To lock the new beliefs in place, the subject must be made to care deeply – and to revile previous beliefs. Watch the video of the Jonestown inhabitants on the night before they killed themselves: you will see the rapture on those doomed faces and hear the thrilled excitement in their voices.

By isolating people, controlling the competing truths they hear, questioning and challenging their previous beliefs, repeating core messages over and over, and manipulating their emotions, the worst kind of ideological and religious Misleaders have gained extraordinary control over the actions of others.

Corporate creed

Following the 2008 financial crisis and various scandals in industry and the media, much effort has been expended to change the cultures of numerous organizations. Millions of dollars have been spent on training courses and consultants to make bankers, pharma executives and journalists behave more ethically. Culture change is also an essential component of many corporate transformation programmes. Companies facing disruption often need to persuade their people to make major behavioural changes, for example being more willing to try new ideas or collaborate with other teams.

Culture change experts have long known that we cannot usually bring about behavioural change simply by asking people to behave differently. Instead, leaders have to understand and shift the beliefs that drive behaviours. Consultants liken organizational culture to an iceberg: isolated behaviours are visible to all, but they rest on the much more substantial 'submerged' shared beliefs of the organization. 'Changing culture thus requires change at the beliefs level,' advises consulting firm Deloitte.[6]

General Electric (GE) used to be notorious for its unforgiving

culture of 'ranking and yanking' employees based on tough performance metrics. Under its legendary boss Jack Welch, GE nurtured
a set of powerful beliefs around using challenge and confrontation
to eliminate mistakes and improve quality. Commenting on the
performance-based ranking of GE employees that many saw as
'cruel', Stanford business psychology professor Bob Sutton said,
'Jack believed in it like a religion.'[7] A decade later, the focus under
a new CEO was on innovation, and consequently imagination,
courage and inclusiveness were valued. Now, GE has different
strategic goals and needs to shift its culture again. To that end, the
company has instituted 'the GE Beliefs':

Customers determine our success
Stay lean to go fast
Learn and adapt to win
Empower and inspire each other
Deliver results in an uncertain world[8]

If a list of generic corporate slogans brings out the sceptic in you,
it's worth knowing that the GE Beliefs were crowd-sourced from
employees. These are the things GE people *want* to believe. But
they are also consistent with the company's strategy.

Not all beliefs are so constructive. Here are some beliefs commonly held in organizations:

My hard work makes no difference in the end.

The management are just in it for themselves.

Customers are idiots and don't know what they want.

Women don't make good engineers.

Such negative, counter-productive or destructive beliefs demoti-
vate employees or lead to behaviours that harm the organization

and diminish its performance. Where leaders identify such beliefs within their organization, they should attempt to change them.

This is easier said than done.

A culture change consultant might first seek to establish the causal link between underlying beliefs and undesirable behaviours. Understanding why such beliefs might have arisen, and the purpose they may have once served, leaders can acknowledge their past truth or value even as they make the case that the beliefs are no longer valid or helpful. Relevant anecdotes that show the damage caused by toxic beliefs may help to dispel them. Influencers – the colleagues people listen to around the water cooler – can be enlisted to propagate new, more constructive beliefs.

Corporate memos, events and initiatives are used to repeat and reinforce the new beliefs. Leaders act as role models, demonstrating in their words and deeds their own commitment to the new beliefs, while disowning the old beliefs. Employees who visibly live by the new beliefs are recognized and rewarded. Recruiters select candidates who share – or are amenable to – the new beliefs.

You might notice a few parallels between this process of corporate culture change and the cultish brainwashing techniques identified by Kathleen Taylor. The critical differences lie in the freedom of corporate employees to abstain or leave, the lack of isolation, and the generally benevolent intentions of business leaders. We could no doubt imagine tyrannical corporate environments where culture change programmes might approach brainwashing, but most that I have witnessed are fairly benign. Nevertheless, fiddling with other people's beliefs is a delicate business that needs to be approached with great care and responsibility.

Interpreters of the faith

No one who has watched the videos of the 9/11 attacks, studied the history of the Crusades or heard reports of faith-based violence in Kashmir, Myanmar or Syria, among many other examples, can be in any doubt as to the power of religious beliefs to influence human behaviour. Less conspicuous but much more widespread are the acts of kindness, charity, forgiveness and stewardship inspired by such beliefs. Faith drives action.

Yet while co-religionists may share some central beliefs, they often differ substantially on the details. They hold competing truths about their shared faith. Christians agree about the virgin birth, the crucifixion and the resurrection but disagree about transubstantiation and the nature of the Trinity. Buddhists agree on the Four Noble Truths concerning suffering but disagree as to the best way to attain Nirvana. Muslims agree that Muhammad was the last of the prophets but disagree about his rightful successor.

That Christianity generates competing beliefs is not surprising, as the Bible offers four alternative versions of Jesus's life, written by different people at different times for different audiences. The gospels are not intended to be objective journalism; they are selective accounts – stories – that deliberately emphasize different events and different moral or ideological tenets, and that sometimes conflict with one another. Jesus claims to be God in the gospel according to John, but not in Matthew, Mark or Luke. Matthew's Sermon on the Mount – which gives us many of the core Christian ideals – is relocated to a 'level place' by Luke and missed entirely by Mark and John. Judas betrays Jesus with a kiss in Mark but not in John; he hangs himself in Matthew, but in Acts (written by Luke) he dies by falling over and bursting open. That is the gospel truth.

But even where there is only one account of events or one moral position advanced in a holy scripture, there is scope for multiple interpretations, particularly with regard to social issues or technologies that did not exist when the scripture was written. Does the Qur'an endorse gender equality? Does the Bible outlaw abortion? These are questions for which the sacred texts do not provide clear, unambiguous answers. Symbolic or allegorical language muddies the scriptural waters still further. Yet deciding which truths to draw from their holy books has a profound influence on the choices and actions of billions.

> **Beliefs tactic #4**
> *Selective interpretation of sacred texts*

While Mohandas Gandhi was studying law in late nineteenth-century London, he was introduced to an English translation of the Bhagavad Gita. He was 19 years old and had never read the Hindu sacred text. The man who would go on to become the spiritual father of independent India was a rebel as a teenager, eating meat, drinking alcohol and chasing women. The Gita – a dialogue between Prince Arjuna and Krishna (an incarnation of the supreme God Vishnu) – was a revelation to him. Some of its verses 'made a deep impression in my mind, and they still ring in my ears,' Gandhi wrote in his autobiography. The Gita helped inspire his campaign of non-violent civil protest. 'Today the Gita is not only my Bible or my Koran,' he said in 1934, 'it is more than that – it is my mother.'[9] He devoted considerable time to translating the work into Gujarati.

'The text from the Bhagavad Gita shows to me how the eternal principle of conquering hate by love, untruth by truth can and must be applied,' he wrote to the independence activist Bal Gangadhar Tilak.[10]

At first glance, this is really rather odd, because the Gita is no pacifist's manifesto. It consists in large part of a compelling argument for war.

The setting of the Gita is a military chariot on a battlefield between two armies. Prince Arjuna, a great warrior, is reluctant to fight in a war of succession that will pit him against his own family and friends. 'Murder most hateful, murder of brothers!' as he puts it. Krishna argues that he must: it is his duty as a soldier, and he is the instrument of Krishna's deadly will.

> Arise! obtain renown! destroy thy foes!
> Fight for the kingdom waiting thee when thou hast vanquished those.
> By Me they fall – not thee! the stroke of death is dealt them now,
> Even as they stand thus gallantly; My instrument art thou!

It's hard to think of a more forceful call to arms. And it works. By the end of the text, Arjuna has picked up his weapons and is ready for a battle that will leave almost everyone dead. Indeed, it was the Gita that Robert Oppenheimer quoted when reflecting on the first detonation of a nuclear weapon in the New Mexico desert: 'Now I am become Death, the destroyer of worlds.'

So how did Gandhi interpret it as a text of truth and love? He viewed the battlefield setting as a metaphor for the internal struggles we all face. Arjuna has to fight – not literally, but figuratively, as must we all. For Gandhi, the fight was a non-violent struggle for an independent India that would embrace all faiths. The central message of the Gita was not one of war but of non-attachment to the fruits of one's actions; while it is perfectly normal to feel happy at a good outcome to one's work, the main thing is to do that work well without fixating on the results. Non-attachment, for Gandhi, led logically to a creed of non-violence.

In fact, Gandhi said of the Mahabharata, the colossal, blood-soaked poem of which the Gita is just one episode, 'I have maintained in the teeth of orthodox Hindu opposition that it is a book written to establish the futility of war and violence.'[11]

Unsurprisingly, others have interpreted the Gita quite differently. Men like Tilak saw the Gita as an exclusively Hindu book that sanctioned violence in the cause of righteous struggle – whether against British colonialists or Muslim neighbours. Among Indian freedom fighters locked up by the British in the early twentieth century, the Gita was the most popular book. One of them was Lala Lajpat Rai, who wrote that the Gita's injunction that a warrior should 'take up arms and risk his life' obliged Indians to risk their lives to fight British rule.[12] Violence, for such men, was endorsed by the Gita so long as those committing violence did not crave the 'fruits of their actions'.

Today, the governing Bharatiya Janata Party and other champions of the fundamentalist Hindutva ideology draw inspiration and legitimacy from the Gita. The chief of the militant Hindu organization Rashtriya Swayamsevak Sangh has recently called for Indians to 'imbibe and practise' the teachings of the Gita, in order to make India a world leader.[13] Prime minister Narendra Modi, the man who as chief minister of Gujarat state in 2002 seemed to stand by while close to a thousand Muslims were murdered, said after presenting a copy of the Gita to his Japanese counterpart, 'I don't think that I have anything more to give and the world also does not have anything more to get than this.'[14]

Jawaharlal Nehru, the first prime minister of India, observed, 'The leaders of thought and action of the present day – Tilak, Aurobindo Ghose, Gandhi – have written on [the Gita], each giving his own interpretation. Gandhi ji bases his firm belief in non-violence on it; others justify violence and warfare for a righteous cause.'[15]

Another man who formed a more violent interpretation of the Gita was Nathuram Godse. He wrote, 'Lord Krishna, in war and otherwise, killed many self-opinionated and influential persons for the betterment of the world, and even in the Gita He has time and again counseled Arjun to kill his near and dear ones and ultimately persuaded him to do so.'[16] On 30 January 1948, Godse took a Beretta semi-automatic pistol to Birla House in Delhi and fired three bullets at close range into the chest and abdomen of one such influential person, Mohandas Gandhi. At his trial, Godse quoted from the Gita, and he took a copy of the book to his execution. His truths were drawn from the same sacred text as those of the man he murdered, but they could not have been more different.

'These traditions do not speak with a single voice,' observed philosopher Kwame Anthony Appiah of the major faiths. 'To have mastery of the scriptures is to know which passages to read *into* and which to read *past*.'[17] He is, of course, describing the tactics of omission and selectivity that we encountered in Part One. As different scriptural masters can choose to read past (omit) different passages, they will inevitably generate competing truths about what their holy book is saying and steer their followers towards different actions. Even if you believe the Bible or the Qur'an is the word of God, there are plenty of opportunities for human intermediaries to shape His message. Indeed, religious leaders are sometimes obliged to find new interpretations to keep their faith relevant as social mores change; modern views on slavery and homosexuality demand new ways of understanding texts like Ephesians and Leviticus.

Judaism seems at times positively to encourage competing truths. When two leading schools of Jewish law disagreed profoundly in the Talmud, a 'divine voice' declared of their conflicting opinions, 'Both these and those are the words of the living God.' Of this passage, Rabbi Marc D. Angel has written:

> In such debates, a ruling must be reached so that people will know what the law requires. Yet, the 'losing' side has not really lost. His opinion is still quoted, still taken seriously. While it did not prevail then, it might prevail at another time or in another context.[18]

Jonathan Sacks, who was for many years the chief rabbi in the UK, also sees a place for different versions of the truth:

> Truth on earth is not, nor can be, the whole truth. It is limited, not comprehensive; particular, not universal. When two propositions conflict it is not necessarily because one is true the other false. It may be, and often is, that each represents a different perspective on reality . . . In heaven there is truth; on earth there are truths.[19]

Amen to that.

God only knows

The one thing we can all agree on, it is commonly observed, is that most other people are wrong about religion. Perhaps everyone is wrong. Certainly, not everyone can be right. Many of these beliefs must be false. But until we can prove them false, they remain compelling truths for the faithful.

'Every man seeks for truth; but God only knows who has found it,' wrote Lord Chesterfield to his son in 1747, in an attempt to temper the boy's scorn for 'the credulity and superstition of the Papists'.

We can respect some rival beliefs as competing truths. That doesn't mean we have to embrace them. We are within our rights to try to persuade others to change their beliefs by presenting them with moral or rational arguments, or even by making emotional appeals. In societies torn apart by conflicting beliefs, or organizations contaminated by destructive beliefs, we absolutely should try. So long as we stop short of attempting to brainwash those in our employ or subject to our influence, evangelism in service of the right goals can be a valuable endeavour.

In practice

• If you want to change the negative behaviours of those around you, identify and challenge the beliefs that underpin those behaviours.

• Strengthen groups and organizations by establishing and celebrating positive shared beliefs.

But watch out for . . .

• Brainwashers isolating people and controlling the competing truths they hear.

• Groups that try to shape beliefs through pressure to conform.

• Misleaders trying to convince you of a dangerous or extreme interpretation of a sacred text.

EPILOGUE
Final Truths

> No one could call him a liar. And this was mainly because the
> lie was in his head, and any truth coming from his mouth carried
> the color of the lie.
>
> JOHN STEINBECK, *East of Eden*

In this guide to truth, I have said very little about why truth
matters. If you don't already prefer truth to the alternative, I doubt
you'll have bothered to read this far. Instead, what I have sought
to emphasize throughout is the importance of selecting, communicating and embracing the *right* truth.

We've explored an alarming number of ways in which politicians, marketers, journalists, campaigners and even government
bureaucrats can mislead us with the truth. It is up to us to catch
them at it, call them out and resist dancing to their tune. Misleading truths are not always obvious; they can be found in advertising
copy, your Twitter feed, newspaper editorials, gossip, office memos
and charity leaflets. Some are deliberately designed to be all but
invisible. 'We are governed, our minds molded, our tastes formed,
our ideas suggested, largely by men we have never heard of,' wrote
Edward Bernays, one of the pioneers of public relations, in 1928.

Misleading truths are all around us. The checklist in Appendix 1 may help you spot them.

Misleaders depend on unquestioning acceptance. Once they are challenged, it is very hard to keep misleading while remaining truthful. So challenge them where you can. Demand clarification and confirmation. Leave no wiggle room. If you suspect something has been omitted, ask about it. If numbers have been presented in a misleading way, posit alternative interpretations. Query the relevance of emotive stories and names. Ask what moral or belief assumptions an argument is based upon. Demand a formal definition of terms.

'I wasn't lying,' insisted Rob Ford, the late crack-smoking mayor of Toronto, to a room of reporters. 'You didn't ask the correct questions.'[1]

We try to hold leaders and commentators to account for their lies. We are less good at holding Misleaders to account when their statements are technically true. If they are able to argue that they have only spoken truth, we tend to let it go, despite a nagging sense that justice has not been done. This allows Misleaders to keep pulling the same tricks. We shouldn't let them.

One of our difficulties is a lack of shared terminology to denounce Misleaders. If a politician claims wages have gone up, and can point to a clever statistical interpretation of the facts to give herself cover, we can't call her a liar. So what do we say?

My suggestion for social media is **#misleadingtruth**. Let's call out **misleading truths** wherever we see them. Let's label the people who use them **Misleaders**.

You can also refer misleading truths to the most relevant fact-checking organization (see Appendix 2). Fact-checkers alone will not solve our post-truth woes; the misleading claims of popular politicians and celebrities have far greater reach than the counter-claims of the fact-checkers. Nevertheless, these organizations provide a useful foundation of relatively objective fact on which we can anchor our efforts to correct the public record and reinforce a more accurate representation of reality.

With increasingly sophisticated personalized mass-communications techniques, it is now possible for political campaigns, companies, activists and even foreign disinformation operatives to target particular groups with tailored messages that are invisible to the media and fact-checkers. Selective truths are delivered via email, Facebook messages or online advertisements that the rest of the population never sees. This substantially reduces the risk to Misleaders of being found out and publicly shamed, increasing the likelihood that they will indulge in such behaviour. If you receive a targeted message containing a misleading truth, call it out. Otherwise, we may never know about it, and the Misleaders will grow ever bolder.

Ultimately, misleading truths are best combated with more representative and complete truths. We have to take responsibility for understanding issues more fully and drawing on the most reliable data we can find to judge which are the most honest and relevant truths. This is hard work. It takes effort to go beyond our instinctive reaction to an event or to test the first claims made about a breaking story. It takes discipline to avoid confirmation bias and maintain an open mind. But in a fragmented, biased media landscape, it is the only way we can discover and propagate the most honest truths.

Our truths need to be well researched and fact-checked before we put them up in opposition to misleading truths. They need to be clearly stated and supported with evidence. And they need to be concise and pithy to cut through the noise and stand a chance of being widely shared. The more of us that share these 'truer' truths, the more likely they are to take root.

Let's finish by putting the Misleaders to one side and remembering the positive aspects of competing truths. We have achieved staggering things by working together. Eliminating diseases, feeding billions, building global companies, defending nations, developing miraculous technologies, connecting the world: all of this has been done by humans cooperating, and that cooperation is built on the ideas we share – the truths we tell each other.

The people who engineered these great achievements did so by choosing their truths carefully and then sharing them effectively. They used inspiring predictions and beliefs, persuasive opinions of what was desirable, tailored versions of history, compelling stories, dire assessments of threats, and bold visions of new social constructs, to build a following and drive action. Communicators make everything happen.

Choosing the right competing truths to share has always been a fundamental requirement of good leadership and transformational advocacy, but it's also important if we are to achieve the most basic cooperation in our families and workplaces. Your chosen truth should be honest, of course, but it also needs to be effective.

Some truths are just more instantly believable than others. They *ring true*. Even if you think you can prove your truth with data and logic, will you get the chance? In the Brexit referendum, those campaigning to leave the EU often seemed to have a better instinct for choosing truths that made sense on first hearing than those arguing to remain. The most persuasive competing truths are those that appear self-evidently true.

The format of your truth matters if you want people to hear it. Use simple messaging, surprising insight, eye-catching numbers, compelling stories and colourful visions to make an impression. 'American women earn just 74 cents for every $1 a man earns' beats any number of speeches about discrimination in the workplace. Minimalist messages make memorable memes (especially with some alliteration). Try to present your message in a format that can be grasped in a glance.

By definition, there will be alternatives to your competing truth, and you may face opposition founded on rival truths. Even if you have the power to silence valid truths, as head teacher or CEO perhaps, this is rarely the smartest strategy. A more respectful and engaging approach is to provide a structured forum in which rival truths can be voiced and publicly answered. Take time to demonstrate you have understood the alternative point of view before putting your counter-arguments. Your competing truth should win on its merits.

Messages often don't fully sink in on first encounter; they need to be heard or read multiple times to shift opinions and establish new mindsets. Repetition is also a good way of countering rival truths, which are more likely to take root in a communications vacuum. But the problem with repetition, outside of cults, is that it can feel like nagging. Or, as happened during the 2017 UK election with Theresa May's recurring promise to provide 'strong and stable' government, it can turn people off or become the subject of ridicule. To avoid this outcome, communicators need to find new and interesting ways to say the same thing.

We can think of communications like a composer might approach a 'theme and variations'. The composer begins with a short musical idea – the theme: a melody that is rarely more than a couple of minutes long. He then plays with that melody, adding or removing notes, varying the rhythm, moving to a different key or time signature, introducing ornamentation, changing the tempo or the instrumentation. Each variation takes on a different character and may sound completely different to the original melody, but the underlying theme is always there. Organizations can take the same approach: agree the core truth – the theme – but then allow people to express it in their own way, as interesting variations that keep the theme in everyone's minds.

You can see this whole book as variations on a theme:

There is usually more than one true way to talk about something. We can use competing truths constructively to

engage people and inspire action, but we should also watch
out for communicators who use competing truths to mis-
lead us.

That's my theme. I hope you've enjoyed all the variations.

In the coming years, competing truths are going to proliferate. Complexity is growing with every new connection between people and organizations, subjective truths are multiplying as the retreat of authoritarianism allows more individuality and self-expression, new artificial truths are being created every second, and unknown truths will only increase as we look further into the future or wrestle with ever more abstract concepts.

We should not be afraid of competing truths. Our progress depends on the interplay of truths. Science, politics and the arts thrive when we allow a dialectic between different truths. We should welcome competing truths as the raw materials of new thinking, of creativity, of innovation. In fact, we should be wary of anyone who tries to assert the one 'true' truth and deny all others. Who needs conversation, judgement or debate when there is one truth and everything else is heresy?

Our recognition that multiple truths can coexist should not make us overly suspicious of others' words. There has been a general decline in trust, and it has contributed to the post-truth malaise. We need to watch out for misleading truths, but we shouldn't doubt the motives of everyone who picks their truths carefully. As I have tried to illustrate throughout this book, competing truths are widely used for good as well as ill. I have included hundreds of my own competing truths in the preceding chapters: some are obvious, others more subtle; none are intended to mislead readers or cause harm. I would hope you can trust most of what I've written, even though I admit to having selected my truths carefully in order to offer you a particular impression of reality.

The democratization of information brings responsibilities as well as power. In the past, authorities like the Church or totalitarian governments decided what was true. More enlightened times saw trusted media take on that role. But there is so much more information out there now, coming at us from so many more sources. We can no longer rely on organizations like the *New York Times* and the BBC to curate the world's information for us and tell us which truth is more relevant and which is misleading. There are no gatekeepers any more. We have to do it for ourselves and help those around us do it too. We need to be more aware of how the truths we hear shape our mindsets and can entrench partisan divides. To escape our echo chambers and filter bubbles, we should seek out competing truths that challenge our mindsets and our tribe's beliefs.

It has never been more important for each of us to recognize a competing truth when we see it. Conversely, there has never been more opportunity to make a positive difference with the right competing truth. The tools, the knowledge, the communications channels and the audiences are all there. We just need to choose our truths wisely and tell them well.

ACKNOWLEDGEMENTS

I am a storyteller and a collector of insightful ideas, but I do very little primary research, so I am indebted to all of the journalists, scientists, historians, researchers and writers who put in the hard work of documenting the countless facts referenced in this book. Reflecting my media preferences, a substantial number of the stories in *Truth* began life with BBC Radio 4 (especially *More or Less*), the *Guardian*, *The Economist*, the *New York Times* and the *Washington Post*. Thank you to all the programme-makers, journalists and editors who made the truths I have drawn on so accurate and accessible.

The idea for this book originated in the strategic communications work I have done over the past ten years, and all of that started with The Storytellers. My thanks to Marcus Hayes, Martin Clarkson, Alison Esse and Chris Spencer for showing me that a company's past, present and future can be usefully (if selectively) represented in thirty sentences, and for giving me the opportunity to create narratives for some of the most interesting organizations on the planet. Thank you also to Atkins, Ericsson, Royal Botanic Gardens, Kew, and the Bank of England for allowing me to write about them.

Good friends read early drafts and gave great advice: Dani Byrne, Becky Carter, Martin Clarkson, Imogen Cleaver, Paul Cleaver, Mel Cochran, Rosemary Macdonald, Malcolm Millar,

Bruno Shovelton, Laura Watkins and Andrew Wilson. I am also grateful to Marc Bellemare and Karsten Haustein for their expert advice on quinoa economics and climate change respectively. Any remaining errors or misleading truths are mine.

A lot of people have been, and will be, involved in publishing *Truth*. My thanks to all of them, and in particular to Tracy Behar, Doug Pepper and Doug Young for jointly editing the text with such wisdom, grace and unity. Finally, to Euan Thorneycroft, Richard Pine, Hélène Ferey, Jennifer Custer and everyone at A. M. Heath, thank you for getting me back in the game.

APPENDIX 1
Misleading Truths Checklist

These questions are intended to help us assess a suspicious state-ment and decide whether or not it is a non-trivial misleading truth. It's not a tick-box exercise. We need to use our own judgement and do appropriate research to come to a conclusion.

- Is the statement true?
- Will it change the way I see things?
- Might it affect my behaviour?
- What agenda does the communicator have, and will this statement help them advance it?
- What facts or context might they have left out?
- Have they provided evidence to back up their statement? Is it reliable?
- How else might a particular fact or figure be represented? Would this change its meaning?
- Does the statement depend on a subjective judgement of morality, desirability or financial value?
- Is the communicator defining their terms the same way I would?
- Am I being influenced by their choice of name or an emotive anecdote?

- Does the statement depend on a prediction or belief, and if so are alternative predictions or beliefs more credible?
- Would someone else be able to convey a different but equally truthful impression of reality?

APPENDIX 2
Fact-checking Organizations

Numerous organizations around the world are working to counter the post-truth flood of lies in public discourse with studious fact-checking, and some of them take on misleading truths as well. You may wish to support them or contact them with suggestions of misleading truths to investigate and publicize:

- **PolitiFact** rates US political claims on their Truth-O-Meter, with assessments ranging from 'True' to 'Pants on Fire' for the most ridiculous falsehoods. It was awarded the Pulitzer Prize for its coverage of the 2008 US presidential election. Its 'Half True' and 'Mostly False' ratings would apply to many misleading truths. It pays particular attention to context and wording. http://politifact.com/
- The *Washington Post* **Fact Checker** aims to 'truth squad' the statements of political figures, provide missing context and define 'code words' used by Misleaders to 'obscure or shade the truth'. It awards 'Pinocchios' to misleading or false statements; misleading truths earn between one Pinocchio ('Selective telling of the truth. Some omissions and exaggerations') and three Pinocchios ('Could include statements which are technically correct . . . but are so taken out of context as to be very misleading'). https://washingtonpost.com/news/fact-checker/

- **FactCheck.org** is run by the Annenberg Public Policy Center of the University of Pennsylvania. It monitors the factual accuracy of US political discourse, with a focus on presidential and Senate races. http://factcheck.org/
- **Full Fact** is a UK charity that seeks to correct misleading or unsubstantiated claims on mostly UK political issues. It provides educational tools and a directory of reliable UK data. https://fullfact.org/
- **First Draft** is a coalition of organizations, including Google News Lab, that aims to improve standards of reporting of information and eyewitness content sourced from the Internet and social media. It has now built a partner network that includes CNN, the BBC, BuzzFeed, Bloomberg and numerous other media organizations, academic institutions and NGOs. https://firstdraftnews.com/
- The **International Fact-Checking Network** (IFCN), hosted by the Poynter Institute for Media Studies, provides support and resources for fact-checking organizations around the world. https://poynter.org/channels/fact-checking
- **Snopes.com** is primarily dedicated to busting urban legends, some of which are founded on misleading truths. http://snopes.com/
- The BBC provides an online service, **Reality Check** (http://bbc.co.uk/realitycheck), that examines issues of primarily British political interest and provides objective data and insight. *More or Less* is a long-running BBC Radio 4 programme that analyses the numbers in the news with wit and rigour. The *More or Less* team particularly enjoy slaying 'zombie statistics' and calling out misleading numbers. http://bbc.co.uk/programmes/b006qshd
- **Les décodeurs** is the fact-checking unit of *Le Monde* in France. Its mission is to verify declarations, statements and rumours, and put information in context. *Le Monde* has

developed browser extensions that identify dodgy online stories. http://lemonde.fr/les-decodeurs/

- **Fact Check** is a partnership between Australia's RMIT University and the ABC, which aims to cut through 'the mud of fake news, self-serving spin, misinformation and good old-fashioned fearmongering'. It has advisory panels of experts on climate change, the law and the economy. http://abc.net.au/news/factcheck/

- **CORRECT!V** is a German non-profit carrying out investigative journalism into controversial topics like TTIP and Flight MH17. It has also set up an education programme to provide the tools of investigative journalism to the public. https://correctiv.org/en/

- **Africa Check** is a non-profit based in Johannesburg that tests claims made by public figures across Africa. It also has a French-language site run by a team in Dakar. https://africacheck.org/

- **Chequeado** is Argentina's top fact-checking organization. It has conducted live fact-checking during presidential debates and now has a cable TV show, *50 Minutos*. http://chequeado.com/

This is by no means an exhaustive list. In 2017, the Duke Reporters' Lab identified 114 dedicated fact-checking teams in 47 countries. Look for the organizations most relevant to you online.

REFERENCES

To minimize distracting superscript numbers, only direct quotes and critical/controversial facts are referenced in the text. Other sources are listed below.

The main hyperlinks can also be found at: www.hectormacdonald.com/truth

Introduction: When Truths Collide

Quinoa

http://www.independent.co.uk/life-style/health-and-families/ancient-inca-grain-is-new-health-food-darling-2227055.html

https://www.economist.com/news/finance-and-economics/21699087-fad-andean-staple-has-not-hurt-pooryet-against-grain

The Philosophy of Truth

For example:

John D. Caputo, *Truth: The Search for Wisdom in the Postmodern Age* (London, Penguin Books, 2013).

Blackburn, Simon, *Truth: A Guide* (Oxford, OUP, 2005).

Post-Truth

For example:

Evan Davis, *Post-Truth: Why We Have Reached Peak Bullshit and What We Can Do About It* (London, Little, Brown, 2017).

Matthew D'Ancona, *Post-Truth: The New War on Truth and How to Fight Back* (London, Ebury, 2017).

James Ball, *Post-Truth: How Bullshit Conquered the World* (London, Biteback, 2017).

Ari Rabin-Havt and Media Matters, *Lies, Incorporated: The World of Post-Truth Politics* (New York, Anchor, 2016).

1: Complexity
Amazon
https://www.nytimes.com/2014/11/14/technology/amazon-hachette-ebook-dispute.html

http://authorsunited.net/

Brad Stone, *The Everything Store: Jeff Bezos and the Age of Amazon* (New York, Little, Brown, 2013).

https://www.forbes.com/sites/roberthof/2016/03/22/ten-years-later-amazon-web-services-defies-skeptics/#76f0fd656c44

https://www.srgresearch.com/articles/leading-cloud-providers-continue-run-away-market

Bell Pottinger
https://www.theguardian.com/media/2017/sep/05/bell-pottingersouth-africa-pr-firm

https://citizen.co.za/news/south-africa/1564335/this-is-how-guptas-were-allowed-to-landed-at-waterkloof-airport-report/

https://www.ft.com/content/ce8ddb84-9a01-11e7-a652-cde3f882dd7b

https://www.nytimes.com/2016/03/18/world/africa/south-africa-jacob-zuma-gupta-family.html

https://www.theguardian.com/media/2017/sep/12/bell-pottinger-goes-into-administration

2: History
Coca-Cola
Mark Pendergrast, *For God, Country, and Coca-Cola: The Definitive History of the Great American Soft Drink and the Company That Makes It* (New York, Scribner, 1993).

http://www.snopes.com/cokelore/fanta.asp

Peter Barton Hutt, 'The Image and Politics of Coca-Cola: From the Early Years to the Present' (Harvard Law School, 2001); https://dash.harvard.edu/handle/1/8852150

Murray J. Eldred, *The Emperors of Coca Cola* (2008).

Oubliance

Mark Greengrass, *France in the Age of Henri IV* (Oxon, Routledge, 1995).

Diane Claire Margolf, *Religion and Royal Justice in Early Modern France: The Paris Chambre de l'edit, 1598–1665* (Kirksville, MO, Truman State University Press, 2003).

Bush, PEPFAR and the Environment

https://www.cgdev.org/page/overview-president%E2%80%99s-emergency-plan-aids-relief-pepfar

http://www.telegraph.co.uk/news/worldnews/northamerica/usa/4242376/George-W-Bushs-10-Best-Moments.html

https://www.epa.gov/nepa/what-national-environmental-policy-act

De Gaulle

Timothy Garton Ash, *Free World: Why a Crisis of the West Reveals an Opportunity of Our Times* (London, Allen Lane, 2004).

Denis MacShane, *Heath* (London, Haus, 2006).

Ericsson

https://www.rcrwireless.com/20160727/internet-of-things/ericsson-maersk-industrial-internet-of-things-tag31-tag99

https://www.ericsson.com/en/networked-society/innovation/innovations-with-impact

https://www.ericsson.com/en/about-us/history

Alena V. Ledeneva, *Can Russia Modernise?: Sistema, Power Networks and Informal Governance* (Cambridge, Cambridge University Press, 2013).

China

http://www.bbc.co.uk/news/magazine-30810596

http://www.economist.com/node/21534758

3: Context

Elmyr de Hory

Clifford Irving, *Fake: The Story of Elmyr de Hory* (New York, McGraw-Hill, 1969).

Stephen Armstrong, *The White Island: The Extraordinary History of the Mediterranean's Capital of Hedonism* (London, Black Swan, 2005).

http://www.nytimes.com/2011/04/08/arts/design/elmyr-de-horys-real-identity-its-becoming-less-of-a-mystery.html

http://www.intenttodeceive.org/forger-profiles/elmyr-de-hory/the-artifice-of-elmyr-de-hory/

http://forejustice.org/write/fake.html

Ulrich Kirk, Martin Skov, Oliver Hulme, Mark S. Christensen and Semir Zeki, 'Modulation of aesthetic value by semantic context: An fMRI study', *NeuroImage*, 44 (2009).

http://www.sfgate.com/entertainment/article/Master-Con-Artist-Painting-forger-Elmyr-de-2917456.php

Cultured Meat

https://www.economist.com/news/business/21716076-plant-based-meat-products-have-made-it-menus-and-supermarket-shelves-market

http://www.fao.org/docrep/ARTICLE/WFC/XII/0568-B1.HTM

http://www.theecologist.org/News/news_analysis/1122016/revealed_the_secret_horror_of_the_worlds_mega_factory_farms.html

http://www.sierraclub.org/michigan/why-are-cafos-bad

http://www.bbc.co.uk/news/science-environment-34540193

4: Numbers

Arctic National Wildlife Refuge

http://www.nytimes.com/2001/05/01/us/cheney-promotes-increasing-supply-as-energy-policy.html

http://www.nytimes.com/2002/03/01/opinion/two-thousand-acres.html

http://www.nytimes.com/2005/12/22/politics/senate-rejects-bid-for-drilling-in-arctic-area.html

Irish GDP

https://www.irishtimes.com/business/economy/ireland-s-gdp-figures-why-26-economic-growth-is-a-problem-1.2722170

http://www.independent.co.uk/news/business/news/ireland-s-economy-grows-263-in-2015-as-corporations-flock-to-low-tax-rate-a7133321.html

https://www.irishtimes.com/business/economy/state-s-debt-ratio-falling-at-fastest-rate-in-the-euro-zone-1.2584911

5: Story

Hurricane Katrina

http://www.politico.com/story/2012/10/10-facts-about-the-katrina-response-081957

http://usatoday30.usatoday.com/news/nation/2005-09-07-firefighters-ga-katrina_x.htm

http://www.nytimes.com/2005/09/28/us/nationalspecial/when-storm-hit-national-guard-was-deluged-too.html

http://news.bbc.co.uk/1/hi/world/americas/4707536.stm

http://www.washingtonpost.com/wp-dyn/content/article/2005/09/15/AR2005091502297.html

http://www.nbcnews.com/id/9323298/#.V5s2QZMrLBI

Nike

https://www.fastcompany.com/38979/nike-story-just-tell-it

6: Morality
Dissoi Logoi

Quotations are from the translation by Rosamond Kent Sprague, published in *Mind: A Quarterly Review*, Vol. LXXVII, 306 (1968). A copy can be found at http://myweb.fsu.edu/jjm09f/RhetoricSpring2012/Dissoilogoi.pdf

Moral Foundations

Jonathan Haidt, *The Righteous Mind: Why Good People are Divided by Politics and Religion* (New York, Pantheon, 2012).

https://blogs.scientificamerican.com/guest-blog/jonathan-haidt-the-moral-matrix-breaking-out-of-our-righteous-minds/

Drugs

Tom Feiling, *Cocaine Nation: How the White Trade Took Over the World* (New York, Pegasus, 2010).

Organ Donation

http://www.bbc.co.uk/programmes/b08nq6fh

Public Health

https://medicalxpress.com/news/2011-06-doctors-health-dilemmas.html

Joshua Greene, *Moral Tribes: Emotion, Reason and the Gaps Between Us and Them* (New York, Penguin Press, 2013).

Business Morality

http://news.bbc.co.uk/1/hi/business/7528463.stm

http://www.bbc.co.uk/news/business-39194395

http://www.bbc.co.uk/news/business-38644114

http://money.cnn.com/2017/08/31/investing/wells-fargo-fake-accounts/index.html

https://www.bloomberg.com/news/articles/2017-10-13/kobe-steel-scam-hits-planes-trains-automobiles-quicktake-q-a-j8pto39q

Los Angeles LGBT Center

http://science.sciencemag.org/content/352/6282/220

http://www.sciencemag.org/news/2016/04/real-time-talking-people-about-gay-and-transgender-issues-can-change-their-prejudices

Aristotle

Nicomachean Ethics Book II (350 BCE), quotation from translation by W. D. Ross http://classics.mit.edu/Aristotle/nicomachean.2.ii.html

7: Desirability

Obesity

http://www.who.int/mediacentre/factsheets/fs311/en/

https://www.mckinsey.com/mgi/overview/in-the-news/the-obesity-crisis

Wine study: http://www.caltech.edu/news/wine-study-shows-price-influences-perception-1374

Stanford Food Names Experiment: Bradley P. Turnwald, Danielle Z. Boles and Alia J. Crum, 'Association Between Indulgent Descriptions and Vegetable Consumption: Twisted Carrots and Dynamite Beets', *JAMA Internal Medicine*, 177 (8) (August 2017).

Immigrants

http://www.independent.co.uk/news/people/katie-hopkins-and-the-sun-editor-reported-to-police-for-incitement-to-racial-hatred-following-10190549.html

TÁRKI Social Research Institute study on Hungarian attitudes: http://www.tarki.hu/hu/news/2016/kitekint/20160330_refugees.pdf

http://www.bbc.co.uk/news/world-europe-34131911

http://www.dailymail.co.uk/wires/ap/article-3397194/The-Latest-Rights-monitor-Hungary-asylum-seekers-risk.html

http://www.bbc.co.uk/news/world-europe-37310819

8: Financial Value

Penicillin Mould

http://www.bonhams.com/auctions/23259/lot/1057/

https://www.theguardian.com/education/2017/mar/01/penicillin-mould-created-alexander-fleming-sells-over-14000-bonhams

Rarity Valuations

https://www.nytimes.com/2016/06/09/theater/hamilton-raises-ticket-prices-the-best-seats-will-now-cost-849.html

http://news.bbc.co.uk/1/hi/entertainment/4623280.stm

https://www.theguardian.com/film/2011/jun/19/marilyn-monroe-dress-debbie-reynolds

http://abcnews.go.com/Business/hostess-twinkies-sell-60-box-ebay/story?id=17739110

Diamonds

Edward Jay Epstein wrote the definitive article on diamond marketing for *The Atlantic* in 1982: https://www.theatlantic.com/magazine/archive/1982/02/have-you-ever-tried-to-sell-a-diamond/304575/

http://www.capetowndiamondmuseum.org/about-diamonds/south-african-diamond-history/

http://www.nytimes.com/2013/05/05/fashion/weddings/how-americans-learned-to-love-diamonds.html

https://www.washingtonpost.com/opinions/why-a-diamond-is-forever-has-lasted-so-long/2014/02/07/f6adf3f4-8eae-11e3-84e1-27626c5ef5fb_story.html

http://www.debeersgroup.com/content/dam/de-beers/corporate/documents/Reports/Insight/FlashData/Diamond%20Insight%20Flash%20Data%20April%202016.pdf/_jcr_content/renditions/original

https://www.theatlantic.com/international/archive/2015/02/how-an-ad-campaign-invented-the-diamond-engagement-ring/385376/

Pricing

William Poundstone, *Priceless: The Hidden Psychology of Value* (Oxford, Oneworld, 2010).

Robert H. Frank, *The Economic Naturalist* (London, Virgin Books, 2007).

Tim Harford, *The Undercover Economist* (London, Little, Brown, 2006).

Gig Economy

http://www.bbc.co.uk/news/business-11600902

http://theweek.com/articles/631927/inside-japans-booming-rentafriend-industry

http://www.huffingtonpost.com.au/2016/07/04/meet-the-1m-man-who-s-making-a-killing-from-freelancing_a_21423270/

9: Definitions

My dictionary, from which various definitions are drawn, is the *Concise Oxford English Dictionary.*

Famine

http://www.un.org/apps/news/story.asp?NewsID=39113#.WdofsROPJAa

https://www.theguardian.com/global-development/2017/feb/20/famine-declared-in-south-sudan

https://www.dec.org.uk/press-release/dec-east-africa-crisis-appeal-reaches-a-staggering-%C2%A350-million-in-just-3-weeks

http://www.npr.org/sections/parallels/2014/08/27/343758300/when-do-food-shortages-become-a-famine-theres-a-formula-for-that

Rwanda

https://www.theguardian.com/world/2004/mar/31/usa.rwanda

http://www.bbc.co.uk/news/world-11108059

https://www.theatlantic.com/magazine/archive/2001/09/bystanders-to-genocide/304571/

https://treaties.un.org/doc/publication/unts/volume%2078/volume-78-i-1021-english.pdf

https://www.cnbc.com/id/100546207

Monica Lewinsky

http://www.washingtonpost.com/wp-srv/politics/special/clinton/icreport/6narritiii.htm

http://www.washingtonpost.com/wp-srv/politics/special/clinton/icreport/7groundsi.htm

Gender

http://www.npr.org/2016/06/17/482480188/neither-male-nor-female-oregon-resident-legally-recognized-as-third-gender

https://www.americandialect.org/2015-word-of-the-year-is-singular-they

https://www.theguardian.com/society/2015/aug/18/bisexual-british-adults-define-gay-straight-heterosexual

10: Social Constructs
Ceuta and Melilla
http://www.independent.co.uk/news/world/europe/refugee-crisis-migrants-ceuta-fence-climb-hundreds-mass-spain-mediterranean-record-deaths-a7586436.html

http://www.aljazeera.com/indepth/inpictures/2016/01/earning-living-border-morocco-spanish-enclave-160128090148249.html

https://www.pri.org/stories/2015-05-14/along-morocco-s-border-spanish-enclave-these-women-shoulder-twice-their-weight

Human Rights
https://www.libertarianism.org/publications/essays/excursions/jeremy-benthams-attack-natural-rights

https://www.history.org/Almanack/life/politics/varights.cfm

https://www.archives.gov/founding-docs/declaration-transcript

http://www.conseil-constitutionnel.fr/conseil-constitutionnel/english/constitution/declaration-of-human-and-civic-rights-of-26-august-1789.105305.html

http://www.un.org/en/universal-declaration-human-rights/index.html

http://www.dailymail.co.uk/news/article-3201918/One-three-cases-lost-Britain-European-Court-Human-Rights-brought-terrorists-prisoners-criminals.html

China's Social Credit System
https://www.economist.com/news/briefing/21711902-worrying-implications-its-social-credit-project-china-invents-digital-totalitarian

http://www.independent.co.uk/news/world/asia/china-surveillance-big-data-score-censorship-a7375221.html

http://www.bbc.co.uk/news/world-asia-china-34592186

11: Names
Megan's Law
http://www.nydailynews.com/news/crime/parents-girl-inspired-megan-law-recall-tragedy-article-1.1881551

https://usatoday30.usatoday.com/news/nation/2007-11-18-homeless-offenders_N.htm

http://www.cjcj.org/uploads/cjcj/documents/attitudes_towards.pdf

https://www.congress.gov/bill/104th-congress/house-bill/2137/actions

Dementia Tax

https://www.theguardian.com/commentisfree/2008/jul/13/mentalhealth.health

http://www.telegraph.co.uk/news/2017/05/26/conservative-poll-lead-cut-half-dementia-tax-u-turn/

Snowflake

https://www.collinsdictionary.com/word-lovers-blog/new/top-10-collins-words-of-the-year-2016,323,HCB.html

https://www.ft.com/content/65708d48-c394-11e6-9bca-2b93a6856354

Changing Names

http://www.telegraph.co.uk/finance/4469961/The-muck-stops-here.html

https://www.ft.com/content/b7bb4a8a-a8d2-11e5-955c-1e1d6de94879

http://www.dailymail.co.uk/news/article-2525775/Mugabe-orders-Victoria-Falls-renamed-smoke-thunders-rid-colonial-history.html

http://www.ntlis.nt.gov.au/placenames/view.jsp?id=10532

https://www.theguardian.com/politics/blog/2010/jun/14/obama-britain-bp-michael-white

Chilean Sea Bass

G. Bruce Knecht, *Hooked: Pirates, Poaching, and the Perfect Fish* (Emmaus, PA, Rodale, 2006).

Ralph Keyes, *Unmentionables* (London, John Murray, 2010).

https://www.wsj.com/news/articles/SB114670694136643399

http://news.nationalgeographic.com/news/2002/05/0522_020522_seabass.html

http://www.washingtonpost.com/wp-dyn/content/article/2009/07/30/AR2009073002478.html

http://www.independent.co.uk/life-style/food-and-drink/news/when-is-a-pilchard-not-a-pilchard-when-its-a-sardine-sales-of-the-once-neglected-fish-are-booming-9833601.html

http://usa.chinadaily.com.cn/epaper/2014-10/13/content_18730596.htm

https://cantbeatemeatem.com/2904-2/

http://news.bbc.co.uk/1/hi/world/middle_east/4724656.stm

http://www.twincities.com/2014/04/27/asian-carp-gets-a-name-change-in-minnesota-senate/

Frank Luntz

https://www.theatlantic.com/politics/archive/2014/01/the-agony-of-frank-luntz/282766/

https://www.irs.gov/businesses/small-businesses-self-employed/estate-tax

http://prospect.org/article/meet-mr-death

12: Predictions

Pre-emptive War

Priscilla Roberts (ed.), *Arab-Israeli Conflict: The Essential Reference Guide* (Santa Barbara, CA, ABC-CLIO, 2014).

http://news.bbc.co.uk/1/shared/spl/hi/guides/457000/457035/html/nn1page1.stm

Jean Lartéguy, *The Walls of Israel* (Lanham, MD, Rowman & Littlefield, 2014).

https://history.state.gov/milestones/1961-1968/arab-israeli-war-1967

https://www.foreignpolicyjournal.com/2010/07/04/israels-attack-on-egypt-in-june-67-was-not-preemptive/

http://www.washingtoninstitute.org/policy-analysis/view/the-six-day-war-and-its-enduring-legacy

Global Warming

The 2017 Climate Science Special Report is available at https://assets.documentcloud.org/documents/3914641/Draft-of-the-Climate-Science-Special-Report.pdf

http://e360.yale.edu/features/investigating-the-enigma-of-clouds-and-climate-change

https://www.ipcc.ch/publications_and_data/ar4/wg1/en/ch8s8-6-3-2.html

https://www.ipcc.ch/pdf/assessment-report/ar5/wg1/WG1AR5_Chapter07_FINAL.pdf

http://edition.cnn.com/2017/09/15/us/climate-change-hurricanes-harvey-and-irma/index.html

https://www.nytimes.com/2017/08/07/climate/climate-change-drastic-warming-trump.html

https://www.nytimes.com/2017/09/24/us/puerto-rico-hurricane-maria-agriculture-.html

13: Beliefs

Jim Jones

Larry D. Barnett, 'Anti-Miscegenation Laws', *The Family Life Coordinator*, 13 (4) (October 1964).

http://www.in.gov/library/2848.htm

http://www.nytimes.com/1992/01/05/books/how-the-klan-captured-indiana.html

Valrie Plaza, *American Mass Murderers* (Lulu, 2015).

http://indianapublicmedia.org/momentofindianahistory/jim-jones/

http://www.indystar.com/story/news/history/retroindy/2013/11/18/peoples-temple/3634925/

http://content.time.com/time/arts/article/0,8599,1859903,00.html

http://www.latimes.com/world/africa/la-me-jonestownarchive19-2003nov19-story.html

http://people.com/archive/four-years-after-surviving-jonestowns-hell-tim-reiterman-tries-to-explain-how-it-happened-vol-18-no-21/

Group Beliefs

https://www.simplypsychology.org/asch-conformity.html

https://www.theguardian.com/world/2005/oct/08/terrorism.booksonhealth

Bhagavad Gita

Quotation is from the translation by Franklin Edgerton (1944).

http://www.thehindu.com/opinion/op-ed/gita-gandhi-and-godse/article6835411.ece

https://www.theguardian.com/books/2007/aug/16/fiction

http://www.nybooks.com/articles/2014/12/04/war-and-peace-bhagavad-gita/

M. K. Gandhi, *An Autobiography* (Ahmedabad, Navajivan, 1927–29).

M. V. Kamath, *Gandhi: A Spiritual Journey* (Mumbai, Indus Source, 2007).

http://www.hindustantimes.com/punjab/imbibe-gita-teachings-to-make-india-world-leader-rss-chief/story-IGwO1smUgtPyMZMv1gdWtO.html

https://timesofindia.indiatimes.com/india/Mystery-shrouds-ownership-of-pistol-that-killed-Bapu/articleshow/16633870.cms

http://www.nytimes.com/learning/general/onthisday/big/0130.html#article

ENDNOTES

Introduction: When Truths Collide

1 https://www.theguardian.com/lifeandstyle/2007/feb/24/foodanddrink.recipes1
2 http://www.independent.co.uk/life-style/food-and-drink/features/the-food-fad-that's-starving-bolivia-2248932.html
3 http://www.nytimes.com/2011/03/20/world/americas/20bolivia.html
4 https://www.theguardian.com/commentisfree/2013/jan/16/vegans-stomach-unpalatable-truth-quinoa
5 http://www.independent.co.uk/life-style/food-and-drink/features/quinoa-good-for-you-bad-for-bolivians-8675455.html
6 http://www.theglobeandmail.com/life/the-hot-button/the-more-you-love-quinoa-the-more-you-hurt-peruvians-and-bolivians/article7409637/
7 http://intent.com/intent/169482/
8 Marc F. Bellemare, Johanna Fajardo-Gonzalez and Seth R. Gitter, 'Foods and Fads – The Welfare Impacts of Rising Quinoa Prices in Peru', Working Papers 2016-06, Towson University, Department of Economics (2016).
9 http://www.npr.org/sections/thesalt/2016/03/31/472453674/your-quinoa-habit-really-did-help-perus-poor-but-theres-trouble-ahead
10 http://vegnews.com/articles/page.do?pageId=6345&catId=5
11 https://www.theguardian.com/environment/2013/jan/25/quinoa-good-evil-complicated
12 http://www.independent.co.uk/life-style/food-and-drink/features/quinoa-good-for-you-bad-for-bolivians-8675455.html
13 http://vegnews.com/articles/page.do?pageId=6345&catId=5
14 Walter Lippmann, *Public Opinion* (New York, Harcourt, Brace and Company, 1922).

15 http://media.nationalarchives.gov.uk/index.php/king-george-vi-radio-broadcast-3-september-1939/

16 http://news.bbc.co.uk/1/hi/uk/6269521.stm

17 http://www.telegraph.co.uk/news/uknews/1539715/Colgate-gets-the-brush-off-for-misleading-ads.html

18 http://www.pbs.org/wgbh/pages/frontline/shows/persuaders/interviews/luntz.html

19 https://dshs.texas.gov/wrtk/

20 https://www.cancer.org/cancer/cancer-causes/medical-treatments/abortion-and-breast-cancer-risk.html

21 https://www.cancer.gov/types/breast/abortion-miscarriage-risk

22 https://www.washingtonpost.com/news/fact-checker/wp/2016/12/14/texas-state-booklet-misleads-women-on-abortions-and-their-risk-of-breast-cancer

23 Evan Davis, *Post-Truth: Why We Have Reached Peak Bullshit and What We Can Do About It* (London, Little, Brown, 2017).

24 Tony Blair, *A Journey* (London, Hutchinson, 2010).

1: Complexity

1 http://www.publishersweekly.com/pw/by-topic/industry-news/bookselling/article/62785-is-amazon-really-the-devil.html

2 http://www.independent.co.uk/news/people/profiles/james-daunt-amazon-are-a-ruthless-money-making-devil-the-consumers-enemy-6272351.html

3 http://www.csmonitor.com/Books/chapter-and-verse/2012/0607/Ann-Patchett-calls-out-Amazon

4 http://www.independent.co.uk/arts-entertainment/books/news/amazon-the-darth-vader-of-the-literary-world-is-crushing-small-publishers-former-downing-st-adviser-a6888531.html

5 http://www.authorsunited.net/july/

6 James McConnachie, 'What do we think of Amazon?', *The Author*, Winter 2013.

7 https://www.theguardian.com/commentisfree/2014/jun/04/war-on-amazon-publishing-writers

8 https://www.srgresearch.com/articles/leading-cloud-providers-continue-run-away-market

9 https://www.thebureauinvestigates.com/stories/2011-12-07/revealed-the-wikipedia-pages-changed-by-bell-pottinger

10 https://press-admin.voteda.org/wp-content/uploads/2017/09/Findings-of-Herbert-Smith-Freehills-Review.pdf
11 http://amabhungane.co.za/article/2017-06-06-guptaleaks-how-bell-pottinger-sought-to-package-sa-economic-message
12 https://www.nelsonmandela.org/news/entry/transcript-of-nelson-mandela-annual-lecture-2015
13 http://amabhungane.co.za/article/2017-06-06-guptaleaks-how-bell-pottinger-sought-to-package-sa-economic-message
14 http://www.thetimes.co.uk/edition/news/450m-lost-over-failed-green-power-programme-n7hf0h6ht
15 https://georgewbush-whitehouse.archives.gov/news/releases/2002/10/20021007-8.html
16 https://thecaucus.blogs.nytimes.com/2007/07/10/scandal-taints-another-giuliani-ally/?mcubz=0&_r=0
17 http://abcnews.go.com/Blotter/DemocraticDebate/story?id=4443788

2: History

1 https://www.coca-colacompany.com/content/dam/journey/us/en/private/fileassets/pdf/2011/05/Coca-Cola_125_years_booklet.pdf
2 Civil War Preservation Trust, *Civil War Sites: The Official Guide to the Civil War Discovery Trail* (Guildford, CT, Globe Pequot Press, 2007).
3 https://www.washingtonpost.com/local/education/150-years-later-schools-are-still-a-battlefield-for-interpreting-civil-war/2015/07/05/e8fbd57e-2001-11e5-bf41-c23f5d3face1_story.html
4 http://www.nytimes.com/2015/10/22/opinion/how-texas-teaches-history.html
5 http://www.people-press.org/2011/04/08/civil-war-at-150-still-relevant-still-divisive/
6 https://www.washingtonpost.com/local/education/150-years-later-schools-are-still-a-battlefield-for-interpreting-civil-war/2015/07/05/e8fbd57e-2001-11e5-bf41-c23f5d3face1_story.html
7 http://www.latimes.com/opinion/editorials/la-ed-textbook27jul27-story.html
8 http://news.bbc.co.uk/1/hi/8163959.stm
9 http://news.bbc.co.uk/1/hi/world/africa/7831460.stm
10 http://abcnews.go.com/blogs/politics/2013/04/george-w-bushs-legacy-on-africa-wins-praise-even-from-foes/

11 http://www.nytimes.com/books/97/04/13/reviews/papers-lessons.html

12 http://www.nytimes.com/2015/04/25/opinion/will-the-vietnam-war-ever-go-away.html

13 http://news.bbc.co.uk/1/hi/world/asia-pacific/716609.stm

14 Ken Hughes, *Fatal Politics: The Nixon Tapes, the Vietnam War and the Casualties of Reelection* (Charlottesville, VA, University of Virginia Press, 2015).

15 http://www.theguardian.com/news/2015/apr/21/40-years-on-from-fall-of-saigon-witnessing-end-of-vietnam-war

16 Walter Lord, *The Miracle of Dunkirk* (New York, Viking, 1982).

17 http://www.bbc.co.uk/history/worldwars/wwtwo/dunkirk_spinning_01.shtml

18 https://theguardian.com/books/2017/jun/03/hilary-mantel-why-i-became-a-historical-novelist

3: Context

1 The Infinite Mind, 'Taboos' Program Transcript: https://books.google.co.uk/books?id=Z2jn-Txy5xIC&lpg=PA10

2 https://blogs.spectator.co.uk/2014/11/the-tribal-view-of-voters-illustrated-through-downing-streets-cats/

3 https://www.cbsnews.com/news/masterpieces-of-deception-some-fake-art-worth-real-money/

4 https://issuu.com/onview/docs/on_view_04-06.2014?e=1593647/7308241

5 https://www.economist.com/news/business/21716076-plant-based-meat-products-have-made-it-menus-and-supermarket-shelves-market

6 https://www.smithsonianmag.com/smart-news/biotech-company-growing-meatballs-lab-180958051/

7 http://www.nowtolove.com.au/news/latest-news/are-you-for-real-all-men-panel-at-the-global-summit-of-women-6288

8 https://twitter.com/rocio_carvajalc/status/479023547311202305

9 https://twitter.com/KathyLette/status/478980823014576128

10 https://www.globewomen.org/about/aboutus.htm

11 http://www.globewomen.org/ENewsletter/Issue%20No.%20CCXIV,%20December%202018,%202013.html

12 https://www.nytimes.com/2016/02/16/us/politics/ted-cruz-ad-goes-after-donald-trumps-stance-on-planned-parenthood.html

4: Numbers

1 S. Coren and D. F. Halpern, 'Left-handedness: a marker for decreased survival fitness', *Psychological Bulletin*, 109 (1) (1991).
2 http://www.nytimes.com/1991/04/04/us/being-left-handed-may-be-dangerous-to-life-study-says.html
3 http://www.bbc.co.uk/news/magazine-23988352
4 http://www.bbc.co.uk/news/magazine-19592372
5 http://uk.businessinsider.com/trump-says-94-million-americans-out-of-labor-force-in-speech-to-congress-2017-2?r=US&IR=T
6 https://www.washingtonpost.com/politics/2017/live-updates/trump-white-house/real-time-fact-checking-and-analysis-of-trumps-address-to-congress/fact-check-ninety-four-million-americans-are-out-of-the-labor-force/?utm_term=.54286ee433ca
7 http://www.nbcnews.com/politics/2016-election/trump-says-places-afghanistan-are-safer-u-s-inner-cities-n651651
8 http://www.forbes.com/sites/niallmccarthy/2016/09/08/homicides-in-chicago-eclipse-u-s-death-toll-in-afghanistan-and-iraq-infographic/#7fe711792512
9 http://watson.brown.edu/costsofwar/costs/human/civilians/afghan
10 https://blogs.spectator.co.uk/2017/10/theresa-mays-conservative-conference-speech-full-text/
11 http://www.independent.co.uk/news/uk/politics/theresa-may-housing-policy-new-homes-per-year-low-a7982901.html
12 http://www.iihs.org/iihs/topics/t/general-statistics/fatalityfacts/state-by-state-overview
13 http://www.forbes.com/sites/timworstall/2013/07/10/apples-chinese-suicides-and-the-amazing-economics-of-ha-joon-chang/#2c2fd5e36d1c
14 http://www.nsc.org/NSCDocuments_Corporate/Injury-Facts-41.pdf
15 http://edition.cnn.com/2013/04/18/us/u-s-terrorist-attacks-fast-facts/index.html
16 https://www.plannedparenthood.org/files/2114/5089/0863/2014-2015_PPFA_Annual_Report_.pdf
17 https://www.cdc.gov/mmwr/volumes/65/ss/ss6512a1.htm
18 http://www.oecd.org/dac/development-aid-rises-again-in-2016-but-flows-to-poorest-countries-dip.htm and http://election2017.ifs.org.uk/article/the-changing-landscape-of-uk-aid
19 http://www.express.co.uk/news/royal/484893/Proof-our-sovereign-really-is-worth-her-weight-in-gold

20 https://inews.co.uk/essentials/news/doctors-warn-lifesaving-breast-cancer-drug-costing-just-43p-denied-thousands/
21 https://popularresistance.org/when-someone-says-we-cant-afford-free-college-show-them-this/
22 http://www.parliament.uk/business/publications/written-questions-answers-statements/written-question/Lords/2015-12-03/HL4253
23 http://renewcanada.net/2016/federal-government-announces-additional-81-billion-for-infrastructure/
24 https://twitter.com/DanielJHannan/status/608733778995998720
25 https://www.gov.uk/government/news/hm-treasury-analysis-shows-leaving-eu-would-cost-british-households-4300-per-year
26 https://www.childrenwithcancer.org.uk/stories/cancer-cases-in-children-and-young-people-up-40-in-past-16-years/
27 http://www.telegraph.co.uk/science/2016/09/03/modern-life-is-killing-our-children-cancer-rate-in-young-people/
28 http://www.cancerresearchuk.org/about-us/cancer-news/press-release/2015-11-26-childrens-cancer-death-rates-drop-by-a-quarter-in-10-years
29 http://www.bbc.co.uk/programmes/p04kv749
30 http://www.cancerresearchuk.org/health-professional/cancer-statistics/childrens-cancers#heading-Zero
31 Lance Price, *The Spin Doctor's Diary: Inside Number 10 with New Labour* (London, Hodder & Stoughton, 2005).
32 Danny Dorling, Heather Eyre, Ron Johnston and Charles Pattie, 'A Good Place to Bury Bad News?: Hiding the Detail in the Geography on the Labour Party's Website', *Political Quarterly*, 73 (4) (2002) http://www.dannydorling.org/wp-content/files/dannydorling_publication_id1646.pdf
33 https://qz.com/138458/apple-is-either-terrible-at-designing-charts-or-thinks-you-wont-notice-the-difference/
34 http://www.telegraph.co.uk/news/politics/9819607/Minister-poor-families-are-likely-to-be-obese.html
35 https://www.gov.uk/government/statistics/distribution-of-median-and-mean-income-and-tax-by-age-range-and-gender-2010-to-2011
36 http://www.newstatesman.com/2013/05/most-misleading-statistics-all-thanks-simpsons-paradox
37 https://www.ft.com/content/658aba32-41c7-11e6-9b66-0712b3873ae1
38 https://www.jfklibrary.org/Research/Research-Aids/Ready-Reference/RFK-Speeches/Remarks-of-Robert-F-Kennedy-at-the-University-of-Kansas-March-18-1968.aspx

5: Story

1   Mervyn King, *The End of Alchemy: Money, Banking and the Future of the Global Economy* (London, Little, Brown, 2016).
2   Nassim Nicholas Taleb, *The Black Swan: The Impact of the Highly Improbable* (London, Random House, 2007).
3   Naomi Klein, *The Shock Doctrine: The Rise of Disaster Capitalism* (London, Penguin, 2007).
4   https://www.theguardian.com/uk-news/2017/mar/28/beyond-the-blade-the-truth-about-knife-in-britain
5   https://www.bbc.co.uk/education/guides/zyydjxs/revision/4
6   http://www.independent.co.uk/news/james-purvis-has-lost-his-job-and-his-faith-in-politicians-but-hes-hanging-on-to-the-sierra-1358104.html

6: Morality

1   http://www.larouchepub.com/eiw/public/1999/eirv26n07-19990212/eirv26n07-19990212_056-stand_by_moral_truths_pope_urges.pdf
2   http://www.margaretthatcher.org/document/107246
3   http://www.phlmetropolis.com/santorums-houston-speech.php
4   http://articles.latimes.com/1990-09-06/news/mn-983_1_casual-drug-users
5   Julia Buxton, *The Political Economy of Narcotics: Production, Consumption and Global Markets* (London, Zed Books, 2006).
6   http://query.nytimes.com/mem/archive-free/pdf?res=9901E5D61F3BE633A2575BC0A9649C946596D6CF
7   David F. Musto, *The American Disease: Origins of Narcotic Control* (New York, OUP, 1999).
8   Stephen R. Kandall, *Substance and Shadow: Women and Addiction in the United States* (Cambridge, MA, Harvard University Press, 1999).
9   Timothy Alton Hickman, *The Secret Leprosy of Modern Days: Narcotic Addiction and Cultural Crisis in the United States, 1870–1920* (Amherst, MA, University of Massachusetts Press, 2007).
10 Susan L. Speaker, '"The Struggle of Mankind Against Its Deadliest Foe": Themes of Counter-subversion in Anti-narcotic Campaigns, 1920–1940', *Journal of Social History*, 34 (3) (2001).
11 http://www.theguardian.com/society/2016/mar/08/nancy-reagan-drugs-just-say-no-dare-program-opioid-epidemic

12 https://harpers.org/archive/2016/04/legalize-it-all/

13 https://www.theguardian.com/us-news/2017/may/12/jeff-sessions-prison-sentences-obama-criminal-justice

14 http://abcnews.go.com/ABC_Univision/Politics/obama-drug-czar-treatment-arrests-time/story?id=19033234

15 S. L. A. Marshall, *Men Against Fire: The Problem of Battle Command in Future War* (New York, William Morrow, 1947).

16 Peter Kilner, 'Military Leaders' Obligation to Justify Killing in War', *Military Review*, 82 (2) (2002).

17 John Stuart Mill, *On Liberty* (1859) http://www.econlib.org/library/Mill/mlLbty1.html

18 http://www.nytimes.com/2013/02/03/opinion/sunday/why-police-officers-lie-under-oath.html

19 https://www.youtube.com/watch?v=BmXWQm3d2Lw

20 http://www.nytimes.com/2012/03/14/opinion/why-i-am-leaving-goldman-sachs.html

21 http://www.theguardian.com/sustainable-business/2016/jan/18/big-banks-problem-ethics-morality-davos

22 https://www.theguardian.com/culture/culture-cuts-blog/2011/feb/15/arts-funding-arts-policy

7: Desirability

1 http://www.ft.com/cms/s/0/cb58980a-218b-11e5-ab0f-6bb9974f25d0.html

2 Yuval Noah Harari, *Sapiens: A Brief History of Mankind* (London, Harvill Secker, 2014).

3 Rajagopal Raghunathan, Rebecca Walker Naylor and Wayne D. Hoyer, 'The Unhealthy = Tasty Intuition and its Effects on Taste Inferences, Enjoyment, and Choice of Food Products', *Journal of Marketing*, 70 (4) (2006).

4 http://www.caltech.edu/news/wine-study-shows-price-influences-perception-1374

5 Andrew S. Hanks, David Just and Adam Brumberg, 'Marketing Vegetables: Leveraging Branded Media to Increase Vegetable Uptake in Elementary Schools' (10 December 2015). https://ssrn.com/abstract=2701890

6 Brian Wansink, David R. Just, Collin R. Payne and Matthew Z. Klinger, 'Attractive names sustain increased vegetable intake in

schools', *Preventative Medicine*, 55 (4) (2012). https://www.ncbi.nlm.
nih.gov/pubmed/22846502

7 https://www.theguardian.com/lifeandstyle/2016/jan/05/diet-detox-art-
healthy-eating

8 https://www.theguardian.com/careers/2016/feb/11/why-i-love-my-job-
from-flexible-working-to-chilled-out-bosses

9 https://www.glassdoor.com/Reviews/Employee-Review-Aspen-Valley-
Hospital-RVW10555388.htm

10 https://www.glassdoor.ie/Reviews/Employee-Review-NBCUniversal-
RVW11687972.htm

11 https://sliwinski.com/5-loves/

12 http://www.gallup.com/poll/165269/worldwide-employees-engaged-
work.aspx

13 https://www.theguardian.com/sustainable-business/2014/nov/
05/society-business-fixation-profit-maximisation-fiduciary-duty

14 http://www.tarki.hu/hu/news/2016/kitekint/20160330_refugees.pdf

15 http://www.bbc.co.uk/news/world-europe-37310819

8: Financial Value

1 https://www.theatlantic.com/magazine/archive/1982/02/have-you-
ever-tried-to-sell-a-diamond/304575/

9: Definitions

1 http://www.bbc.co.uk/news/world-us-canada-14199080

2 ibid.

3 http://www.theguardian.com/global-development-professionals-
network/2014/aug/04/south-sudan-famine-malnutrition

4 ibid.

5 https://www.theatlantic.com/magazine/archive/2001/09/bystanders-
to-genocide/304571/

6 http://nsarchive2.gwu.edu/NSAEBB/NSAEBB53/rw050194.pdf

7 https://www.unilever.co.uk/brands/our-brands/sure.html accessed
8/10/17

8 http://abcnews.go.com/Business/dannon-settles-lawsuit/story?id=
9950269

9 http://nypost.com/2003/06/20/suit-poland-spring-from-dubious-
source/

10 https://www.theguardian.com/uk/2004/mar/19/foodanddrink

11 http://adage.com/article/cmo-strategy/sierra-mist-changing/301864/

12 George Orwell, 'Politics and the English Language' (1946). http://www.orwell.ru/library/essays/politics/english/e_polit/

13 http://england.shelter.org.uk/news/november_2013/80,000_children_facing_homelessness_this_christmas

14 https://england.shelter.org.uk/donate/hiddenhomeless

15 http://slate.com/articles/news_and_politics/chatterbox/1998/09/bill_clinton_and_the_meaning_of_is.html

16 Lance Price, *The Spin Doctor's Diary: Inside Number 10 with New Labour* (London, Hodder & Stoughton, 2005).

17 http://www.cbsnews.com/news/poll-womens-movement-worthwhile/

18 http://www.theguardian.com/theobserver/2013/jun/30/susan-sarandon-q-and-a

19 https://www.facebook.com/WomenAgainstFeminism/info/ accessed 8/10/17

20 http://www.huffingtonpost.com/joan-williams/feminism_b_1878213.html

21 http://www.elleuk.com/life-and-culture/news/a23534/david-cameron-afraid-feminist-shirt-meaning/

22 http://www.independent.co.uk/voices/comment/feminists-should-weep-at-the-death-of-margaret-thatcher-and-why-would-that-be-exactly-8567202.html

23 https://www.instagram.com/p/2WJAqmwzOQ/

10: Social Constructs

1 Yuval Noah Harari, *Sapiens: A Brief History of Mankind* (London, Harvill Secker, 2014).

2 http://www.standard.co.uk/news/politics/eu-referendum-what-is-the-eu-trends-on-google-hours-after-brexit-result-announced-a3280581.html

3 http://www.un.org/ga/search/view_doc.asp?symbol=A/HRC/32/L.20

4 http://www.express.co.uk/comment/expresscomment/414006/This-human-rights-ruling-flies-in-the-face-of-UK-justice

5 http://www.bbc.co.uk/news/world-asia-china-34592186

11: Names

1 https://www.theguardian.com/environment/2016/aug/29/
declare-anthropocene-epoch-experts-urge-geological-congress-human-
impact-earth

2 http://www.economist.com/node/18744401

3 http://www.nature.com/news/anthropocene-the-human-age-1.17085

4 http://e360.yale.edu/feature/living_in_the_anthropocene_toward_a_
new_global_ethos/2363/

5 https://www.aeaweb.org/articles?id=10.1257/0002828042002561

6 http://www.emeraldinsight.com/doi/abs/10.1108/02683940810849648

7 https://insight.kellogg.northwestern.edu/article/name-letter_branding

8 Kate Fitch, 'Megan's Law: Does it protect children? (2) An updated
review of evidence on the impact of community notification as
legislated for by Megan's Law in the United States' (NSPCC, 2006).

9 http://www.nj.com/news/index.ssf/2009/02/study_finds_megans_law_
fails_t_1.html

10 https://www.bjs.gov/content/pub/pdf/saycrle.pdf

11 Kate Fitch, 'Megan's Law: Does it protect children? (2) An updated
review of evidence on the impact of community notification as
legislated for by Megan's Law in the United States' (NSPCC,
2006).

12 Brian Christopher Jones, 'From the Innocuous to the Evocative: How
Bill Naming Manipulates and Informs the Policy Process', available
at https://dspace.stir.ac.uk/bitstream/1893/9206/1/Thesis%20
Examination%20Copy%20-%20New%20-%20Final.pdf

13 Alzheimer's Society, 'The Dementia Tax 2011', June 2011.

14 https://support.google.com/glass/answer/4347178?hl=en-GB accessed
8/10/17

15 https://sites.google.com/site/glasscomms/glass-explorers

16 https://www.ft.com/content/af01ff78-c394-11e6-9bca-2b93a6856354

17 http://www.independent.co.uk/arts-entertainment/read-bret-easton-
ellis-excoriating-monologue-on-social-justice-warriors-and-political-
correctness-a7170101.html

18 http://www.washingtonpost.com/wp-dyn/content/article/2009/07/30/
AR2009073002478.html?sid=ST2009073002982

19 http://www.telegraph.co.uk/news/politics/ukip/10656533/Ukip-
should-be-dismissed-as-a-modern-day-CND-says-Lord-Heseltine.html

20 David Fairhall, *Common Ground: The Story of Greenham* (London,
IB Tauris, 2006).

21 https://www.theatlantic.com/politics/archive/2014/01/the-agony-of-frank-luntz/282766/

22 http://prospect.org/article/meet-mr-death

23 Frank Luntz, *Words that Work: It's Not What You Say, It's What People Hear* (New York, Hyperion, 2007).

24 http://www.nytimes.com/2009/05/24/magazine/24wwln-q4-t.html

25 Steven Poole, *Unspeak* (London, Little, Brown, 2006).

26 https://www.theguardian.com/environment/2014/may/27/americans-climate-change-global-warming-yale-report

27 http://www.pbs.org/wgbh/pages/frontline/shows/persuaders/interviews/luntz.html

12: Predictions

1 https://www.ft.com/content/d646b090-9207-311c-bdd1-fca78e6dd03e

2 https://www.theguardian.com/politics/2016/may/22/david-cameron-defence-minister-penny-mordaunt-lying-turkey-joining-eu

3 http://www.ipcc.ch/pdf/assessment-report/ar5/wg1/WG1AR5_SPM_FINAL.pdf

4 https://www.scientificamerican.com/article/10-ways-climate-science-has-advanced-since-an-inconvenient-truth/

5 https://www.forbes.com/forbes/2006/1225/038.html

6 https://www.thegwpf.org/matt-ridley-global-warming-versus-global-greening/

7 https://www.ecb.europa.eu/press/key/date/2012/html/sp120726.en.html

8 https://www.ft.com/content/45de9cca-fda7-3191-ae70-ca5daa2273ee

9 https://futureoflife.org/ai-principles/

10 http://www.bbc.co.uk/news/technology-30290540

11 http://www.huffingtonpost.com/entry/humankinds-greatest-threat-may-not-be-global-warming_us_59935cdde4b0afd94eb3f597

12 https://www.theguardian.com/technology/2014/oct/27/elon-musk-artificial-intelligence-ai-biggest-existential-threat

13 http://www.vanityfair.com/news/2017/03/elon-musk-billion-dollar-crusade-to-stop-ai-space-x

14 http://www.vanityfair.com/news/2017/04/elon-musk-is-seriously-starting-a-telepathy-company

15 https://qz.com/911968/bill-gates-the-robot-that-takes-your-job-should-pay-taxes/

13: Beliefs

1   https://www.theatlantic.com/national/archive/2011/11/drinking-the-kool-aid-a-survivor-remembers-jim-jones/248723/
2   http://edition.cnn.com/2008/US/11/13/jonestown.jim.jones/index.html
3   ibid.
4   https://www.theatlantic.com/national/archive/2011/11/drinking-the-kool-aid-a-survivor-remembers-jim-jones/248723/
5   https://www.archkck.org/file/schools_doc_file/curriculum/religion/religion-updated-8/3/15/Fifty_Truths_Every_Catholic_Teen_Should_Know_snack.pdf
6   https://www2.deloitte.com/us/en/pages/finance/articles/cfo-insights-culture-shift-beliefs-behaviors-outcomes.html
7   https://www.theatlantic.com/politics/archive/2015/08/how-millennials-forced-ge-to-scrap-performance-reviews/432585/
8   https://hbr.org/2015/01/ges-culture-challenge-after-welch-and-immelt
9   M. V. Kamath, *Gandhi: A Spiritual Journey* (Mumbai, Indus Source, 2007).
10 http://thehindu.com/opinion/op-ed/gita-gandhi-and-godse/article6835411.ece
11 https://theguardian.com/books/2007/aug/16/fiction
12 http://nybooks.com/articles/2014/12/04/war-and-peace-bhagavad-gita/
13 http://www.hindustantimes.com/punjab/imbibe-gita-teachings-to-make-india-world-leader-rss-chief/story-IGwO1smUgtPyMZMv1gdWtO.html
14 http://timesofindia.indiatimes.com/india/Narendra-Modi-gifts-Gita-to-Japanese-emperor-takes-a-dig-at-secular-friends/articleshow/41530900.cms
15 http://thehindu.com/opinion/op-ed/gita-gandhi-and-godse/article6835411.ece
16 http://nybooks.com/articles/2014/12/04/war-and-peace-bhagavad-gita/
17 http://downloads.bbc.co.uk/radio4/transcripts/2016_reith1_Appiah_Mistaken_Identies_Creed.pdf
18 https://www.jewishideas.org/healthy-and-unhealthy-controversythoughts-parashat-korach-june-25-2011
19 Jonathan Sacks, *The Dignity of Difference* (New York, Continuum, 2002).

Epilogue: Final Truths

1   http://www.cbc.ca/news/canada/toronto/rob-ford-s-crack-use-in-his-own-words-1.2415605

INDEX

INDEX